Michael Gibbs

All or nothing
and other pages

Edited by Gerrit Jan de Rook & Andrew Wilson

Uniformbooks 2016

First published 2016
Uniformbooks in association with Boekie Woekie,
with support from Soledad Senlle, Amsterdam.
Copyright © Estate of Michael Gibbs, individual contributors
ISBN 978-1-910010-13-6

Uniformbooks
7 Hillhead Terrace, Axminster, Devon EX13 5JL
www.uniformbooks.co.uk

Boekie Woekie
Berenstraat 16, 1016 GH Amsterdam
www.boekiewoekie.com

Trade distribution in the UK by Central Books
www.centralbooks.com

Printed and bound by T J International, Padstow, Cornwall

Contents

Introduction by Andrew Wilson	7
1. *The Art of Forgetting—the Lost Idealism of the Sixties*	13
2. *Destruction in Art Symposium*	19
3. *Words to be looked at*	20
4. *Mr Fluxus*	23
5. *SomeVolumesFromTheLibraryOfBabel*	26
6. *Documentary and its discontents*	38
7. *Graph of photography*	46
8. *Back to Basics*	57
9. *Superchannel*	61
10. *Net Working*	64
11. *Stalking the Web*	67
12. *Virtual Artworlds*	70
13. *Locative Media*	73
14. *All or nothing—an anthology of blank books*	76
15. *Poems, publications, performance, and photography*	95
Donald Gardner: *Subverter of Categories*	173
Gerrit Jan de Rook: *Concrete poetry and language art*	175
Guy Schraenen: *The Bloody Alphabet, or how to crack it*	183
Marga van Mechelen: *Performances*	190
John Held Jr.: *Michael Gibbs & the Development of a Network...*	200
Henriette Dingemans: *Why not sneeze?*	203
Rob Perrée: *The dialectical view of Michael Gibbs*	206
Bas Vroege: *Being one and the other*	210
Biography	214
Contributors	221

ANDREW WILSON

Introduction

Michael Gibbs was a gentle and tolerant believer in the worth of art—its social, cultural, political and aesthetic worth. Art excited him and was the core of his life. In September 1966, aged just seventeen, he attended events at the *Destruction In Art Symposium*. For the teenager, the flyers for these events, even a fragment of Yoko Ono's Biba dress that he had cut from her, exerted a talismanic power. He had resolved at that point to be a particular sort of artist and he kept these artefacts near him for the rest of his life. Those events in 1966 marked his immersion in what he called "a genuinely 'underground' culture… which owed nothing to the official art establishment". Towards the end of his life, largely ignored by that establishment, he was nevertheless content that his archives, including the materials he had saved from *DIAS*, were to be preserved in the collection of the Tate Archive; these detail a nuanced and critical life lived in and through art, identified by an absolute generosity of spirit, an embrace of the positive possibilities of exchange, discussion, learning, criticism and collaboration.

DIAS in effect set the stage for his world. In the early 1970s he embarked on research at the American Arts Documentation Centre at the University of Exeter and was at the heart of the small community—'Fluxus West'—that ran the experimental Beau Geste Press, organising the related touring exhibition *Fluxshoe* that between 1972 and 1973 reintroduced Britain to the delights of Fluxus. If in the late 1960s Gibbs had resolved to become an avant-garde concrete poet (following the twin examples of Guillaume Apollinaire and Dom Sylvester Houédard), it was in the context of the Exeter community that he first flourished as an artist. In 1975 he relocated to the Netherlands in search of an alternative to his Exeter life.

Gibbs' work through the 1970s—predominantly poems, performance, film, books, magazines, mail art—was largely predicated on play and his engagement with the avant-garde spirit of chance operations. By the 1980s and 1990s he was also producing photo-text pieces that owed much to the work of Allan Sekula and Martha

Rosler. These were artists he wrote about in the Dutch magazine *Perpektief*, affecting a generation of Dutch artists and photographers. In fact his publishing—from *Kontexts* (1967–77) and *Artzien* (1978–82) and on to his critical writing, primarily in *Art Monthly*, had one aim of realising the potential of art to have an effect in not only encouraging people to see the world differently but also act differently within the world as well. Using the words of George Maciunas, Gibbs reminds us that one of the aims of Fluxus was to "promote living art, anti-art, promote NON ART REALITY to be grasped by all peoples, not only critics, dilettantes and professionals". The generosity of these words, and the implication that art should have the capacity to affect anybody and everybody, indicates the core of his work. It was also absolutely consistent that his critical position entailed little contact with the art market—his main income coming characteristically from translation and teaching.

The spirit of the 1960s can be identified in the setting up of webs or networks surrounding different communities. The key behind his self-publishing of *Kontexts* and *Artzien* through the 1970s and early 1980s was distribution. It was with this in mind that he also collaborated with the book spaces both of Ulises Carrión (Other Books and So, 1975–78) and Jan Voss, Henriëtte van Egten and Rúna Thorkelsdóttir (Boekie Woekie, since 1986). It was also at the heart of his involvement with the mail art community, a network that was predicated on the free sharing of ideas through a distribution that was only limited by the imagination and the extent of the international mail services. In the 1990s his vision of community, play, and the avant-garde's social and aesthetic commitment—successively realised through the examples of Fluxus, publishing, writing and performance—was extended to the Internet, about which he wrote regularly for *Art Monthly* (for which he had been a contributor since 1986) and his own Internet art magazine *Why Not Sneeze?* (1996–99, archived at nondes.home.xs4all.nl/sneeze/frame.html).

Gibbs' writing was grounded in the form of the exhibition and book review, and this is true for *Art Monthly* as much as it is for *Perspektief*, but one clear exception to this is an article written in 1992 for the Dutch magazine *Kunst & Museumjournaal*. This text, 'The Art of Forgetting—The Lost Idealism of the Sixties', questions the recuperation of radical art practices of the 1960s and 1970s by the institutions of art, be they museums or marketplace. He mourns both the loss of the avant-garde as it becomes "a theory divorced from practice" and the disappearance of play as it has been similarly transformed into an application of strategy. Written three years after the breaching of the Berlin Wall and the collapse of communism Gibbs suggests that "radicalism has ceased to be regarded as a viable presence. Except, perhaps, for a radicalism of the Right: a resurgence of the capitalist market economy and a radical abandonment of socialist values. Artists are more concerned today about whether their work will sell, or whether they'll be given another subsidy, than about how their work may engage with society... The motivation to create new forms of art in the sixties and seventies stemmed from a need to express a desire for change". This position was strongly drawn in most of his reviews—whether of Anselm Kiefer's survey exhibition at the Stedelijk Museum in Amsterdam in 1987 or a profile of Superflex's Superchannel project in 2001.

The piece on Superchannel is useful also for detailing how Gibbs' involvement in the Internet was absolutely a reflection of his belief in the power of art's social responsibility, which he had recognised so early on as a teenager at *DIAS* and also through his later exposure to Fluxus. He equates Superflex's activities both with "Maciunas' promotion of 'non art reality' and his advocacy of social commitment and communal projects", as much as in "Beuys' notions of 'social sculpture' and economic reform"—both important examples for Gibbs' himself. 'Superchannel' also usefully illustrates Gibbs' own position with regard to the Internet, as the final sentences of his profile make abundantly clear. He understands the project as "evidence of a return to the spirit of community that characterised the early years of the Internet with its bulletin boards, discussion lists and MOOs. True, it was only textual then, but it was essentially democratic and participatory, qualities that are all too much in danger of being lost in the corporate-driven visions of e-topia. Cities are built of bricks as well as bits, and are inhabited by people whose immediate concerns are local rather than global".

However, as his 1992 polemic makes clear (and this ends with his suggestion "until it regains its radical edge, let's forget art"), Gibbs was always highly tuned aesthetically and his criticism was not without teeth if he felt that social and aesthetic responsibility was falling short. For instance, in 2001 he noted that "the net art community is growing rapidly but, like the mail art movement that preceded it, it tends to abjure criticism in favour of promiscuous groupings and linkings, and a potentially infinite address book. Building topologies... may simply mean that another index is added to what is already indexical, so that, in a very real sense, Baudrillard's 'the map precedes the territory' is becoming true. Ultimately, we may end up spending more time trying to read and decipher the map than actually going anywhere, let alone arriving at any desired destination".

The connectivity of the Internet was for Gibbs positively instable and ephemeral—just as were the vulnerabilities of the free exchange of mail art, and the essentially event-based nature of Fluxus in their respective offering of a challenge to orthodoxies. Above all, however, Gibbs loved books and words and the spaces between words and letters on pages—and those pages being turned and the letters, words and spaces being read by many different readers. Despite his love for a distribution of ideas and art, it might be surprising that much of what he wrote, published and exhibited is about disappearance and erasure—most notably in his brilliant study of blank books *All or Nothing*, published in 2005. Its subject returns him to the beginnings of his life in art: to *DIAS* and also to John Cage, whose use of the random qualities of chance fuelled his early research in Exeter. In this book he declared clearly his understanding that "There can be no space that is completely empty nor... is there any such thing as absolute silence... Blankness is as much a state of mind as it is a material condition and as such it can be deceptive, hallucinatory, intentional, poetic or spiritual. It can be legible or illegible, present or absent, perfect or imperfect. But it is never empty".

An earlier version of this introduction originally appeared in *Art Monthly*, 333, February 2010. With grateful acknowledgements to *Art Monthly*, *Perspektief*, and *Kunst & Museum Journaal* for permission to republish the following essays.

1

The Art of Forgetting—the Lost Idealism of the Sixties

One evening, about twenty-five years ago, I ventured into the basement of Better Books in London's Charing Cross Road, where it had been announced that a 'Book Plumbing Event' by the artist John Latham would be taking place. The walls of the basement were lined with untidy piles of newspapers and a number of kettles pouring out constant clouds of steam. In the middle of the space stood a bookcase filled with a variety of paperbacks. A stepladder was set up in front of the bookcase and a nude girl climbed to the top where she sat with an open book covering her lap. As the 'Event' progressed, the books slowly began falling out of the bookcase, apparently propelled by lengths of pneumatic plastic tubing emitting a nasty-looking greenish goo. I remember being slightly appalled by the sight of all those quite readable books being irrevocably damaged, but I recognised that it was all being done for a good cause, namely that of 'experimental' or 'avant-garde' art. Indeed, John Latham had something of a reputation as a biblioclast—a few months previously he had performed one of his notorious book-burning ceremonies as part of the *DIAS* Festival in London. Latham's book-burnings (he made towers of books which he then set alight, calling the actions 'SKOOB', books spelled backwards) were not seen as manifestations of bigotry, as they would today perhaps, bearing in mind the recent Salman Rushdie affair, but as genuine artistic expressions involving play, experiment and a healthy spirit of provocation.

A new sense of adventure was in the air in London in the mid-sixties. Fuelled by the emerging youth culture and the wave of political protest opposing the Vietnam War and Britain's Nuclear Bomb, the sixties saw a convergence of idealism, protest and sheer adventurous anarchism that has not been witnessed since (except for a brief reprise—though minus the idealism which had long turned sour—during the heyday of the Punk era).[1] Art events were organised in the unlikeliest of locations—the playground of the

London Free School, for instance, where some of the *DIAS* events took place, or venues like the Africa Centre which hosted two evenings of performances by Yoko Ono. *DIAS* (*Destruction in Art Symposium*) was organised on a shoe-string budget by the sound poet Bob Cobbing (at that time manager of Better Books and one of the founders of the London Filmmakers Co-op) and the anarchist painter/architect Gustav Metzger, who was often to be seen 'leading' the London Anarchists contingent at the many protest marches that were taking place in London at that time. It was anarchist ideals that united the experimental poets and artists in London with the activities of the Provos in Holland, the Aktionisten in Vienna, the Happening artists in New York and the International Situationists. A genuinely 'underground' culture had emerged, which owed nothing to the official art establishment, taking its cue instead from Dadaism and the burgeoning youth revolt. Alex Trocchi, a key figure within the British counter-culture and instigator of the Situationist-inspired 'Project Sigma', coined the term "astronauts of inner space" to describe the representatives of this new consciousness.

It is all too easy to look back at this period with nostalgia. It is not my intention in writing this piece to look fondly back at the sixties and say "those were the days" or something equally inane, but to pose the question of what has happened to the idealism and sense of adventure that we felt at the time. I was young then—just seventeen—literally a child of the times, and perhaps such freewheeling optimism and enthusiasm is simply the prerogative of youth. But what attracts adolescent would-be artists today? What are they inspired by, what do they identify with? And what has happened to that sense of play that so characterised the 'avant-garde' of the sixties and early seventies?

I have just introduced two terms—'play' and 'avant-garde'—that seem antithetical to the type of art that is being produced today and the way it is received. Indeed, the words sound almost anachronistic: art takes itself and the world much more seriously nowadays, and the avant-garde has long been consigned to the safe territory of art history. The confluence of experimental art and social radicalism that marked not only the historical avant-garde movements of Dadaism, Russian Constructivism and Surrealism, but also the Happenings and Events of the sixties, has almost totally evaporated. Its last manifestation was perhaps embodied in the career of Joseph Beuys.

During the last decade, with the unimaginably swift collapse of Communism, radicalism has ceased to be regarded as a viable presence. Except, perhaps, for a radicalism of the Right: a resurgence of the capitalist market economy and a radical abandonment of socialist values. Artists are more concerned today about whether their work will sell, or whether they'll be given another subsidy, than about how their work may engage with society. Even much of the so-called 'socially-committed' art that has been emerging in the US recently seems more committed to publicity and art market mechanisms than to any broad-based social idealism. The experimental art of the sixties and seventies was born in (and borne upon) a wave of revolutionary fervour that now seems to have totally subsided. When we hear the word 'revolution' today it is more likely to be in the context of an advertisement for a new car or some other product of consumer technology.

What has happened is that most of the new, challenging art forms and ideas of the sixties—visual and sound poetry, performances, artists' books, 'alternative' spaces, 'Free Universities', etcetera—have either been consigned to oblivion or valorised by the art market and museum economy. Fluxus, for example, was virtually ignored by dealers and curators until its driving force, George Maciunas, died in 1978, whereupon they appropriated the movement, sanitised it of Maciunas's revolutionary anarchism and remoulded it in their own image in the form of revivals and retrospective survey exhibitions, all of which coincidentally served to vastly increase the market value of Fluxus multiples that were once ridiculously cheap or even free. Fluxus today means nothing more than a section of the 'collectables' market; like the other historical avant-gardes, it has been reduced to items in dealers' catalogues.

Perhaps because they lacked a catchy name, like 'Fluxus', other new forms of art that developed in the sixties, including concrete poetry, mail art and artists' books, have fared less well. The self-congratulatory title of the recent exhibition at the Amsterdam Fodor Museum devoted to the career of Ulises Carrión and his bookshop Other Books & So—*"We have won! Haven't we?"*—sounds to me rather hollow, begging more questions than it answers. What, in any case, is (or was) there to win? Fame and fortune? A guaranteed place in art history? This, I think, is far from what Ulises was hoping to achieve. The mail art network he was involved in never had any pretensions to winning any stakes in the art world, yet it generated a tremendous amount of activity, uniting more artists in a sort of international fraternity than any mega-event like *Documenta* could ever hope to.

These invisible, transient, ephemeral networks (linking concrete poets, performance artists, Conceptualists, social activists...) can never be fully documented or archived—to attempt to do so would, in any case, be a boring and futile task. Lucy Lippard's book *Six Years*, a cross-reference compilation of the *dematerialization of the art object from 1966 to 1972*, simply and chronologically lists hundreds of conceptual events and publications that took place all over the world during that brief period of six years. In 1973, when the book was first published, most of the events were still fresh and capable of inspiring a new generation of artists. Yet such inspiration was to be short-lived; only the 'major' Conceptualists like Huebler, Kosuth, Nauman, Weiner and Buren managed to survive the changing art market conditions of the seventies and the 'return to order' represented by the revival of painting. If Conceptual Art remains a force today, it is perhaps largely because its early champions are now in positions of curatorial authority. The career of John Latham, the artist I mentioned at the beginning of this essay, is another case in point. In 1966 Latham founded the Artists Placement Group, an organisation dedicated to the idea that artists could collaborate with administrative bodies and government institutions not in order to produce 'aesthetic' works but to take part in an interactive, creative process. British artists such as Ian Breakwell and Stuart Brisley took up 'placements' and initiated projects that had genuine and far-reaching social relevance. Attempts to introduce similar placements in Europe, however, have so far failed, and the APG has more or less dissolved. Latham, meanwhile, has continued to pursue his complex theories of 'Time Base' art and to show his book-objects in chic New York galleries like Josh Baer.[2] I do not wish to begrudge Latham his art world success (he certainly deserves it more than most artists showing in the New York gallery scene), but the shift of emphasis from active and intangible process to marketable product in many ways typifies the new conditions of art in the nineties.

The sense of communality, naive and unfocussed though it was, that characterised the experimental art of the sixties has steadily dissipated as the centralising influence exerted by cultural administration has increased. This influence has created fixed spatial co-ordinates within an art world axis that spans New York, London, Paris and various competing cities in Germany, replacing the unfixed, immaterial, more genuinely international co-ordinates within which concrete poetry, Fluxus and performance art, for example, developed. The art world today is just that: a self-enclosed, hegemonic world geared to producing products to be consumed within the cultural economy. It is an industry that constantly needs to be fed by the turnover of products and the generation of publicity. Everyone—artists, galleries, museums, critics, subsidising bodies, consumers—is involved in this industry. Art's sole role, it seems, is to feed the insatiable mills of the art industry. The result is that only that art gets circulated that fits within the processes and mechanisms of the machines.

If my words seem reminiscent of the critique against the culture industry launched by the Frankfurt School during the thirties, then it would seem that the ideas of Walter Benjamin, Theodor Adorno, Max Horkheimer and Herbert Marcuse have maintained their validity. That they were powerless to halt the expansion of the culture industry does not invalidate their idealism, but it does bring it into sharper relief. These writers were also popular among artists twenty years ago, when the ramifications of the culture industry became evident again after the early demise of the sixties avant-garde. The failure of the student revolts of 1968 and the privatisation of hedonism beginning in the early seventies (the shift from communal joy to the narcissism of the Me generation), followed by the deadening effects of AIDS on gay (in the general sense of the word) sensibilities, marked the exhaustion of idealism and the end of communality. The hope invested in the idea of an avant-garde has also disappeared. The very notion of an avant-garde has become just that: a theory divorced from practice, a loss to be mourned instead of a living presence. According to one recent account, the very discourse surrounding any discussion of the avant-garde already articulates its death.[3] The dialectical double bind that fatally affects the avant-garde also conditions any avowal of an 'oppositional' or 'idealist' art. Perhaps the only beneficiaries of this dilemma are the theorists and art historians for whom art is already dead matter.

But why should we continue to accept the concept of an avant-garde? Simply because of its historical validity, as something that keeps the art industry moving? What if the avant-garde never really existed? That it was simply an invention of critics and apologists for the bourgeoisie seeking to justify the Modernist demand to "Make it new!". The art of the sixties and seventies was not self-consciously avant-garde; it was radical because the times were radical, in the same way that Dada emerged not as an art 'movement' but as a direct, radical response to the cultural situation of Europe during the First World War, or the way that Russian Constructivism grew not from an art programme but from a genuinely revolutionary crisis.

The motivation to create new forms of art in the sixties and seventies stemmed from a need to ask questions about life and society, a need to express a desire for change. It did not rely on galleries, glossy magazines, state support or wealthy collectors for its circulation, since it possessed its own dynamic. Nor did it enjoy the level of social and economic acceptance that art receives today; most often it was regarded with disdain, if not outright hostility.

The conditions are perhaps not yet right for a renewal of the arts, or a revival of idealism. We may still be impatient for change, but the crisis is yet to come. In the meantime, let's forget the sixties, the seventies, the eighties. And, if necessary, at least until it regains its radical edge, let's forget art.

1 The best account of the British 'underground' culture in the sixties, written by an insider, is Jeff Nuttall's *Bomb Culture*, published in 1968.

2 A useful survey of Latham's career is provided in *John Latham, Art after Physics*, Museum of Modern Art Oxford and Edition Hansjorg Mayer, Stuttgart, 1991. On the Artists Placement Croup see 'Papers and Proceedings of the discussion held at the Apollohuis Eindhoven January 16, 1982'.

3 Paul Mann, *The Theory-Death of the Avant-Garde*, Bloomington: Indiana University Press, 1991.

This article originally appeared in *Kunst & Museum Journaal*, vol.3, no.6, 1992.

Destruction in Art Symposium

I didn't attend all the *DIAS* events in London in September 1966, but the one that was the most memorable was Yoko Ono's performance evening at the Africa Centre, an unlikely venue, but perhaps no more so than the London Free School Playground in Notting Hill where most of the outdoor *DIAS* events took place. Before the evening began, or it may have been after the intermission, a number of changes to the programme were announced. *Sky Piece*, *Touch Poem* and *Fly Piece* were scrapped, and *Wall Piece* added. During the first half, Yoko and her 'assistant', Anthony Cox, performed *Bag Piece* by climbing into a large black bag and (reportedly) exchanging their clothing. Three years later, I saw Yoko perform the same piece, this time with John Lennon, at the 'Alchemical Wedding' evening at the Royal Albert Hall. I wonder if they used the same bag?

After the intermission there were two 'audience participation' pieces. For *Wall Piece* the audience was invited to bang their heads against the nearest wall. I good-naturedly joined in, but couldn't help feeling rather foolish. Was this really what avant-garde art was all about? But then, thinking of Dada pranks half a century earlier, I supposed it had a sort of legitimacy. Anyway, it was something to tell my schoolmates about, I was only seventeen at the time and had just become a sixth former. I remember trying to describe *Bag Piece* to my friends and sticking a cloth guitar case over my head to demonstrate.

I had the same trepidation about taking part in *Cut Piece*. There was Yoko kneeling on the stage wearing a colourful Biba dress, inviting members of the audience to come up on stage and cut her clothes off. Was she wearing underwear, I wondered? I decided to play safe and cut off a small piece of her dress before the situation got any more embarrassing. I am afraid I do not remember if her underwear was cut away as well, but the piece concluded with someone handing her a hand-lettered sheet of cardboard which she held in front of her. It said, "The body is the scar of the mind".

This article originally appeared in *Art Monthly*, 212, December 1997–January 1998.

3

Words to be looked at

Liz Kotz's study of the turn to language in the experimental art being produced, mostly in New York between 1958 and 1968, begins not, as one might expect, with Allan Kaprow's 1961 *Words* environment, but with an elucidation of the music of John Cage, specifically his famous 1953 'silent' composition *4'33"*. (*Words To Be Looked At: Language in 1960s Art*, Cambridge, Mass., 2007) Cage's conception of music as existing within the expanded field of sound was later to find its parallel in the idea of poetry as an expanded field of language, but it was also his increasing use of graphic scores and chance procedures that was to strike a chord with both visual artists and poets. In the late fifties Cage taught a class in experimental composition at the New School in New York, whose members included George Brecht, Jackson Mac Low and Dick Higgins. It was there that Brecht developed his idea of 'event scores', an extension of music into indeterminate actions involving everyday objects. A couple of years later George Maciunas would print these and similar events by such composers as La Monte Young and Yoko Ono in the form of boxed sets of cards under the Fluxus imprint. While Fluxus was clearly indebted to a Cagean aesthetic, Maciunas's interests extended beyond the confines of New York's avant-garde to embrace experimental art being produced contemporaneously in Europe. Maciunas himself was living in Wiesbaden in Germany in the early sixties, while his closest collaborator in Fluxus, the American poet Emmett Williams, was living in nearby Darmstadt. A link was thus established with European artists like Daniel Spoerri and Wolf Vostell, while Williams also provided contacts with the emerging school of concrete poetry, which had its origins in the Swiss artist Max Bill's notion of concrete art. Concrete poetry certainly fits the description of "words to he looked at" yet Liz Kotz dismisses it as "a reliance on rather quaint illustrational or pictorial modes—as in poems that take on the shape of their subjects", leaving it "out of touch with changing paradigms in the visual arts". Admittedly, concrete poetry never really took off in the US (unlike in Europe where it forged links with Op Art and

Kinetic Art), but at least in the persons of Mac Low, Williams and Higgins it certainly played a vital role in the emerging avant-gardes in sixties New York.

In discussing the chance-generated poems of Mac Low, Kotz takes a different tack, comparing them with a poem titled 'Europa' by John Ashbery, which was published in his 1962 book *The Tennis Court Oath*. In both cases there is a use of found material, but Ashbery's concerns are far from Mac Low's Cage-inspired use of chance structures; indeed, Ashbery himself dismissed his experimental efforts at the time as 'transitional', whereas Mac Law's non-syntactical texts served as the basis for an extremely conscious and precise oral delivery. One of the values of Kotz's close reading of the sixties New York art scene is the discovery that several people primarily known as artists actually started out as poets, notably Dan Graham, Vito Acconci and Carl Andre. It is unfortunate that Andre refused to allow his poems to be reproduced in this book, but Kotz manages to include enough quotes to give us an idea of his minimal, serially structured texts that parallel his other experiments in the early sixties with objects and materials. "Whole poems are made out of the many single poems we call words", he once wrote. Acconci, on the other hand, saw poetry as "a field of force, a field of encounter", and in the pages of his magazine *0 to 9* he confronted the reader with columns of almost unreadable prose interspersed with random punctuation marks. Acconci would later expand his linguistic field to confrontational performances and installations that often relied upon taped audio or video recordings of his own speaking voice—language to be listened to rather than looked at.

It was with Conceptual Art *pur sang* that language really made its mark in New York in the sixties—Graham's magazine pieces, Joseph Kosuth's ideas as art, On Kawara's telegrams, Douglas Huebler's 'Variable Pieces', Art & Language's 'Index Works' and, of course, Lawrence Weiner's 'statements'. As Kotz notes, these artists recognised Minimalism's linguistic potential as exemplified by its processes of reduction, placement and iteration. "It is no historical accident", she writes, "that self-consciously conceptual and linguistically oriented art emerged from prolonged engagements with Minimalism, rather than directly from Cagean or neo-Dada practices". Lawrence Weiner epitomises the transference of minimalist sculptural terms into language, deliberately eschewing any content that could be described as 'poetic' or 'metaphorical'. Yet the art/literature boundaries were not that well drawn, even in the sixties. The American poet Robert Lax, for example (whom Kotz does not even mention) was producing minimalist poem sequences that bear a remarkable resemblance to Weiner's work.

Despite my reservations, Kotz's book is an excellently researched archaeology of the emergence of Conceptualism in New York in the sixties and a reminder of the extraordinary fecundity of the dialogues that were occurring in avant-garde circles at that time. As the sixties came to a close, poststructuralism started to impose a new order, constraining linguistic experimentation within a perceived crisis of representation. It is perhaps fitting that the last chapter in the book is devoted to Andy Warhol's *a: a novel*, published by Grove Press in 1968, an unrelenting 450 page transcription of recordings of twenty-four hours of Warhol and his superstar Ondine on speed. Although it embodies many of the precepts that Kotz has been discussing in her book—indeterminacy, mechanical recording, readymade material—it remains eminently unreadable. Words to be looked at, indeed, rather than read.

This article originally appeared in *Art Monthly*, 324, March 2009.

Mr Fluxus

Fluxus was probably the last genuinely international avant-garde art movement of the twentieth century. It is worth remembering the military origin of the term avant-garde, for George Maciunas, the founder of Fluxus, clearly saw himself as the commander-in-chief of a motley, somewhat undisciplined band of foot soldiers who were waging a sort of guerrilla war against the institutions of High Art. It was in fact while working as a designer for the US Army in Wiesbaden that Maciunas organised the first. Fluxus festivals in 1962, which were quickly followed by similar events in Copenhagen, Paris, Düsseldorf and Amsterdam. The European wing of Fluxus, as represented by Addi Kopcke, Wolf Vostell, Tomas Schmit and Ben Vautier, had a distinctly more anarchic and bohemian attitude than its American counterparts who had mostly emerged from the John Cage school of experimental music. But Maciunas himself was of European origin. having been born in Lithuania; he had emigrated with his mother to the US after the war and, as this 'collective portrait' of George Maciunas makes clear (*Mr. Fluxus: A Collective Portrait of George Maciunas 1931–1978*, edited by Emmett Williams & Ann Noël, London, 1997), there were innumerable contradictions and inconsistencies to his character which were to influence the way that Fluxus was to develop. He was often dictatorial, purging people from Fluxus when they dared to disagree with his political and artistic doctrines, yet at the same time he could be as non-egotistical and generous as a saint. Like many despots, Maciunas was obsessive: he liked to keep things in impeccable order (like the complex charts he devised showing the art historical genealogy of Fluxus), yet most of his attempted business enterprises were dismal failures.

After returning to New York in the mid-sixties, Maciunas started producing Fluxus newspapers, cards, boxes, and games and opened a Fluxshop on Canal Street, but failed to sell a single item. Maciunas was clearly, and problematically, ahead of his time: the art world hadn't yet heard about Multiples, let alone Fluxus. But Maciunas was uncompromising and, as his 1963 *Fluxus Manifesto* makes clear, he wasn't even aiming at an art audience. He wanted to "promote living art, anti-art, promote NON ART REALITY to be grasped by all peoples, not only critics, dilettantes and professionals". All his life he dreamed of unleashing a revolution that would "fuse the cadres of cultural, social & political revolutionaries into united front & action".

That this terminology is not dissimilar to that used by the promoters of the Chinese Cultural Revolution later in the sixties is perhaps not accidental. One of Maciunas's closest colleagues was Henry Flynt who authored a Fluxus pamphlet called *Down with Art*, and co-authored with Maciunas another pamphlet called *Communists Must Give Revolutionary Leadership in Culture*. Several of the letters published in *Mr Fluxus* reveal that Maciunas was hoping to interest the Soviet authorities in Fluxus and in his designs for prefabricated housing, and he was not amused when Eric Anderson and other 'renegade' Fluxists perpetrated a hoax on Maciunas by informing him that they had performed outrageous Fluxus events in various cities in Russia. Maciunas was definitely fond of gags, but not when he was the victim.

He became the unwilling victim in other ways too, as in his pioneering attempts to organise cooperative studio lofts in SoHo, which earned him a severe beating at the hands of Mafia thugs and continual harassment from the law enforcement authorities who were not impressed with Maciunas's unconventional business methods.

There is nothing Maciunas liked more than to play the clown, to dress up and organise extravagant Fluxsports, Fluxtours, Fluxmeals and so on. Indeed, his vision of a Fluxworld embraced just about everything, from Fluxmedicins and Fluxclothes to Fluxflags and Fluxclocks. What is amazing is that many of these products and services were actually realised, although they never circulated much beyond a small circle of participants.

Other projects, however, were more grandiose. Having failed to establish a Fluxhouse in SoHo, Maciunas decided to look for an island to set up a Fluxus community. He almost found one, but, inevitably, the deal fell through (probably to the relief of people like John Lennon and Yoko Ono who had been persuaded to support this particular scheme). In 1976 he purchased a farm in Massachusetts which had several buildings and outbuildings, giving it the appearance of a medieval village. None of his New York artist friends, however, came to live there, and he only received the occasional visitor. Many people were undoubtedly put off by the dictatorial rules of the house. Smoking, for instance, was vigorously prohibited on the entire estate.

A year later he was diagnosed as suffering from cancer and he died in 1978 at the age of forty-seven.

Fluxus, of course, has in the meantime become eminently marketable and has been the subject of innumerable books, catalogues, revivals and exhibitions. Yet none of it would have happened without Maciunas, and it is to the credit of his life-long colleague, Emmett Williams, that this book of reminiscences, letters, and documents has been put together and published. Some of the material has been reprinted from other, sometimes obscure, sources, but the bulk of it is original material conveyed to Williams through letters. It is an excellent companion volume to Emmett Williams own insider's view of Fluxus, *My Life in Fluxus–and Vice Versa*. What emerges is a portrait of an elusive crusader who refused to take life, or art seriously. He was a benign conspirator, an underground organiser, a talented graphic designer, an entrepreneur, a Don Quixote tilting against the windmills of the art establishment.

He never wanted to be an artist, and hopefully he will not be remembered as one. Fluxus, he wrote, "forgoes artist's indispensability, exclusiveness, individuality, ambition, forgoes all pretension towards significance, rarity, inspiration, skill, complexity, profundity, greatness, institutional and commodity value".

That it has since achieved many of these values is not Maciunas's fault. Fluxus effectively died in 1978. May it rest in peace.

This article originally appeared in *Art Monthly*, 216, May 1998.

5

SomeVolumesFromTheLibraryOfBabel

"There is nothing outside of the text."—Jacques Derrida

Jorge Luis Borges, the blind librarian and inventor of treatises on mythical books, describes in his story *The Library of Babel* a possibly infinite universe consisting of hexagonal galleries filled with books:

> "Five shelves correspond to each one of the walls of each hexagram; each shelf contains thirty-two books of a uniform format; each book is made up of four hundred and ten pages; each page of forty lines; each line, of some eighty black letters."

Though uniform, each book is different as it contains just one part of all the possible combinations of the letters of the alphabet, the period, the comma, and the space. The Library is total; it contains everything that is possible to express in writing:

> "the minute history of the future, the autobiographies of the archangels, the faithful catalogue of the Library, thousands and thousands of false catalogues, a demonstration of the fallacy of these catalogues, a demonstration of the fallacy of the true catalogue, the Gnostic gospel of Basilides, the commentary on this gospel, the commentary on the commentary of this gospel, the veridical account of your death, a version of each book in all languages, the interpolations of every book in all books."

To which we might add all the masterpieces of literature as well as every third-rate novel ever published. Borges' vision begins to resemble the Strand Bookstore in New York where millions of unsellable second-hand books occupy several miles of shelf space. Borges, however, is less interested in the mundane status of books than in their ontological and metaphorical aspects. The Library he postulates represents the absolute sum of knowledge, including both fact and fiction, truth as well as falsehood, and as such it is beyond human comprehension. Realising this, many of the inhabitants of Borges' Library are driven insane; others persist in searching for the total book which would be the cipher and compendium of all the rest.

Religious mystics have long maintained that their scriptures—the Bible, the Koran, etc.—embody the Book of Books, whose secrets it is their duty to unravel. In Jewish tradition, for example, "the whole Torah is nothing but the great name of God"; exegesis is therefore equivalent to the direct experience of God. The earliest books were codifications of religion, and there soon developed what Jacques Derrida calls "the encyclopaedic protection of theology". The logo centricism of these authorless (or divinely-authored, which amounts to the same thing) books represents a defence against the "aphoristic energy" of writing, which continually threatens to disrupt the "natural totality" of the signifier, to which the idea of the book always refers. Mallarmé, too, saw the book as the "total expansion of the letter", whose usage is "capable of infinity almost to the point of sanctifying a language". Indeed, if we calculate the number of possible combinations of the twenty-six letters of the alphabet, we arrive at a finite figure* although when we include the possibility of letters repeating, and of books containing 410 pages, then we might as well attempt to count the proverbial grains of sand on a beach.

Texts, and sometimes whole books, consisting of all the permutations of a single word or line of words exist from as way back as the thirteenth century. Barnard Bauhus's *Unius Versi Librum*, published in Antwerp in 1617, consisted of page after page of permutations of Latin sentences, as though desperately searching for a mystic meaning in the face of the obdurate obstinacy of words. The Jewish mystic Abraham Abulafia used the Permutations of the four-letter name of Jehovah (YHVH) as a means of meditation, not unlike the Buddhist mantra. The writing and speaking of all the possible variations of the Name of God indicates an absolute identification with the signifier in order to attain the ineffable. Borges, in *The Library of Babel*, mentions "a blasphemous sect" who spent their time shuffling letters "until they succeeded in composing, by means of an improbable stroke of luck, the canonical books". The idea is similar to that of the hypothetical room of monkeys with typewriters, who, if given enough time, could eventually manage to write the works of Shakespeare. With the processing power of computers, such experiments become more feasible. Simon Biggs' *Book of Books 1* uses a computer programme to generate random words and insert them into a never expanding text, which becomes progressively smaller and smaller until it is finally (after a considerable period of time) reduced to a one pixel font size,

---

* According to Massin (*Letter and Image*, London, 1970) the number of possible combinations of the twenty-six letters of the alphabet is 620,448,401,733,239,439,360,000. However, after painstaking calculation my own estimate comes to 403,291,461,126, 605,635,584,000,000.

"at which point it resembles our new universal language, binary code". Designed for display on the World Wide Web [www.littlepig.org.uk], the piece is directly inspired by Borges' story as well as by the original Biblical story of Babel where the unity of man's language has been destroyed and divided in to innumerable other languages.

Another operation is to take all the words from an existing book and rearrange them, which is what Karen Reimer (writing as Eve Rhymer) has done in her book *Legendary, Lexical, Loquacious Love* published by Sara Ranchouse Publishing, Chicago, in 1996. Chapter One begins with "A" and Chapter Twenty Four, the last one, ends with "Y-y-you're". In between, all the words of an existing pulp romance novel have been arranged alphabetically (presumably using computer technology), thus providing the reader with a lexical rather than a literary experience. Interestingly, the word 'sex' only appears three times.

A far more ambitious attempt to embrace the totality of language is *The Complete Dictionary* by Tine Melzer, realised in printed and digital versions in 2003. Twenty-six volumes from A to Z, each containing 1,600 pages, list fifty million words. Two restrictions apply to the project: only words from one to six letters are generated, and all words have to be pronounceable. Strictly speaking, this is a lexicon (from the Greek *lexikos*=word) rather than a dictionary, since no meanings of the words are given. To whom do these words belong, then? To language itself, perhaps, and to its infinite possibilities. As the inventor of cut-ups, Brion Gysin, observed, "Writers don't own their words". Gysin and William Burroughs' experiments in the 1960s with cut-up and permutational methods achieved startling poetic juxtapositions, showing that chance operations can at least be serendipitous if not definitive or *authoritative*.

Colin Sackett has produced a number of small books in which letters and words are extracted from various sources including maps and radio transcripts and then subjected to repetitions, elisions and permutations, so as to provide new meanings through a combination of verbal play and typographic design. Sackett himself describes this as "the processes of 'making' words *appear*". *Theenglshalphabet*, published in 2002, consists of twenty-six pages, each featuring a running-on eleven by eleven block of letters making up real or abbreviated words such as KEYBDS or YETTY. UPTURN becomes NUPTUR, as sequences turn into involuntary permutations.

Emmett Williams shuffled the letters of a single word to produce 140 pages of a book titled *sweethearts* (Something Else Press, New York 1967). Here the visual permutations result in an extraordinary wealth of meaning: "all the free variations, and the pure concrete sequences, and the narrative, and the lyricism, the animated sexual metaphors, the erotic flights of fancy" (Emmett Williams, interview in *West Coast Poetry Review*, Reno 1977). The title in fact contains the whole book, which almost amounts to a reversal of the Jewish belief mentioned above.

Perhaps the one true book in Borges' Library is the blank book, the one composed purely by chance of nothing but spaces, but we won't venture into this at the moment as it's the subject of a much longer essay which has now been published concurrently with the one you are reading (*All or nothing*, Cromford: RGAP, 2005). [see p.76] In the absence of any other 'true' book that would definitively explain the existence of the Library, and that would demonstratively not be an imperfect facsimile, or in any way false, we must turn, like the father of Borges' narrator, to those books which exhibit a system, if not a meaning, like the book that was "composed of the letters MCV perversely repeated from the first line to the last". A book remarkably similar to this is José Luis Castillejo's *The Book of 18 Letters* (first published in Madrid in 1972 with the Spanish title *El Libro de las Dieciocho Letras*). Each one of the book's 360 pages contains fifteen unbroken lines of two printed letters which change every three pages, with one of the pair being retained in the subsequent set. Castillejo is a diplomat by profession, having been stationed in Germany for a number of years, but since the mid-sixties he has also been a member of the Zaj group, which was founded around 1964 in Madrid by the musicians and composers Juan Hidalgo and Walter Marchetti. The spirit of Zaj is closely akin to that of Fluxus, as the texts and manifestos printed in *A Zaj Sampler* (Something Else Press 1967) make clear. In his introduction to this little pamphlet Castillejo refers to the "allusionless" quality of Zaj works which are "devoid of all symbolism and connotation. They are not dangerous nor do they have any hidden meanings". This statement should deter any cryptographers among the inhabitants of Borges' Library who might be tempted to decipher the lines of *The Book of 18 Letters* as a binary code, although, of course, it is conceivable that a hidden message, provided by God, could lie in the book, unbeknownst to the writer. In another contribution to the *Zaj Sampler* Castillejo gives an example of *closed writing*: a self-generating text which exemplifies the idea that "writing consists of putting letters on a piece of paper, and hoping to have someone read them". This definition recalls Maurice Denis' famous dictum that "a picture—before being a war horse, a nude woman, or some anecdote—is essentially a plane surface coloured with colours arranged in a certain order". Ironically, Denis was one of the founders of the Symbolist style in painting. Castillejo promises his readers nothing—no allusions, no symbolisms. He thanks them for their perseverance, but he himself is just interested in continuing his task: the cultivation of his *black and white garden*. If *The Book of 18 Letters* offers at least some variety of black and white species, Castillejo's second book *The Book of the i's* (Bonn 1969) is more like a row of identical shoots. Each page contains a large letter 'i' placed in the centre, and each page is the same. In its capital form the letter 'i' denotes ego, the personality of the writer or narrator. True to his allusion-less principle Castillejo has produced the absolutely impersonal book, as stark and implacable as his listing of the years of a man's life as his life history in a short text titled 'Don Federico'.

Outwardly, Castillejo's books are quite ordinary-looking while their contents are utterly divorced from the normal experience of reading. Guy de Cointet, whose books also clearly belong to the Library of Babel, stays closer to the customary characteristics of the book, with discernable chapters, paragraphs, sentences and words, although what is written is as 'unreadable' as an unknown language. One of his books bears the title *Espahor ledet ko uluner!*, and the author's name seems to be Qui No Mysxdod. Nowhere is the real author's name given, but if *d*=t, and *o*=e, then we are possibly dealing with a book composed entirely in code. If we could manage to decipher it we would find out who *Gizellal* and *Gha* are, as these appear to be the coded names of the main characters of the tale, and what happens to them. It might even turn out to be a well-written story. As Jean Cocteau once remarked, "The greatest literary masterpiece is no more than an alphabet in disorder". De Cointet's fictive language is also to be seen in another book, *A Few Drawings*, which at least bears the author's name as well as its date of publication (1975). Here, instead of a developing narrative, each page is a discrete piece (as in a 'normal' book of drawings) composed of letters and numerals, superficially resembling concrete poetry, but offering no meaning beyond an apparently arbitrary arrangement of elements.

DeCointet's books may be highly ordered, but it is a hidden or disguised order, while for Gerald Ferguson language already possesses its own formal structure which he highlights in his book *The Standard Corpus of Present Day English Language Usage Arranged by Word Length and Alphabetized Within Word Length*, which was typed, stencilled and published by Ferguson in 1970 at the Nova Scotia College of Art & Design. A second edition, offset-printed, was published by the College in 1978. The book begins with Length 1 (the letters A–Z and the numerals 1–10, arranged in a single column) and ends with Length 20 (the last two words are: *TWENTY-FIRST-CENTURY* and *TWENTY-FIVE-YEAR-OLD*); fourteen pages are devoted to Length 7, ten pages to Length 11, and so on. The book contains a total of 50,000 words. I could well have done with a copy of the book during my school days when I once had to write out, as a punishment, 1000 nine-letter words! Ferguson's work belongs within the aesthetic framework of Conceptual Art, which also produced around that period such other deadpan publications as N.E. Thing Co's *A Portfolio of Piles* (1968), consisting of piles of chains, logs, barrels, etc., photographed in situ, and Ed Ruscha's photo-book *Every Building on the Sunset Strip* (1966). The desire for an all-inclusive representation of phenomena can also be seen in Douglas Huebler's *Variable Piece #70 (In Process) Global* (1971) which was a proposal to photographically document the existence of everyone alive, or Robert Barry's equally conceptual piece, *All the things I know but of which I am not at the moment thinking—1.36pm, 15 June 1969.* Compared to these pithy ideas, Ferguson's opus represents a maximum of effort and dedication, and is closer in spirit to a work such as Hanne Darboven's *One Century in One Year* which consists of 365 volumes of 100 hand-written pages each. In methodically inscribing every day's date Darboven is primarily concerned with the physical experience of the time span spent in both the writing and the reading of her work. The material she chooses to structure, time, is very much like Ferguson's use of language, in that both are 'given' and virtually limitless.

Numerals, letters, and punctuation marks are all linguistic signs, elements which are semantic as well as graphic. Together they comprise, pull together, the text, although punctuation more often serves as interruption: break, period, dislocation (in the case of quotation marks and parentheses), emphasis, or interrogation. Punctuation is a limited form of speech notation, but perhaps more importantly for the structure of text, it is also a reminder of the difference between writing and speech. Quotation marks, in particular, introduce us to this difference, to this 'other' voice embedded in the text belonging to the writer. We make a pause before quotation marks as though to concede the other's voice, acknowledging the privilege of precedence. To what 'other', then, are we being introduced in the title of Jaroslaw Kozlowski's book "*Reality*" (Poznan, 1972). Is it the concept we know by the word 'reality', i.e. reality; or our memory of that concept; the dictionary definition of the word; or the idea of using it as a title? And who is the real author: "Jaroslaw" "Kozlowski" (as the cover states), or Jaroslaw Kozlowski, or "Immanuel" "Kant" [author of] *"Kritik" "der" "reinen" "Vernunft"*, this being the inscription contained on the book's inside back cover. The actual text (presumably Kant's) is absent—all that's left on the book's twenty-four pages are its traces: arrays of punctuation marks, mostly periods and commas, but also others that Borges neglects to include: the hyphen, the stroke, the bracket, the colon, the semi-colon, and quotation marks. We perceive an echo of a voice within these constellations, something musical, wordless, a stuttering broken tempo of measures without harmony. Everything is distanced, perhaps alienated, from this text: Kant, Kozlowski, and language itself. Kozlowski continues this strategy of atomising linguistic structure in order to disclose its properties in another book titled *Lesson* (Beau Geste Press, Cranleigh 1975). Taking as his base text a beginner's English language lesson— "This is a man. He is John Brown; he is Mr Brown. He is in his sitting room.", etc.—Kozlowski has photographed each situation described in the sentences (thereby providing visual, phenomological evidence of the event), while re-structuring the sentences into their logical components: single letters, words without spaces, letters joined with hyphens, words in quotation marks, the whole sentence in quotation marks, and the sentence as it stands. Each version makes linguistic sense. Finally, on every page, there is an exercise: to say the sentence phonetically, and *to think:...* implying that beside the voices of the writer, and of the language, there is the third voice of the reader to consider. In *22 Questions* appended to the *Lesson*, Kozlowski interrogates text, reality, drawing, photography, speech, and thought, asking for example, "what is a text in the presence of reality? / what is reality in the presence of a text?", which only begs further questions: are these concepts in(ter) determinate? Is the one justified, or mediated, by the other? And what about the reality of the text in *"Reality"* which is simultaneously presence and absence?

For Dieter Roth, language is unquestionably a matter of presence. In the second half of the twentieth century he produced a phenomenal number of idiosyncratic books, enough to fill almost a whole hexagram of the Library on his own. Most of his books, from the earliest handmade editions which he simply titled *Book V*, *Book 21*, etc. to the endless series of collected works published by Hansjörg Mayer in Stuttgart, not to mention in numerable photocopied editions, are instalments of Roth's constant outpourings of drawings and writings. In addition there are several volumes of his *Collected Shit*, published under the imprint of the anonymous-sounding 'Verlag' (Edition), which exemplify Roth's complete disregard for any distinction between verbal and visual material. "The word is just a cheap image", he has commented, while Emmett Williams affirms that "Roth's quest for objectivity... is so compulsive that he has never written about anything since his coming of age as an artist". His aim is just to produce more books, with the emphasis on quantity rather than quality. Taking literally and to extremes the dictionary definition of a book—"a portable written or printed treatise filling a number of sheets fastened together"—Roth has been busy filling pages of books (or at least instructing a printer to do so) with repetitions of a single sentence, a single word, or single letters. These are his 'essays' of which six volumes have appeared so far. The first, *112 Problems of Our Time* (Verlag, Reykjavik 1971) stretches an essay of sixty words and punctuation marks over sixty pages. The second, an essay on Franz Eggenschwiler, dispenses with words altogether, the text being represented by scribbled lines. The most bulky of the essays bears the equally cumbersome and tongue-in cheek title ON THE RELATION OF THE GENERAL TO ORDER A SPECIAL OR THE GENERAL ORDERING A SPECIAL I.E. THE SPECIAL ORDERING A GENERAL (Verlag, Reykjavik, 1972). Each of the book's 474 pages contains only one letter, space or punctuation mark from a 76-word text which states "that which is here should want to express something neither better nor different as that which has already been said or written on the theme dealt with or not dealt with here". (my translation). On a visual level this book is similar to Castillejo's *Book of 18 Letters*, but whereas the latter is primarily concerned with structure and appearance, Roth's book does have an extricable message, even if the result is virtually meaningless. One is reminded of Kant's definition of art: "purposiveness without purpose", or, as Dieter Roth observes, "There are two sides to nonsense: sense and nonsense". Besides the large body of stretched text, ON THE RELATION OF THE GENERAL... also contains long prefaces and after words written by Roth in what seems to be an opaque mixture of ungrammatical, mis-spelt German peppered with Icelandic. As though to further frustrate the perplexed reader, the texts refer for 'explanation' to each other! In his obsessive objectivity (or is it an uncompromising subjectivity?), his not caring a damn for what words mean, Roth has completely internalised language, thoroughly digested it until it becomes a formless pulp, and then passed it out again as waste product.

Frank Kuenstler worked for twelve years (1952–64) on his book *Lens* (published by Film Culture, New York, 1964), filling page after page with words, letters and full-stops, without any regard for syntax or sense. Two lines taken at random read:

"secretary. Aryan. mesa, Smith. yes. Titty. himmler. Amaya. carne. Avril. crone.
State. reap. Lied. book. Aaron. villon. I. ggg. Artifact. demise. Lermontov"

Every one of the book's eighty pages is densely packed, alleviated only by divisions of three or four paragraph spaces. Like a dictionary in disorder, or a crossword-puzzle, the words assail the reader with the force of hard objects. Frank Kuenstlers's background as a film maker is evident in the title: the lens is all-embracing, registering everything. The world becomes the word which becomes the book, in which, to paraphrase Mallarmé, everything ends up that is in the world: "the art-life theme, Culture, Music, poetry & prose, Marxism, the Movies, epistomology, History, psycho-analysis, the Enlightenment, et al". It is a cornucopia of language, a monumental word hoard, offering as much pleasureable delving in to as *Finnegans Wake*. Like Joyce, Kuenstler is fond of puns (in the lines quoted above, for example, we have "yes. Titty" for 'yesterday', and "demise. Lermontov", Denise Levertov being a well-known American poetess and Lemontov a deceased Russian writer), though the reader of Kuenstler's book is more likely to make his/her innocent connections and personal recognitions out of the chaos of words than to concentrate on mining the meanings intended by the determinate craft of an author like Joyce.

We have already seen how perseverance is needed to compose page after page of text to complete these volumes from the Library of Babel, and this applies also to Jeff Instone's work. In his book *Script 1976–1978*, published by Matt's Gallery, London, in 1980, every one of the book's ninety-seven pages contains columns of repetitions of single words, with different typefaces used for each word, and with a few words lined up in another typeface separating each set of columns. All the words seem to have been chosen arbitrarily, although usually the separating words will contain a word from one of the adjacent columns. Instone did not type out the text for the book himself (someone else is credited with that task), but he has made drawings by handwriting the words on to huge sheets of paper, writing over and over until the paper is a blackened fragile tissue. The example reproduced in the centrefold of the book measures five feet by twenty-one feet, and contains 69,000 words. The paper is ripped in places by the sharpness of the pencil, and there is the visible outline of a brick wall which was used to support the paper. Instone's dedication, as well as his concern for the resultant surface effect, is reminiscent of the Polish artist Roman Opalka who has for several decades been carrying out the awesome task of painting numerals from one to infinity onto large canvasses. As he progresses slowly from canvas to canvas he lightens the tone of his paint, so that the series, if it is ever finished (and Opalka has declared that he will continue as long as he is able to hold a brush), will show visually the passage of time, which is also the measure of the artist's life.

Borges relates the difference between handwriting and printing to the distance between the human and the divine, comparing the "rude tremulous symbols" scribbled by his "fallible" hand with the letters contained in a book, "exact, delicate, intensely black, inimitably symmetric". Somewhat more melodramatically, Mallarmé regarded the letters on a page as "the shadow scattered in black characters" which becomes spread out "like a wreckage of mystery" when the page is opened. He complained, too, about the "incessant successive coming and going" involved in reading lines of text from left to right and back again. Mallarmé's solution was to vary the typography and the positions of words, and to exploit the white space of the page as an active element of composition. The result was *Un Coup des Dés*, in which the words are dotted like constellations over the infinite surface of double pages. Mallarmé also dreamed of expanding the form of the book by creating a randomly determined sequence of printed material which would be narrated, sung, acted, or mimed before invited audiences. Unfortunately he never got beyond writing notes for the structure of this project, which he referred to as his "Great Work", probably aware that this term also has an alchemical connotation: from base linguistic material he would create a 'total book' which would express the sum of everything in the world.

In a footnote to *The Library of Babel* (and expounded more fully in another fable, *The Book of Sand*), Borges postulates a more metaphysical sort of 'total book': "a volume of ordinary format, printed in nine or ten type body, and consisting of an infinite number of infinitely thin pages". Such a book would be manifestly as impossible to read as all the books in the Library of Babel. One can, however, easily imagine a book whose every page is taken from another book: page one (and the verso, page two) from book A, pages three and four from book B, and so on. My book *Pages* (Kontexts Publications, Amsterdam, 1976) was assembled in this manner. After obtaining a supply of more than a hundred second-hand books, including volumes in French, Spanish, Dutch, English and German, I first removed all the covers and cut off the spines. The task of collating one hundred sequential leaves from different books, plus new title and colophon pages, was akin to playing a monstrous game of 'Patience'. Each one of the hundred resulting copies of Pages is unique. The reader progresses through a randomised world of literary fragments: a page from the Spanish novel *Rubén Dário*, followed by a page of philosophy in Dutch, and then a piece of the French *Conte de Fée de Banlieuell*. Typographies, margins, paper tone and quality, elements of the book which we normally take for granted and hardly notice, are now emphatic in their diversity. If *Pages* is a microcosm of books, then Dirk Larsen's *White Library* represents the macrocosm. Larsen's strategy involved negating the author(ity) of books, by removing the title pages from a large number of cheap paperbacks which were on their way to be pulped and already had their covers ripped off, and then rebinding them in white covers. All the books that pass through this treatment are thereby rendered anonymous: one doesn't know what one is going to read, whether it's a crime-thriller or a romance, whether its author is well-known or not. All that's left is the fiction: "Words, words, words", as Hamlet said.

Larsen's treatment also recalls the standardisation of bookbinding which used to be prevalent in the eighteenth and nineteenth centuries, when gentlemen could furnish their libraries with elegant rows of identically bound books, a practice which survives today only in the binding styles used for encyclopaedias and law books (both of which, it's worth noting, epitomise the authority and systematisation of the written word). This is in marked contrast to today's average private library which displays such a wide range of colours and sizes that one is tempted to suggest that one *can* indeed judge a book by looking at its cover. Despite these considerations, the book is essentially a uniform object, as fixed in its generic form as each individual grain of sand or atomic nucleus. All books are rectangular, have covers and title pages, and contain sequentially ordered (and usually numbered) pages which are printed with horizontal lines of letters and punctuation marks which combine to form words, sentences and paragraphs. Even the artists who contributed to the upsurge of 'artists' books' during the 1970s hardly succeeded in expanding these limits, except by substituting images for words, and very few of them responded to the challenge of redefining the essence and function of books, or of the act of reading, in order to investigate new possibilities. The authors of the volumes I have selected from the Library of Babel exaggerate the given nature of the book by pointing to the absurdity of trying to imprison language in a finite container.

The world to which their letters and words refer is not the one *out there*, which the reader is accustomed to perceive through the dissolving window of the page, but the world which *is* language, resting opaquely on the page. The world mediated by language is greater than that perceptible to man since it encompasses all that is imaginable by all men, as well as everything that, in Wittgenstein's words "is the case". Like the universe, it exceeds the power of human comprehension. Borges may be right when he suspects that "the human species is on the road to extinction, while the Library will last on forever: Illuminated, solitary, perfectly immovable, filled with precious volumes, useless, incorruptible, secret".

Bibliography

Bernard Bauhus *Unius Versi Librum*, 1617; Simon Biggs *Book of Books 1*, 2003; José Luis Castillego *The Book of 18 Letters*, 1972; Guy de Cointet *Espahor ledet ko uluner!*, n.d.; Gerald Ferguson *The Standard Corpus of Present Day English Language Usage Arranged by Word Length and Alphabetized Within Word Length*, 1970; Michael Gibbs *Pages*, 1976; Jeff Instone *Script 1976–1988*, 1980; Jaroslaw Kozłowki *"Reality"*, 1972; Frank Kuenstler *Lens*, 1964; Tine Melzer *The Complete Dictionary*, 2003; Karen Reimer *Legendary, Lexical, Loquacious Love*, 1996; Dieter Roth *ON THE RELATION OF THE GENERAL TO ORDER A SPECIAL OR THE GENERAL ORDERING A SPECIAL I.E. THE SPECIAL ORDERING A GENERAL*, 1972; Colin Sackett *Theenglshalphabet*, 2002; Emmet Williams *Sweethearts*, 1967.

SomeVolumesFromTheLibraryOfBabel was originally published in 1982 by Editions Ex Libris, Amsterdam. The text was typewritten entirely without word-spacing (apart from quotations and titles of works), as was the revised and expanded typeset version published by RGAP (Research Group for Artists Publications) Cromford, Derbys, 2005. This version of the latter has been typeset conventionally.

6

Documentary and its discontents

At the end of the nineteenth century the newly emerged technology of photographic documentation began to be applied to the exposure of social injustices, an area that previously had been represented only by illustrators and a few painters. The camera had already recorded the triumphs of industrialisation, the factories, bridges, railways, etc, as well as the members of the new entrepreneurial class who where responsible for them, but had ignored the other, less pleasant side of the story—slum housing conditions, child labour and the exploitation of ethnic minorities. The social reformist photography of Jacob Riis and Lewis Hine, who documented these abuses, depended on the eliciting of an emotional response, in a word, to function as propaganda, and as such it managed to notch up some notable successes, being instrumental in the passing of reformist legislation. The practice of 'concerned' photography continued through the thirties with the work of the Farm Security Administration in America, to Eugene Smith's exposé of chemical poisoning in the village of Minamata. Nowadays, however, despite such praiseworthy efforts as David Bailey's portrayal of Ethiopian famine victims, it is more likely to be a TV special which succeeds in alerting public attention to a particular social or humanitarian issue, thus rendering documentary photographers somewhat redundant, but at the same time more free to indulge in 'personal expression'. Of course, not all documentary photography is committed to social reform; many, if not most, photographers are less interested in changing society than in knowing it, to 'see' the world, as Henry R. Luce proposed, instead of questioning it. But knowledge is never innocent; there are always interests that are being served, whether public or private. Taking their cue from John Grierson's thirties definition of documentary (film), "the creative treatment of reality", documentary photographers aim at technical perfection and at achieving those 'decisive' moments that will grace their portfolios and possibly earn their work a place in the museums of photography. There are plenty of photographic theories to support whatever creative decisions they may make, and 'reality' will always supply them with more than enough subjects to deal with, but until recently there has been a marked lack of *documentary* theory. Grierson's bland definition may well have sufficed for the '30s when documentary film and photography enjoyed an unproblematical relationship with actuality, but in today's society, which is as much 'immaterial' as 'material', the issue of 'reality' has to be seen as much more complex. We have shifted from a society geared to *production*, which enabled objects and people to be represented as fully present material constituents of the 'real' world, to one oriented to consumption, involving the subjective, passive *reception* of a represented world. As one writer recently put it, "tourism has replaced imperialism". Photographs are now admired, no longer feared as they were when Lewis Hine was active.

The narrative

Consumption is measured by time. Thus the documentary photographer's desire to capture 'the times' by means of a telling, 'typical' image which ignores the *specific* in the hope of transcending it in the name of a timeless realism. The 'decisive moment' immobilises and annuals narrative discursive time altogether, in favour of an intuitive subjectivity linked by a meagre caption to a vague place and date. According to John Szarkowski, "photography has never been successful at narrative… (Photographs) give the sense of the scene, while withholding its narrative meaning".[1] But behind the photograph, if not in it, there always lies a text, or rather a multiplicity of texts: the story of why the photographer chooses to depict this or that scene, the meanings inherent in the image itself (which may or may not add up to the legendary 1000 words), and the conditions under which the photograph is later viewed. The main narrative thrust of documentary photography lies in its supposed realism, its adherence to the principle of 'photographic truth'. But this 'truth' is nothing more than a valorised presence, a privileged representation of what Michel Foucault calls a 'regime of truth', or what others would call 'ideology'. As John Tagg argues in his essay 'Power and Photography', "Truth itself is already power, bound to the political, economic and institutional régime which produces it. We must forget the claims of a discredited documentary tradition to fight 'for' 'truth' or 'in favour' of 'truth' and see that the battle is one that should be directed at the rules, operative in our society, according to which 'true' and 'false' representations are separated".[2]

We should not forget, however, that the photograph as 'true' document made its historical appearance during the days of the Paris Commune when the police forces took photographs in order to identify, and later convict, revolutionaries. The photographs taken by Riis and Hine were likewise presented as evidence designed, in Walter Benjamin's words, "to uncover guilt and name the guilty". Thus the reformist photographer and the police appear to share a common task: to 'identify' abuses and injustices in the name of the just and the true, to reveal that which is hidden, and to bring delinquent or 'marginal' cultures under the surveillance of the 'eye of power', whether that power be disciplinary or benevolently reformist. The practice and the apparatus of documentary photography are suffused with ideological rules and constraints. Photographers usually know what they want to depict before they find it, they have certain preconceptions and stylistic preferences of their own, and they may also have to take into account the views of those providing the assignment. Are these then the conditions for the production of 'truth'? And whose truth does it become?

'Personal vision'

Each year the Dutch History Department of the Rijksmuseum in Amsterdam commissions two documentary photographers to cover a particular social 'issue'. Subjects in previous years have included 'The Changing Church', 'Women in Action' and 'Other Cultures in Holland'. In 1983 the topic was 'Youth' and the assignment was awarded to the photographers Maya Pejić (aged forty-eight) and Han Singels (aged forty-one). The results of their work were recently exhibited at the Rijksmuseum and a selection published as a book.[3] From their pictures one could surmise that young people in Holland are living in society in a state of more or less happy equilibrium, with sufficient space for individuality and the freedom to enjoy their own life-style. We see punks looking after their babies like other normal parents, military conscripts uncomplainingly undergoing their first day of duty, holidaymakers having a good time, students decorously partying in evening wear, and so on. Even the couple captioned 'unemployed' are smiling, despite the fact that, as we are told elsewhere in the book, the economic position of Dutch youth has worsened considerably during the last five years. A working eighteen year-old today, for example, receives almost 30% less than he would have done in 1979. None of the realities of the current socio-economic situation, nor of the specific effects these have on young people, are evident in these photographs. Pejić and Singels have recorded nothing more than the superficial display of life-*styles*, those most visible aspects of contemporary youth cultures.

Questions of the accuracy of this documentary project are left by the staff of the Rijksmuseum to the judgement of *future* historians; what matters more for them in determining the value of these pictures is the 'personal vision' expressed by the photographer and the extent to which this ill-defined concept is able to lend a *zeggingskracht*, a power of saying, to the work. Having been removed from history, from specificity, and above all from any say in the discourse imposed upon them, the subjects of this project have been effectively silenced, trapped within the outworn practices of the accepted documentary apparatus. Documentary photographers are often drawn to subjects at the margins of society—gypsies, psychiatric patients, penitentiary pilgrims, immigrants, youth cults, etc.—because within the terms of the bourgeois hegemony (to which most photographers happen to belong) these groups represent 'difference' from the norm. They stick out, almost begging to be photographed. But just as the individual subject has become fragmented and diffused in modern society, so too have these 'others' begun to lose the significance of their difference. Sociology is no longer a favoured discipline, and there are signs of a growing disenchantment with traditional documentary photography. The social issues that interest people nowadays are precisely those that, so far at least, lie outside the acceptable reach of the photographer. Subjects such as incest, stress, adultery, hyperventilation, etc. A recent issue of the Dutch documentary photography magazine *Plaatwerk* offers us one photographer's solution to the problem: Johan Vigeveno hires models to act out the scenes he, or the magazine he works for, requires. The result, unfortunately, is much closer to advertising photography than to documentary.

New strategies

If the real cannot be represented except by illusion, and if the 'true' somehow always manages to escape us, what strategies are possible now for the 'concerned' photographer? Again it is John Tagg who has put forward radical proposals for re-vitalising the 'discredited' documentary tradition: "We must pinpoint those strategic kinds of intervention which can both open up different social arenas of action and stretch the institutional order of the (photographic) practice by deploying or developing new modes of production, distribution and circulation; by exploiting different formats; by evolving different formal solutions; by cutting different trajectories across the ruling codes of pictorial meaning; and by establishing different relationships both with those who are pictured and those who view the pictures".[4] These are heavy demands, and so far there seems to be little evidence that documentary photographers are heeding them, preferring instead to rely on traditional practices of representation and photographic discourse. Rarely do we see work that is both oppositional (in social terms) and innovative (in both theory and praxis). Some artists in the United States, Canada, and Britain, however, having observed the discrepancies and failures of modernism, in eluding the modernist appropriation and appraisal of photography, are turning to the disruptive strategies of 'postmodernism' in order to 're-invent' documentary. It is no accident that most of these artists are also acute theorists, but it would be misleading to suggest that their work therefore suffers from programmatisation. It should be seen rather as a continuation of the concerns with language and with the deployment of art within a social context that characterised the conceptualist movements beginning in the late sixties. Martha Rosler's *The Bowery in Two Inadequate Descriptive Systems*[5] takes as its subject those well-known and much-photographed bums and winos who inhabit the Bowery district of New York. Not one of them is to be seen in Rosler's photographs however; what we are shown instead are dilapidated shopfronts and littered sidewalks, with only the occasional trace of the bums existence visible in the form of a discarded bottle. Rosler is clearly intimating that photography is an inadequate system for describing the Bowery. Traditional exposés of social misery use a combination of photography and text, the latter most often in the form of a survey or report. But is this language any more adequate as a descriptive system as long as it remains the language, as well as the system of its dissemination, identified with capitalism's hegemony over its unfortunate 'victims'? Relinquishing the imposition of both a photographic language and a descriptive language, Rosler alternates her photographs with pages of words: a lexicon of words used to describe the state of being drunk, a "poetics of drunkenness". The richness of this language, its playful imagery and metaphors, celebrates the drunks on and in, their own terms, instead of consigning them to the analytical prose of a sociological report or the charitable tones of liberal humanism. Martha Rosler is not offering any panaceas; she is not out to reform, but to challenge preconceptions by dislocating the rules of representation.

Photography against the grain

This is also the aim of Allan Sekula who, like Martha Rosler, is well aware of the need for a photographer and artist (or any other type of worker, for that matter) to be critical-minded, both towards his own practice and towards the society in which he lives. Sekula is one of the very few artists at work in the United States with avowed socialist aims, and whose photographic 'interventions' go a long way towards fulfilling the demands of John Tagg quoted earlier. The Nova Scotia College of Art and Design recently published a collection of Sekula's essays and photoworks, *Photography against the Grain*. As the title suggests, Sekula's work runs counter to prevailing notions of photographic theory and practice, particularly to "the formalist closure inherent in the American modernist project" which rests on the aesthetic autonomy of the work of art and its privileged author(ity), at the expense of an awareness of its role with him social practice and social history. Sekula's work is, if you will excuse the pun, adamantly *secular*, that is, "concerned with the affairs of this world", as opposed to spiritual. One of the essays included in the book is the by now almost classic and much-reprinted 'On the Invention of Photographic Meaning' which deals with the complex issue of photographic 'discourse': the extent to which meaning is dependent on, and constrained by, the institutional context within which it is communicated. Contrasting two 'historical' photographs of the same subject—immigrants arriving by ship in New York at the beginning of the century—one by Lewis Hine and one by Alfred Stieglitz, Sekula effectively demolishes the aesthetic, symbolist pretensions of the latter and argues in favour of the 'realist', committed approach of Hine. The difference is represented by the contexts in which the images originally appeared: Stieglitz's in the luxurious pages of his own magazine *Camera Work*, Hine's in the reformist journal *Charities and Commons*. Sekula's own photoworks are often designed to be exhibited in universities, colleges and local libraries, as close as possible to the sites in which they intervene, rather than in art galleries or museums. In his essay 'The Traffic in Photographs', he attacks the isolation and reification of photographs by the museological establishment. In exhibitions such as *The Family of Man* photographs are divorced from specific social realities and subjected to a 'universalising' humanist ideology which, in the context of the times (the mid-1950s, for example), is not without political implications. The organiser of that exhibition, Edward Steichen, is also the subject of another of Sekula's essays, 'Steichen at War' which looks into the question of Steichen's aerial reconnaissance photographs taken during the First World War. Sekula points out the discrepancy between the myth of Steichen the great artist and the realities of his career. Allan Sekula's ideas can perhaps be summed up in his statement that "photography is not an independent or autonomous language system, but depends on larger discursive conditions, invariably including those established by the system of verbal-written language. Photographic meaning is always a hybrid construction, the outcome of an interplay of iconic, graphic, and narrative conventions".[6] Hybridisation is certainly characteristic of Sekula's own photoworks, with their commingling of images, narrative texts, and extensive commentaries. *Aerospace Folktales* (1973) deals with his own family background, documenting the results of his father being made redundant at the Lockheed military/industrial factory. In the original presentation 142 photographs and titles were exhibited, together with a spoken sound track (by the artist's mother and father) and an extensive written commentary by the artist. We see images of the factory (reminding one of Brecht's famous comment that a photograph of the Krupp works reveals nothing of what it means), the family, their house (leased from Lockheed), the books on the effects of atomic war his father once used to study, and we read the personal reactions of the mother and the father to unemployment and to the wider social and political situation, as well as the son/artist's comments on the making of the work. The lack of privilege accorded to these different discourse provides a non-ideological, more 'natural' (one is tempted to say 'real') representation of a particular social problem; a documentary in which the subjects are not silenced. A similar practice informs *This Ain't China: A Photonovel* (1974) which confronts another 'local' situation: relations between employer and employees at a fast-food restaurant. The work consists of posed photographs of the workers, their environment and their product, together with narratives written by the artist from the differing viewpoints of the protagonists. Sekula describes it as "a comedy about theatricalised food", a parody of a social-realist novel.

School is a Factory (1980) is much more didactic in scope as Sekula turns to investigating the educational establishment, in which he himself was working at that time as a teacher of photography in a junior college, where training is mostly for the manual and clerical trades. Extensive captions to posed photographs of students outline the bitter realities of their future employment prospects, while an accompanying essay looks pessimistically at the burgeoning division between creative and corporate culture. In all his work Allan Sekula violates the conventional separation of tasks which demands that one is either a photographer or a writer, an artist or a critic. He combines all these functions to construct what he calls a "political geography" of the social systems of which he is much more than a detached observer. By confronting photography in terms of a materialist social history, Sekula and a few other like-minded artists such as Martha Rosler are opening up ways for documentary photography to be re-evaluated, re-invented, and re-invested with direct social relevance.

1 John Szarkowski, *The Photographer's Eye*, Museum of Modern Art, New York, 1966.

2 John Tagg, 'Power and Photography', in *Culture, Ideology and Social Process*, eds. Bennett, Martin, Mercer, Woollacott, London: Batsford, 1981. This essay originally appeared in *Screen Education* no.36, Autumn 1980.

3 De Jongeren, *Fragment Uitgeverij*, Amsterdam, 1985.

4 John Tagg, ibid.

5 Martha Rosler, *3 works*, Halifax: The Press of the Nova Scotia College of Art and Design, 1981.

6 Allan Sekula, *Photography Against the Grain*, Halifax: The Press of the Nova Scotia College of Art and Design, 1984.

This article originally appeared in *Perspektief*, 23, January 1986.

7

Graph of photography

In foregrounding photography's *graph*, its 'scriptural' aspect, as opposed to its relationship to *light*, my aim in this essay is to counteract the emphasis that is usually placed upon photography as an unmediated (or rather, *im*mediate) representation of 'reality'. As with parallel developments in painting and literature, photography did not so much introduce 'new ways of seeing' as institute new ways of *describing*. It is photography's discursive possibilities, rather than its putative 'transparency', that has prompted me to re-examine its history and to discuss the work of a number of artists for whom the photographic image functions as an element of discourse linked not to vision, but to language.

'Photography' literally means 'drawing with light': the light reflected onto objects from the sun (or some other source) is directed through a lens and inscribed, imprinted, onto chemically sensitised plate or film. Before the invention of photography artists had employed the camera obscura as an aid to drawing, but the apparatus was unable to produce a permanent record of the image it produced; the artist's hand was still required to delineate the projected traces of the object. William Henry Fox Talbot, the inventor of the negative-positive process of producing photographic images, referred to the new medium as the 'pencil of nature', predicting that it would enable people who had never made a pencil-sketch in their lives to produce "drawings" that would rival and even excel the "truth and fidelity" achieved by artists of reputation. Talbot not only regarded photography as an adjunct, or possibly an alternative, to drawing, but also recognised its value as a scriptural instrument. Besides being a pioneering scientist, Talbot was a renowned etymologist who saw language as a key to the truth concerning the past. Etymology, he wrote, "is the lamp by which much that is obscure in the primitive history of the world will one day be cleared up".[1] Just as words retain traces of the development of history, so too does the photographic image, and it was a common regret in the nineteenth century that photography had not existed in earlier periods so that we might have had photographs, instead of imprecise and unreliable written descriptions, of historical personages such as Caesar or Christ.

Talbot very early applied his photography to making copies of ancient hieroglyphic inscriptions, thus being one of the first to fulfil the task that Arago described in his famous Report in 1839 to the French Chamber of Deputies on Daguerre's new invention. Arago spoke of the advantages that could have been derived from photography had it existed at the time of the 1798 expedition to Egypt: "To copy the millions of hieroglyphics which cover even the exterior of the great monuments of Thebes, Memphis, Karnak and others would require decades of time and legions of draughtemen. By daguerreotype one person would suffice to accomplish this immense work successfully".[2] Even Baudelaire, in his condemnation of the art of photography, acknowledged that it had value as a means of keeping records: "Let it save crumbling ruins from oblivion, books, engravings, and manuscripts, the prey of time, all those precious things, vowed to dissolution, which crave a place in the archives of our memories".[3] Already, it seems, this 'pencil of nature' was to be used for clerical, archival purposes, for writing the 'already written'. In 1843 Talbot patented a phototypesetting process (involving the photographing of lines of moveable letters). The following year he published the first photographically illustrated book, and it was not long before he invented photogravure as well, which enabled photographs to be reproduced in printed form.

The daguerreotype was a unique object and could not be copied or reproduced, whereas Talbot's negative process allowed any number of prints to be made. This difference underlies the two senses in which we can understand the 'graph' of photography: it can be seen as an originary trace, a chemical and physical process which, in the words of Daguerre, gives Nature "the power to reproduce herself"; or it is already a replication, not of Nature herself, but of an inscription, a representation, a writing. Daguerre's notion of photography as partaking of the ineffable truth of Nature, however, survived as the dominant theoretical underpinning of photography until well into the twentieth century. There is more than a hint of nineteenth century positivism in Andre Bazin's defence of the objectivity and truth-to-nature of photography in his article 'The Ontology of the Photographic Image': "Only the impassive lens, stripping the object of all those ways of seeing it, those piled up preconceptions, that spiritual dust and grime with which my eyes have covered it, is able to present it in all its virginal purity to my attention and consequently to my love. By the power of photography, the natural image of a world that we neither know nor can know, nature at last does more than imitate art: she imitates the artist... The photograph as such and the object in itself share a common being, after the fashion of a fingerprint".[4]

The persistence of this belief in the 'self-evident', 'objective' nature of photography was to have profound implications for the notion of history. Photography was henceforth to be employed for the purpose of indisputably recording the ephemeral, "the transient, the fleeting, the contingent" which Baudelaire saw emerging with modernity. The world was increasingly perceived in terms of the visual, rather than the written. By the mid-twentieth century, with the rise of picture magazines, movies and television, it seemed that the very existence of the word was being threatened, as Berenice Abbott observed in 1951. Walter Benjamin had foreseen this twenty years earlier, when, in his *A Short History of Photography*, he quoted Brecht's comment that "less than ever does the mere reflexion of reality reveal anything about reality. A photograph of the Krupp works or the A.E.G. tells us next to nothing about these institutions".[5] Benjamin acknowledged the essential importance of the caption as a key to reading and understanding photographs, but failed to appreciate fully the discursive and linguistic aspects of the photographic image itself. Photographs are not to be 'read' merely on the basis of a recognition of the visual facts that are presented in them, in correlation with an identifying caption, for any photograph is already a *re*presentation of several layers of meaning, many of which are contingent or hidden. A photograph may be said to contain a polysemous 'floating chain' of signifiers, a hidden agenda of cultural and semiotic texts and linguistic propositions. In this sense, a photograph does indeed reveal something about reality, and this is always *more than* what is purportedly revealed at first glance.

Roland Barthes has pointed to the general resistance that most people feel towards the linguistic nature of the image. This is, he says, "in the name of a certain mythical idea of Life: the image is re-presentation, which is to say ultimately resurrection, and, as we know, the intelligible is reputed antipathetic to lived experience".[6] Barthes may well be referring to *Life* magazine here, a prime example of the unquestioned acceptance of photography's truth to nature. The 'photo essay' developed during the thirties and forties by magazines such as *Life* attempted to organise photographs according to narrative principles, in conjunction with extended captions or journalistic accounts, but in most cases the photographs in fact served little more than as illustrations. Moreover, photographers often found that their message did not always 'read' fluently. Strongly visual photographs tended to interrupt the narrative flow, while a strong narrative was often accompanied by visually weak photographs. By the time of the widely shown exhibition *The Family of Man* in the fifties, the concept of 'lived experience' mythicised through photographs was firmly established within the ideological framework of an all-encompassing, uncritical humanism. The exhibition glorified a 'timeless' and decidedly non political view of mankind, and hence dispensed with identifying captions almost entirely.

As Barthes observes, it is only on the purely denotative level that a photograph is truly a "message without a code", when its reality merely consists of an illusionless "having-been-there". A photograph is simply an image chemically inscribed onto a sheet of paper, bearing gradations of light and dark, which, so long as we know how to perceive a photograph (as opposed to 'reading' it), we recognise to be an image of some person or thing. Someone who has never seen a photograph before might well have difficulty recognising anything on it. The early photographers were charmed by this seemingly magical "real unreality", this absent presence, but this was before the science of language (semiotics) taught us that images are "penetrated through and through by the system of meaning, in exactly the same way as man is articulated to the very depths of his being in distinct languages".[7] Language in this sense is the "totalising abstraction" of the messages emitted and received, and these messages operate according to signifying operations that are frequently ideological in their rhetorical effect. It was this ideological and rhetorical nature of the messages inscribed within images (at a connotative level) that Barthes analysed in his important essay 'Rhetoric of the Image' from 1964. Taking an advertisement photograph as the object of his study, Barthes analysed the various rhetorical codes operating at the level of connotation, showing how even an apparently innocuous image is subject to a complex "intertextuality" of hidden messages. One could add to these the context in which the image is grounded (its appearance in a certain magazine or newspaper), the conditions under which it is perceived (whether its viewer merely glances at it, studies it analytically, or absorbs its message uncritically), as well as other signifying codes dependent on cultural or historical givens. The ostensibly smooth and transparent surface of the photographic image is thus irredeemably marked by the fracture of rhetoric, and so the notion that a photographic image bears some originary, virginal relation to the real world is difficult to maintain. It is rather a *product* of human labour, a cultural object suffused with historical meanings. Photographs, whether used for the purposes of advertising, information or art, are written, are read, are translated. Their 'graph' is scriptural, a panoply of signs and meanings. Light is merely their medium, not their essence.

The phonocentricist argument (from Plato onwards) that privileges speech over writing has its parallel in the importance that is granted to the photographer's *vision* and the *visual* effects created in his photographs. Graininess, contrasts of light and dark, unusual compositions, distortions, etc. are expressive techniques inherent in the medium of photography itself which on a discursive level can be compared to speech acts or gestures. Photographs, like other forms of visual art, are held to 'speak'; what is 'spoken' seems transparently to reveal a guaranteed meaning and authenticity, an originary 'presence' devolving on the photograph's formal characteristics and/or the photographer's intentions. Yet the photograph, like any representational form, merely gives the *illusion* of a certainty of meaning. As Victor Burgin has observed, "In whatever form, meaning is only ever produced within a complex play of differential relationships in which the final *closure* of meaning upon a point of original certainty is endlessly deferred".[8] Jacques Derrida coined the term 'différance' in which are combined the concepts of difference (the fact that linguistic meaning depends on words being different from one another) and deferral (the endless postponement of meaning in any utterance). There can in fact be no originary, unitary presence in any system of representation, nor is there a privileged position from which an author (or a photographer) or a work can 'speak'. All there is is this "complex play of differential relationships".

Within systems of representation, meanings can be seen as 'traces', revealing not the *presence* of things, but their passage through thought. It is not so much that these are traces *of* things; it is not a question of deciphering, but of admitting the absence of the original. "The trace must be thought before the entity", writes Derrida.[9] The photographic 'trace' is the graph, a trail that leads not to a reality that can be captured, but simply something that "marks the passage" (Barthes' "that-has-been"). For Barthes, these traces, this spoor, can have the impact of a *spur*—that which pricks the viewer, bruises him, is poignant. In his book *Camera Lucida* Barthes attempts to analyse the phenomenology of the photograph in terms not of the object that is represented but of time. A photograph's power of representation is exceeded by its power of authentication, which is measured by the extent to which the image is redeemed. "What I see has been there, and yet immediately separated; it has been absolutely irrefutably present, and yet already deferred."[10] In Barthes' case, this separation (which is inextricably linked to his separation from his mother, whose photograph provides the leitmotiv for much of *Camera Lucida*) is linked to mourning and desire, as well as to the fact that a photograph is no more than "a certificate of presence". It is like a bank note (as Oliver Wendell Holmes observed in the nineteenth century) that simply guarantees a promise to pay the bearer. Lacking the immediacy of pure gold, the photograph is merely a token, whose authenticity we have to accept on trust.

The photograph thus 'mimes' immediacy, poses itself[11] as presence in a silent, arrested, impenetrable moment. Unlike the text, the photograph can have nothing added to it. This impenetrability and closure have been challenged by generations of artists seeking to make the photograph 'speak', but the language they want to hear is their own. Alfred Stieglitz photographed cloud formations, believing that he could make them speak an affective language 'equivalent' to his mental states. Many a photographer will say that his images offer an interpretation of reality in terms of its beauty, absurdity, structure, pathos or historical significance, yet without some form of non-visual (i.e. written) commentary, it is often difficult for uninformed viewers to see the point, to see beyond the very intractability of the image itself. A single picture always requires a context for it to become understandable, including not only the context pertaining to the circumstances in which it was taken, but also the conditions under which it is viewed. Thus, despite the fact that the photograph can have nothing added to it, it nevertheless suffers from an irremedial lack; lacking presence, it requires a supplement, another form of writing, another 'graph' inscribed onto the graph of its traces.

It took a long time before photographers began to recognise that there are discursive potentialities of the image that can be expressed and utilised as linguistic elements. The technique of photomontage, developed in Germany and Russia during the 1920s, played with the differential of meanings by subverting the conventional reading of an image, either by juxtaposing it with a discordant text (as in the work of John Heartfield) or by montaging disparate images together as 'floating signifiers'. The latter approach, as practised by Rodchenko and Moholy Nagy, sought to create a constructivist dynamism by organising the movements of objects to create a heterogeneity of new movements, in opposition to the static, harmonious order of composition with its illusion of hermetic unity. The aim, wrote Rodchenko, was "to show the world from all points of view and to teach the ability to see it from all sides".[12] Photomontage was clearly linked to the *word*: it was used to illustrate poetry books (Rodchenko's work in Mayakovsky's *About This*, 1923, being the best example), as book covers (Heartfield) and posters, as well as in what became known as 'factographic' literature on subjects such as Wood, Coal, Iron, etc. Moholy Nagy concentrated on exploring the graphic, formal possibilities of photomontage. In his work we see how the areas of white left between the individual photographic units mimic the formal conditions of signs, the necessity for an exteriority between them. In language this exteriority exists as syntax, which at once connects words and separates them—meaning is created through the syntactical condition of spacing. Cropping photographs is another form of spacing. Photography, in seeming to 'capture' the seamless simultaneity and pure presence of space itself, normally is far from creating this 'linguistic' effect of spacing. In Moholy Nagy's work both forms of spacing are used with found (printed) photographs combined with dynamic, purely graphic elements such as arcs and circles. In the storyboard for his planned, but never realised film 'Dynamic of the Metropolis' text and illustration are united in what he called the "typo-photo".[13] The script demonstrates Moholy Nagy's use of a visual language of association—jungle beasts such as the tiger and lion, for example, are used symbolically. Near the end there is the following sequence: "Stockyard animals / Oxen roaring / The machines of the refrigerating room / Lions / Sausage machine. Thousands of sausages / Head of a lion showing its teeth (close-up) / Theatre. Rigging-loft / The lion's head. TEMPO-o-O / Police with rubber truncheons in the Potsdamer Platz / The TRUNCHEON (CLOSE-UP) / The lion's head gets bigger and bigger until at last the vast jaws fill the screen". In granting equal importance to typography and photography Moholy Nagy emphasised the graphic possibilities of the two media in a highly original manner that has unfortunately been little explored by later generations of artists.

One of the few contemporary artists who appears to have picked up where Rodchenko, Heartfield and Moholy Nagy left off is Barbara Kruger. Kruger has been called a "guerilla semiologist"[14] for the way she juxtaposes 'figured' (stereotyped) images with 'figures of speech' as a means of revealing the cultural ideologies and forms of rhetoric hidden in photographs. Trained as a graphic artist, Kruger simultaneously exploits and subverts the conventions of commercial photography. Her works are instantly legible, yet the insistence of her texts forces the viewer to question and decode what is represented. A reproduced photograph showing a close-up of a mouth with a pair of dentist's tongs extracting a tooth bears the text "You are a captive audience". Such a direct address to the viewer (who is here positioned as both victim and voyeur) is unusual in photographic art. It is a style of address commonly found, however, in advertising. Kruger's interjection of the personal pronouns "I", "You" and "We" are intended not only to address the spectator, but to incorporate him (or her). The "We" in "We won't play nature to your culture", which is combined with a photograph showing a woman's face with leaves covering her eyes, is explicitly addressed to masculine viewers and their stereotyped image of woman as nature as opposed to the patriarchal construction of culture. Kruger reflects stereotypes back on themselves, a form of doubling that results in a disembodiment, producing a *figure* that is "not an empty signifier, but a perpetual ghost".[15] A sense of fracture and obfuscation informs many of Kruger's images, especially those featuring a woman's face, indicating an avowedly feminist approach to the question of identity, to the woman's lack of a self image. Likewise, the texts are fractured across the surface of the image, occasioning a reading that interferes with and is interfered by the image. As Kruger says, "We replicate certain words and pictures and watch them stray from or coincide with your notions of fact and fiction".[16]

Several other artists working with photography within the field that has become known as 'postmodernism' have adopted techniques and approaches similar to Kruger's: the appropriation of mass-media images, a critique of stereotypes, and the use of text as a means of opening discourse.

'Postmodernism' has become such an over-used (and abused) word in recent years that it is perhaps necessary here to discriminate between a reflexive form of postmodernism which merely replicates and simulates an already coded and contextualised 'hyperreality', and a more critical form of postmodernism that questions the systems and symptoms of representation, offering, among other things, a radical re-vision and re-writing of photography's discourse. One of the most influential artists working to advance the latter approach has been Victor Burgin, who has been concerned for many years with "the politics of representation", initially within a socio-critical framework and more lately in terms of representations of gender differences.

Burgin's photo-textual works employ an 'intertextuality' of quotations from Freud, advertising slogans, Marxist literature, film, painting and literature. The images he uses may be his own photographs of street scenes, constructed tableaux, or movie stills. The associations engendered by the images (frequently having to do with expressions of the male 'gaze') are linked to associations of the text, a process that Burgin has likened to poetry, "where meanings occur primarily along chains of associations".[17] More specifically, however, Burgin is interested in evoking a reading of his works that is akin to Freud's description of the 'dream-work', in which the 'primary processes' of the unconscious proceed along metaphorical and metonymical lines. This process is exemplified in Burgin's seven-part work *Gradiva*, which was inspired by Freud's analysis of Wilhelm Jensen's novella of the same title. The story is about a man who becomes obsessed by the image of a woman's gait as depicted in an ancient Pompeian relief. After years of searching he finally encounters a woman with exactly the same gait, and it turns out that she was his old childhood sweetheart; the two are reunited and live happily ever after. In Burgin's version, the story is told from the two different viewpoints of the man and the woman, one running from left to right across the photo series and the other from right to left. The text printed below each photograph is written in a style that Burgin calls 'lapidary', a highly condensed, succinct form adapted to the needs of inscriptions on monuments. Two of the photographs are similarly succinct: they depict a head of an anonymous man and an anonymous woman photographed from a cinema screen. As projected objects of the (cinematic) gaze, they represent ciphers standing for 'the man' and 'the woman'. Rather than using photographs to 'illustrate' his text, Burgin deliberately exploits the rhetorical potentialities of images themselves, using them almost as syntactical elements to build up complex, and condensed layers of meaning. He has emphasised that his work is "neither an *object* to be consumed as 'spectacle', nor an *opinion* to be consumed as 'expression'. The work is not to be *consumed* at all, it is to be *produced* in the active process of looking, reading, composing, interpreting".[18] The viewer/reader is required to *work* (even if, as Burgin claims, this need amount to no more than "to know how to dream"), to 'unpack' the condensations.

Burgin's photographic works are the result of, and the occasion for, a great deal of *reading*. We are not required to admire a supposedly unmediated 'reality' that the photographer has been fortunate to 'capture', nor need we seek to grasp the expression of a pure subjectivity. In this 'postmodern' photography it is not the author/photographer who speaks, but 'the other' that is spoken/is written. The work exists only in the moment of a discourse which is not unitary or ineffable, but disseminated and infinitely deferred.

Burgin and Kruger are not 'photographers' in the usual sense of the word; they employ their art (or rather, *deploy* it), but do not flaunt it. Roland Barthes spoke of "the death of the author"; likewise we can speak of the "death of the photographer": "We know now that a text is not a line of words releasing a single 'theological' meaning (the 'message' of the Author-God) but a multidimensional space in which a variety of writings, none of them original, blend and clash… the reader is the space on which all the quotations that make up a writing are inscribed without any of them being lost; a text's unity lies not in its origin but in its destination".[19]

Both Kruger and Burgin (and many other artists working within Postmodernism) use photography in the form of quotation, in other words as that which is *already read*. Contemporary culture has become a vast encyclopaedia from which the artist draws tissues of quotations, constructs allegories and re-presents representations. Photography has abandoned its excessive claim to 'original' speech, having recognised that, like language, it already contains all texts. We live in a world mediated by fictions, whose authority and authorial function have disintegrated into a welter of 'language games'.[20]

Photography, as a false copy of reality, is in a precarious, but privileged position to deconstruct the simulacrum in that its 'graph' is the very equivocation of language, the deferral/differing that holds reality, and us, at bay. In denying the empiricism of assertions about phenomena, photography is forced to recognise the eternal lack, of which it is itself a sign and a symptom. Perhaps Fox Talbot was right: photography is a pencil, but the traces it leaves are not just those of light. The language of photography has matured in the century and a half since its invention; it no longer even has to draw on itself in order to write itself, since we have learned that it is already written.

---

1 William Henry Fox Talbot, quoted in: Gail Buckland, *Fox Talbot and the Invention of Photography*, David R. Godine, Boston, 1980. p.16.

2 D. F. Arago, 'Report', in: *Classic Essays on Photography* (ed. Alan Trachtenberg), Leete's Island Books, New Haven, 1980. p.17.

3 Charles Baudelaire, 'The Modern Public and Photography', in *Classic Essays on Photography*. p.88.

4 André Bazin, 'The Ontology of the Photographic Image', in: *Classic Essays on Photography*, p.242. Bazin's view reveals a certain belief in the Platonic doctrine of two worlds: the murky world of shadows and illusions, of "spiritual dust and grime", which is the world we are condemned to live in, as opposed to the luminous and perfect 'upper world' of "virginal purity", where meaning is communicated instantaneously, without mediation. Victor Burgin has pointed out the connection between this latter concept of a pure *vision* standing *outside*

discourse and Diderot's use of the term 'hieroglyph' (which Barthes adopts in describing photography's 'pregnant moment', or 'punctum'). The 'figural' nature of the hieroglyph can perhaps be allied to nature's self-becoming, as Bazin understands it, but the "natural image" thus engendered, although potent, is not of the same incontestable order as a fingerprint. A hieroglyph is, after all, a sign something. In whose name, then, can nature be said to imitate the artist? See Victor Burgin, 'Diderot, Barthes, Hieroglyph', in *Talking Back to the Media*, Amsterdam, 1985.

5 Walter Benjamin, 'A Short History of Photography', in: *Germany, The New Photography 1927–33*, Arts Council of Great Britain, 1978, p.73.

6 Roland Barthes, 'Rhetoric of the Image', in: *Image-Music-Text*, trans. Stephen Heath, Fontana Books, London 1977, p.32.

7 Ibid. p.47.

8 Victor Burgin, 'The absence of presence: conceptualism and post modernisms', exhibition catalogue, *1965–1972: When Attitudes Became Form*, Kettles Yard, Cambridge, 1984. Reprinted in Burgin, *The End of Art Theory*.

9 See Jacques Derrida, *Of Grammatology*, trans. Gayatri Chakravorty Spivak, The Johns Hopkins University Press, Baltimore, 1976.

10 Roland Barthes, *Camera Lucida*, trans. Richard Howard, Hill & Wang, New York 1981. p.77.

11 The link with the notion of separation is suggested by the French for 'poses itself': 'se parer'.

12 Alexander Rodchenko, quoted in David Elliott (ed), *Rodchenko and the Arts of Revolutionary Russia*, Museum of Modern Art, Oxford 1979.

13 In the first version, published in the magazine *MA* in 1924, graphic symbols are used instead of the photographs that featured in the second version that concludes his book *Malerei, Photographie, Film* (1925, English version 1969).

14 Jane Weinstock, 'What she means, to you' in: Barbara Kruger, *We won't play nature to your culture*. ICA, London 1983, p.13.

15 Barbara Kruger, interview in *Arts Magazine*, New York, Summer 1987, p.20.

16 ibid. p.13.

17 Victor Burgin, *Between*, ICA, London, 1986. p.82.

18 ibid. p.137

19 Roland Barthes, 'The Death of the Author' in: *Image–Music–Text*, 1977

20 On the loss of the 'master narratives' and 'language games' see Jean-Francois Lyotard, *The Postmodern Condition*, Manchester University Press, 1984.

Published in Dutch translation in *Een Woord voor het beeld*, ed. Van Alphen/Visser, Uitgeverij SUA, Amsterdam, 1989. English version previously unpublished.

8

Back to Basics

Computer programmes are built with software code which usually remains far in the background when one views a piece of computer art or a computer-mediated interactive environment. At this year's 'Ars Electronica' festival in Linz, however, software came to the forefront and digital coding was celebrated not only as "the language of our time" but also as the basic material of art and life. Richard Kriesche, for example, one of Austria's pioneering new media artists, goes so far as to view the human being as a work of data, comparing the information processes of genetic codes with the notion of a 'universal datawork' that has its origins in the idea of the *Gesamtkunstwerk*. Yet his arrays of genetic code sequences tell us little about the person they are supposed to represent; he still needs an old-fashioned photograph to show us what the person actually looks like.

Software in itself is hardly matter for aesthetic enjoyment, no matter how elegantly the code might be written. As Friedrich Kittler has pointed out, code is a script rather than a language. Since programmers cannot even pronounce the code they write, it has become divorced from language. In fact it is more akin to sets of abstract instructions, which puts it more in the performative sphere (with the computer being the performer). As Christiane Paul observes in her excellent new book *Digital Art* (in the Thames & Hudson 'World of Art' series), the idea of rules being a process for creating art, as in the use of instructions in works by Fluxus and Conceptual artists or the principle of random access used by John Cage, is comparable to the procedures of formal instructions known as algorithms that forms the basis of all digital software.

Software has evolved considerably since Jack Burnham curated his groundbreaking *Software* exhibition at the Jewish Museum in New York in 1970, which included a prototype of Ted Nelson's hypertext system and a robot-controlled environment by Nicholas Negroponte as well as a visitors' questionnaire compiled by Hans Haacke and a linguistic piece by Joseph Kosuth. While Burnham's interpretation of software was predicated on a convergence of structuralist theory and Conceptual Art, the current brand of Software Art is exemplified by the two *CODeDOC* shows curated by Paul herself, the first organised for the Whitney Museum's *artport* website in 2002, the second for this year's 'Ars Electronica'. Both shows were based on a specific assignment: "connect and move three points in space". The artists invited were free to use a computer language of their choice, such as Java, Lingo or Perl, and the display of the work included the code that was written as well as its execution. Given the basic, sketch-like nature of the initial premise, it is not surprising that the results are rather meagre, going not much further than the original premise.

Computers are engines that drive abstract, mathematical values which have been embodied in code. What they produce therefore is not art, but meta-art. It is humans who decide whether something is art and whether it is good or bad art. Artists might well be good at writing software code, just as they might well be adept at wielding a brush, a pencil or a camera, but generally what we appreciate is not the process but the result. The *runme* repository (runme.org) includes a large number of categories of online software art, ranging from data transformation to text manipulation, and many of the projects are indeed very imaginative and entertaining, but few of them reveal the underlying code used to produce them.

Computers can do many useful things, but they are not very good at producing noteworthy aesthetic experiences. The history of cybernetic art, from *Cybernetic Serendipity* at the ICA in 1967 to this year's 'Ars Electronica' in Linz, is replete with machines that have been programmed to make drawings, interact with each other or with humans, translating everything into or out of eponymous pixels, bits and bytes. The results are displayed via monitors or projected onto screens, sometimes triggered by audience activity. Computer-generated drawings might even be produced on paper or canvas and framed as traditional works of art, a practice that was pioneered by Harold Cohen in the sixties and which he has continued until today, using increasingly sophisticated versions of his self-authored software. Yet although computers have in the meantime become ubiquitous, computer art has failed to gain admittance into the mainstream art world of museums, markets and collections. To a large extent the genre has been banished to the ghetto of electronic art festivals and the rarefied discourse of computer programming. Museums, of course, tend to be wary of collecting works that demand technical upkeep and that may well cease to function after a while, although this has not stopped them from purchasing equally fragile or complex installations by artists of note. Part of the problem is that computer art, because it is not well represented in museums and prominent galleries, has to a large extent been excluded from critical discourse. Is this because it's not hip or sexy enough, or because few people seem to understand its parameters and aesthetics? Or is it because a lot of computer art goes no further than a performative demonstration of what software can do, whether this be the making of patterns, the establishing of connections or the translation from one sensory medium to another? It is the software driving the computers that causes these processes to become visible and/or audible. Sometimes these processes are interactive, that is, dependent on necessarily arbitrary actions or input on the part of the spectator. Yet such spectators are only empowered to a limited extent; they can only play a pre-established game, whose rules they have to follow. They have to obey the code, not write it.

Computers can certainly produce traditional-looking art, like the abstract 'epigenetic art' coded for pen and brush plotters by Roman Verostko. John Maeda frames his digital art and hangs it in galleries, while Steve Sacks's bitforms gallery in New York includes framed work as well as works displayed on monitors and touch screens. What most of these works have in common, though, is their recourse to a basic language of abstraction, a swirling array of coloured forms and lines generated by software programmes running on a computer. Aesthetically it all looks rather retrogressive and uninspiring.

Much the same can be said for the three dimensional displays that feature in every instalment of 'Ars Electronica', competing for various prizes. The never-ending search for new ways of digitally mediating lived experience or allowing interactions to take place between people and machines seems to be becoming repetitive and predictable. Scott Snibbe's *Deep Walls* takes up Dan Graham's idea of delayed video projection by recording the shadows of viewers and replaying them as loops within a 16-part frame. Marcel·lí Antúnez Roca's pneumatic exoskeleton that reacts to visitors in the space is curiously reminiscent of Bruce Lacey's robots shown at *Cybernetic Serendipity*, if more technologically advanced. Inventive interfaces abound—from a clock that records its own history by using slices of live video feed for the seconds, minutes and hours to mobile phones embedded in pumpkins that transmit heartbeats and puffs of breath. Other practitioners were to be seen laboriously scaling a climbing wall in order to trigger keyboard combinations of programme commands. Or visitors could immerse themselves in *nybble-engine-toolZ* by the Austrian duo Margarete Jahrmann and Max Moswitzer.

This is a complex re-engineering of commercial game software that projects a bewildering array of network commands interspersed with anti-war messages automatically emailed to the White House. Experienced gamers might appreciate its overwhelming effect, but to others it might just represent the revenge of code, a meaningless and self-legitimating impenetrability.

As the electronic environment becomes increasingly controlled and commercialised, its vocabulary is seen to be dependent on ineluctable protocols, regulations and software-based standards and norms. Code is indeed law. The proposed European Union extension of copyright law to new media (digital rights management) threatens to restrict information to those who can pay for it, while Microsoft now wants us to buy computers that will only run legal software (so called 'trusted computing'). The software guardians (not to mention conservative museum directors) may well succeed in halting the what writers like Paul optimistically herald as the 'revolution' in the way we produce and experience art today. The Walker Art Center in America has given the chop to the digital department that Steve Deitz was running so successfully, while several major museums (including Tate Modern) still have no digital art on permanent display. Ten years ago, in 1993, Thames & Hudson published Frank Popper's book *Art of the Electronic Age*. At that time 'electronic art' included video art and laser/holographic art and while the latter has virtually disappeared from public view, the former has undeniably found its place in the art museum context, even though nowadays this tends to be under the aegis of a single artist's oeuvre rather than a wider movement in which other artists participate. Which fate, I wonder, will befall digital art in the future?

This article originally appeared in *Art Monthly*, 271, November 2003.

9

Superchannel

"Superchannel we love you", says the hand-written notice on the door of a room adjoining the offices of Liverpool's Housing Action Trust in the Cunard Building. Inside, there's a group of eight or so elderly men and women, one of whom is operating a digital video camera and another holding a microphone boom. On one side there's a sound mixing panel and a computer. A discussion is in progress: the elderly people, who are all residents or former residents of tower blocks, are being asked about their experiences with the Internet. Their responses are positive, although some have a few reservations, noting that many older people have a sort of mental block when it comes to computers, and that there is a need for more tutors and hands-on training. Above all, they feel a genuine need to communicate—with each other, with their grandchildren, with friends and relatives from afar. Some have stories to tell, like how it was to arrive in England in 1953 as a refugee from Burma and see English sweets and snow for the first time. Others want to be able to air their grievances, especially concerning the condition of their flats and their confrontations with the city council, although one of them is worried about transgressing the laws of libel and slander. Told that the British government plans to have all its services on the Internet within five years, they recognise the imperative for everyone to have access and to feel comfortable in using it.

The whole discussion is being broadcast live over the Internet using Real Player technology, together with a chat line which allows questions or comments to be fed in and answered immediately. This interactive web TV channel goes under the name of Tenantspin, and is the second channel to be set up in Liverpool under the auspices of the Foundation for Art and Creative Technology (FACT) and the Danish artists' group Superflex. The first channel was established last year at Coronation Court, Liverpool's oldest tower block, set up in one of the spare bedrooms of the tenants' association flat. The tenants have complete control of their broadcasting schedule and a number of successful shows have already been aired, with online participation coming from far away. The architect who originally built Coronation Court has been interviewed, as well as the group of Dutch landscape architects appointed to refurbish the area. All the shows are archived on the Superchannel server and website based in Copenhagen [www.superchannel.org], which also hosts a number of other channels such as *The Modern Channel*, broadcasting live music and performance from the Fruitmarket Gallery in Edinburgh, and *The Electric Channel* which covers the Glasgow music scene. Other channels are based in Copenhagen, Vienna, Japan and Bangkok, all initiated, but not controlled by Superflex. Once the operation is set up, usually in cooperation with a wide range of people with their own specific interests and concerns Superflex withdraws and leaves them to continue the project independently. Superflex is keen on allowing anyone to make use of their Superchannel concept, especially as the technology is relatively simple (thanks to their programmer Sean Treadway). Uploading, archiving, scheduling and broadcasting are simplified so that the operators are trained quickly and are then able to concentrate on the content.

Although web TV is already quite widespread on the Internet, it often amounts to no more than a voyeuristic webcam project, or a commercial undertaking virtually indistinguishable from mainstream TV. Superchannel, on the other hand, emphasises the community aspect of broadcasting, transforming the role of the viewer from that of passive spectator to active user. Not only can the archived programmes be viewed at any time, but viewers are also able to post comments whenever they wish. One of Superchannels aims is to demystify Internet technology so that it can become an effective means of communication for social groupings like the aged and those living in tower blocks who probably feel alienated from the sexy whizz-kid world of e-commerce as represented by TV series like *Attachments*. Certainly, there is an element of idealism in the Superchannel project, but Superflex have already demonstrated that they are quite capable of carrying out ambitious projects that fulfil identifiable needs. Two years ago they became involved in the development of a biogas power plant for African villages, which now has financial backing and is successfully operating under the name Supergas. Their entry into digital technology came with the setting up of karlskrona2, a digital copy of the city of Karlskrona in Sweden, whose citizens can adopt avatars and interact with each other via the Internet and a large outdoor projection screen.

The three artists comprising Superflex—Rasmus Nielsen, Jakob Fenger and Bjornsterne Christiansen—insist on creating concrete social interventions in which political, cultural and economic powers and hegemonies are challenged by opening them up to a radical, democratic heterogeneity. Their concerns are discursive rather than aesthetic; the emphasis is on providing services as a means of empowerment for others. It is worth noting, for instance that Christiansen's father is the musician and composer Henning Christiansen who was associated with Fluxus and worked together with Joseph Beuys. The original Fluxus ethos, George Maciunas' promotion of "non art reality" and his advocacy of social commitment and communal projects, is mirrored to some extent in the work of Superflex, as are Beuys' notions of "social sculpture" and economic reform. If artistic practice means "creating conditions for the production of new ways of thinking, acting, speaking and imagining", as Barbara Steiner writes, then the work of Superflex certainly deserves attention. Having already participated in shows such as *Democracy!* at the Royal College of Art in London and *Plan B* at De Appel in Amsterdam, they are fortunate in having forged a strong link with FACT, whose 'Collaboration' programme would seem tailor-made for their needs and aspirations.

Superchannel is evidence of a return to the spirit of community that characterised the early years of the Internet with its bulletin boards, discussion lists and MOOs. True, it was only textual then, but it was essentially democratic and participatory, qualities that are all too much in danger of being lost in the corporate-driven visions of e-topia. Cities are built of bricks as well as bits, and are inhabited by people whose immediate concerns are local rather than global.

This article originally appeared in *Art Monthly*, 243, February 2001.

10

Net Working

Anyone who has ever tried viewing art on the Internet will know that, more often than not, it's an extremely frustrating experience. Even with a fast modem, the vagaries of the telephone networks mean that images trickle down onto the screen at painfully slow speeds, leaving you twiddling your thumbs and getting nervous about the size of your phone bill. What's more, most of the more interesting artists' web projects involve multiple images and texts, and perhaps even sounds, animations and movies which take even longer to download. There's nothing more tedious than staring at an almost blank screen, watching that little clock slowly turn its hands. In such circumstances, the common response is to give up, and zap to another site that will hopefully prove more rewarding. Within the Net community, zapping is sometimes more optimistically called 'surfing', which assumes, of course, that one at least knows how to swim first. Otherwise there is a serious risk of drowning in an endless sea of data. Whatever the case, what it means in effect is that much of the art that is present on the Net is rarely viewed in its entirety.

From the artist's point of view, the Net is an extremely attractive proposition. It offers an inexpensive means of distribution to a potential audience of millions, bypassing museums, galleries and the art press. Yet it's not as simple as that. Making pages of one's artwork for the World Wide Web is very much like do-it-yourself desktop publishing—it's all very well printing thousands of brochures of your work, but how do you get them to the people who might be interested? How do you get your website known to the public at large (at least to those fortunate enough to have a sophisticated computer, an Internet connection and who are interested in art)? In this respect, the role of online galleries, museums and art magazines that have been sprouting on the Net in recent years, simply perpetuates the role that such institutions play in the 'real' art world. An online exhibition is no less selectively organised than its real-world counterpart.

Internet art can be roughly divided into two types: the static and the dynamic. The former espouses the function of information, presenting images and text in a form not that dissimilar from a printed catalogue. Whether it's the Louvre site, or the Museum of Modern Art in New York, all you get are pictures of pictures, reduced to the format of an average computer screen, and pages of text offering background information, descriptions of works, artists' curricula, interviews, and so on. Admittedly, it's considerably cheaper to produce webpages for the Internet than full colour printing on paper, but who enjoys having to read so much text on screen? Most of us still prefer the simple pleasure of holding a book in our hands and turning the pages when we feel like it. Then there's the encyclopaedic nature of the Net. Yes, it's true, it's like having a huge library at your disposal. Just go to one of the many 'search engines' and type in a keyword, say, 'Damien Hirst', and, lo and behold, up pops a list of about 3000 documents all containing some reference to Damien Hirst. After that, of course, the selection is up to you.

In an effort to create 'web-specific' art, there has been a tendency (in true modernist style) for formal issues to dominate. No work is complete without 'hyperlinks', adding a multidimensionality and nonlinearity that often becomes an end in itself rather than an intrinsic conveyor of meaning, while 'interactivity' generally amounts to nothing more than clicking on a mouse, or filling in forms. Fortunately, the days seem to have passed when there were a number of sites where viewers could contribute to the creation of a cumulative artwork, the worst example being Douglas Davis's *The World's First (and probably longest) Collaborative Sentence* (which also earned the dubious title of being the first website to be sold to a collector). One of the best sites currently on offer is run by the Dia Art Foundation in New York, which includes a sound and image work made specially for the web by Susan Hiller, and a collaboration between video artist Tony Oursler, writer Constance de Jong and musician Stephen Vitiello under the title *Fantastic Prayers*. Another interesting New York-based site is *Adaweb*, which features an interactive version of Jenny Holzer's *Truisms* and a multi-layered piece about surveillance by Julia Sher. Veteran multimedia artist Laurie Anderson's recent project for the Stedelijk Museum's *Under Capricorn* exhibition also deserves an honourable mention (although you do need to download certain software in order to view it properly).

Artists wanting to work on the Internet are having to turn themselves into computer programmers, constantly struggling to keep up with the proliferation of software programmes and authoring devices developed by the computer industry. Everything is getting thrown into the pot: texts, images, real-time sound and video, even live video teleconferencing. But the telephone lines that carry all this digitised information are getting clogged up. Because of their low bandwidth, the telephone networks will eventually have to concede defeat to the Cable TV networks, which are much more suited to transmitting high-quality audio and video material. Viewing art on the Net will then be more like viewing a CD-Rom, which promises to be a more rewarding and less frustrating experience than it is at present.

This article originally appeared in *Art Monthly*, 200, October 1996.

11

Stalking the Web

Attempts to define an aesthetics and an ontology of art on the Internet tend to disparage mere visual reproduction in favour of a concern with the network itself as form, agency and concept. While this may smack of Greenbergian modernism and the injunction that art should be determined "through the operations peculiar to itself", the counter argument put forward by T. J. Clark, namely that modernism is also characterised by a resistant negation of its consistency through a pulling apart and an emptying of 'intrinsic' qualities, is perhaps more applicable to much of the innovative work that can be found on the Net. The very volatility and immateriality of the Net militates against permanence and immutability. It is subject to a process of continual mutation as new versions of browsers and the codings they support are being introduced every few months. Art works can easily become obsolescent simply because the technology used to view them has been superseded by a newer version. Art institutions wishing to archive specific examples of Net Art thus face the problem of also having to archive the operating system and software originally used to create the work. Furthermore, since all Net Art is digital it is open to infinite reproduction, manipulation and alteration, which makes it even more difficult to preserve in finite form.

The status of web art as a discrete form of art has received support from a number of institutions, most notably the Walker Art Center in Minneapolis [gallery9.walkerart.org/] which has begun to archive artists projects and to initiate new ones. The pioneering and now defunct New York-based website *Adaweb*, for example, which featured the work of such artists as Jenny Holzer, Julia Sher and Lawrence Weiner, has been preserved in its entirety at the Walker Art Center, where it joins their Digital Arts Study Collection. This collection also includes *Interface*, a compendium of links to more than 40 artists projects (most of which seem to be still online) and a selection of hypertextual essays, including an exhaustive, multi-faceted study of the life and work of Beuys. The Walker Art Center has also commissioned three artists—Janet Cohen, Keith Frank and Jon Ippolito—to collaborate on a re-working of the Adaweb site under the title *The Unreliable Archivist*. This allows viewers to scramble and recombine fragments of Adaweb texts and imagery by using a set of toggle switches that offer alternative texts, images, backgrounds and layouts.

Another example of re-mixing existing web material is the *Shredder* [www.potatoland.org/shredder/] project initiated by Mark Napier. Type a URL (website address) into the *Shredder* and the programme alters the HTML coding before your computer receives it so that you end up with an unreadable jumble of misformed images, texts and coding. The Shredder turns information into art, while Napier's parallel project, the *Digital Landfill* [www.potatoland.org/landfill/], turns it into debris. Viewers are invited to deposit their unwanted digital garbage into the ever-growing landfill, which can then be viewed in cross-sections of ten layers at a time. Just as sifting through someone's garbage can reveal a lot about the person concerned, the *Digital Landfill* offers insight into the actual uses of 'net culture', revealing, for example, the ubiquity of pornography.

One of the reasons for the emergence of these 'alternative' web viewing experiences is perhaps the feeling of sameness that has come to characterise the Net. With only two brands of browsers available, both of which support the same internationally-accepted range of graphics, texts, frames and menus, even the most adventurous web sites are starting to become indistinguishable. Enter the Web Stalker [bak.spc.org/iod/] a totally different kind of web browser developed in London by the members of I/O/D and launched at the end of 1997. What Web Stalker does is map the content of a website, parsing the HTML resources and links, and graphically representing these as circles and lines. Other operations allow users to dismantle a site, store parts of it and extract the raw HTML coding. As Matthew Fuller describes it, "The Web Stalker performs an inextricably technical, aesthetic and ethical operation on the HTML stream that at once refines it, produces new methods of use, ignores much of the data linked to or embedded within it, and provides a mechanism through which the deeper structure of the web can be explored and used". Instead of images and texts, what the Web Stalker produces are beautiful filligree-like patterns that can easily lay claim to be art.

'Speculative software' like the Web Stalker is designed to break the limits imposed by proprietary operating systems and their associated browsers, analogous perhaps to contesting the dominance of the frame and the gallery/museum contexts that condition how we view art. Thousands of copies of the Web Stalker have been freely downloaded from the I/O/D site, and it was awarded the title of Mr. Net Art in 1998. Previous I/O/D projects involved developing free software that played havoc with the generally accepted Graphical User Interface (how things are arranged on your computer screen), or simply presented a black screen that responded to mouse movements with fragments of sound. In the first five or so years of its existence Net Art has clearly sufficiently established itself to warrant the creative re-use of its materials, pulling itself apart in order to be reconstructed, recombined, and reinvented.

This article originally appeared in *Art Monthly*, 223, February 1999

12

Virtual Artworlds

Nowadays you don't have to physically travel in space and time to visit art exhibitions, experience installations or chat to fellow artlovers. You can do all this while sitting in front of your computer and logging into one of the 'Palace' environments that have sprung up all over the world during the last year. Essentially, they are an extension of the text-based MUD (Multi-User Dungeon) and MOO (Multi-Object Oriented) environments, which, in the early days of the Internet, offered visitors the possibility of navigating around 'virtual worlds' that consisted purely of verbal descriptions like "You are standing outside the Library; press X to enter". Once inside the various rooms, you could chat to fellow guests and describe actions that you wish to take. Although everything was mediated through whatever you typed on your keyboard, and this involved knowing a fairly long list of keyboard commands, the MOOs and MUDs managed to instil an uncanny feeling of presence. I once 'attended' a ball at the MediaMOO hosted by the Massachusetts Institute of Technology, and really felt that I was in a ballroom surrounded by other guests whom I could talk to if I wished. I could even order drinks, but, of course, managed to stay sober the whole time!

As with the rest of the Internet, these virtual worlds have now become graphical, so that you can see the space you're in, or at least a detailed graphic, or sometimes photographic, representation of it. But something has become lost: with the textual descriptions of places you had to use your imagination to visualise them. It was more like being immersed in a novel, whereas the graphical worlds are more like watching a film. It comes as no surprise that the company responsible for creating the current generation of visual worlds known as Palaces is Time-Warner Inc. The software necessary for viewing Palaces is available free, and anyone can enter the environments as a guest, but if you want to become a member, which allows you to create your own 'avatar' and do other 'cool' things, then you'll need to pay a $25 registration fee. Otherwise, when you log in, you appear on the screen as an ubiquitous Smiley figure, although there are a series of props that you can don. It's also a good idea, if you have a Mac computer at any rate, to use the text-to-speech software so that you don't have to keep reading the little speech balloons that relay what all the visitors are saying. Sometimes, however, this can get pretty cacophonous, especially when you find that half a dozen people are talking simultaneously in different languages!

Since its inception nearly two years ago there are already hundreds of Palace environments all over the world. Most of them are chat and/or entertainment oriented—you can visit an Alice in Wonderland environment, for example, or 'take part' in a soap opera—but there are at least two that are related to the art world. One of these is *Thingworld*, set up by the New York-based *Thing* website. Their world actually consists of a series of photographs of a gallery, including the back room and the office, and other images such as Peter Halley's studio and a landscape painting by Gerhard Richter. You can wander freely from room to room, and if you're lucky you might encounter another Smiley or an avatar and then you can initiate a discussion, but my own experience is that there's usually nobody else around. Quite the typical gallery in fact!

Lawrence Weiner's *Homeport* [adaweb.walkerart.org/project/homeport] uses the Palace environment as a novel means of presenting his textual and graphical works. Appropriately, the work was included in the exhibition *Port: Navigating Digital Culture* held recently at the MIT List Visual Arts Center. A page on the Adaweb website (who sponsored the project) explains Weiner's thinking behind his concept: "Once within *Homeport* there is no means of proceeding without mixing what is perceived as (a) reality & what we must consider dream space or reality based on assumptions not necessarily correct". Weiner compares navigating through *Homeport* as a voyage through uncharted seas, where all assumptions have to be left behind. Prospective voyagers should not be put off by the censorious voice that announces "Sorry, Members Only" as you enter, nor by the built-in avatars that tell you to fasten your seat belt and ask if you want coffee, tea or milk. Once you start to find your way around and discover the nine hidden passageways (or 'portholes') that are embedded in the various pages, you pass through a series of well-known Weiner formulations in various typographic styles and embellished with the artist's typical lines, arrows and boxes. "STARS DON'T STAND STILL" leads to "IN THE SKY" and then "FOR ANYBODY". Or "WHEN IN DOUBT PLAY TIC TAC TOE & HOPE FOR THE BEST".

Weiner has always been concerned with working in what he calls the "public domain". Here he continues his engagement with popular media that has already seen a steady stream of books, comics, posters, films, t-shirts, buttons, and, most recently, a superb CD called *Monsters from the Deep* produced in collaboration with Ned Sublette, on which professional rock and jazz singers and musicians perform the lyrics of Lawrence Weiner. If anyone deserves the epithet 'pop artist', rather than the label of 'conceptual artist' which he is usually saddled with, then it must be Lawrence Weiner.

This article originally appeared in *Art Monthly*, 205, April 1997.

13

Locative Media

"Where are you?" is the first question that many people ask when talking to someone on a mobile phone, as though to suggest that location is somehow an important context-defining component of communication. At the same time, Internet use is becoming de-localised. allowing you to log in anywhere at any time. The chip manufacturer Intel has even designed a surfboard containing an Internet-enabled computer, so that you can surf the waves and the Internet at the same time (although reception is reported to be poor when the board is underwater).

The Intel corporation is also interested in exploring other possibilities of wireless technologies. Noting that nearly 400 million new mobile phones are scheduled to be sold worldwide this year alone, while wireless networks (WiFi) hardware is being deployed at the rate of one every four seconds globally, Intel's research department at Berkeley is researching ways to connect 'familiar strangers' wirelessly, using an application for mobile phones that can distinguish the locational proximity of other people, in particular people you've seen before but whose identity you don't know. The idea, it seems, is to make us feel less lonely in urban crowds (and more afraid of 'unfamiliar' strangers?). So perhaps now the first thing we'll be asking is "Who are you?".

The widespread use of mobile phones, Global Positioning Satellite enabled Personal Digital Assistants and WiFi is also generating a new media art form that has quickly acquired the label of Locative Media, and as such is being vigorously pursued and promoted as the latest form of artistic intervention in public space. Locative Media involves the overlaying of digital information onto real space. 'Cellspace', as it is known, is invisible but not seamless or impervious. While surveillance extracts data from physical space, cellspace augments it with a mesh of conversations, messages, instructions, information, music. etc. Wireless technology already enables shoppers to be tracked and addressed with special offers. Free, public wireless nodes are popping up in such sanctioned spaces as public libraries or schools, while private nodes without encryption are leaking from offices and homes, enabling Internet access to be hacked and pirated. A new area of contested space has arisen.

Several media artists have been drawn to this new public arena, recognising the potential for spatial authoring, social networking and artistic interventions. Moreover, it is genuinely site-specific and is less dependent on the screens and projections that feature in most presentations of new media art. Pioneers include the Blast Theory group, with their games of electronic hide and seek, and Janet Cardiff's non-networked, Walkman-based pedestrian explorations of urban environments. The Canadian *locative.net* site lists a large number of Locative Media events and workshops taking place in various countries, including Latvia, Iceland and Norway.

Some of these focus on new applications (preferably using open source software) for notions of mobile geography, collaborative mapping and social organisation. A group of psychogeographers in the Netherlands, associated with the *socialfiction.org* site, uses algorithms to explore the city, in derive-like fashion, on the basis of instructions like "first street left, second street right, etc". The Real Time software developed by the Waag Society in Amsterdam allows traces of walks to be made and projected in real time. In 2002 a number of Amsterdam inhabitants were able to create their personal cartographies of the city, revealing the routes they took on a daily basis. The same GPS tracking technology has also been used for a project by artist Esther Polak and Latvian researcher Ieva Auzina, mapping routes of several small-scale Latvian milk farms and of milk transportation throughout Europe. Interesting if you want to know where the powdered milk in your coffee might have originated.

The Futuresonic04 festival in Manchester earlier this year had a special section called 'Mobile Connections', devoted to art projects for wireless environments. *(Area) code*, a collaboration between centrifugalforces and Jem Southern, used an SMS mapping system to allow mobile phone users to submit virtual graffiti to five urban sites in Manchester. Another event, 'mobile clubbing' involved participants wearing headphones to listen to their favourite music and turning up at prearranged places for a dance session, unheard by all other bystanders. Using GPS-enabled laptops, visitors could wander around Manchester, participating in user-driven narratives and soundscapes.

Mobility (and a certain passivity as well as technical know-how) seems to be essential to all these projects, with little opportunity offered for reflection, critical or otherwise. In exploring the *Mobile Connections* site, it came as some relief to discover a piece by Jody

Zellen that introduces itself as "a meditation on the nature of public space". *Disembodied Voices* is a web project that offers a visual representation of the global social reality of mobile telephony. Formally similar to Zellen's earlier *Ghostcity* project and with a sense of humour sadly lacking in many locative media projects, it uses photographs of urban sites and situations, with rollovers producing visual tricks and snatches of sound. Icons float at random across a white screen, accompanied by a cacophony of telephone voices. Other sections use textual transcripts of calls, historical photographs of railway stations and postcard views of world cities, all interspersed with fragmented telephone conversations in different languages. With the advent of mobile phones, space has become translocal. The boundary between public and private space is effaced as, oblivious to our surroundings, we now have private conversations in public. In fact, it no longer matters where one is, as long as one is connected.

This article originally appeared in *Art Monthly*, 280, October 2004.

All or nothing—an anthology of blank books

Robert Rauschenberg once said that a canvas is never empty. Shadows, real or imagined, fall on it all the time. Nature abhors a vacuum, and there can be no space or area that is completely empty nor, as Rauschenberg's colleague John Cage pointed out, is there any such thing as absolute silence. The pristine, virgin page may have caused many a writer distress; they sit before their typewriter, staring at the new page, knowing that to make a mark is to commit themselves irretrievably. For a number of writers and visual artists, however, the very blankness of the page provides a metaphorical paradigm of the possibility of saying everything and/or nothing. A book of blank pages is a book about everything (*qua* Mallarmé) or nothing (*qua* Zen). During the last century, from the advent of modernist experiments at the beginning of the twentieth century to the irony and cynicism characteristic of late twentieth century postmodernism, there has been a variety of blank (or almost blank) books by such artists as Piero Manzoni, Herman de Vries, Sarkis and Allan Ruppersberg, the visual poets Jiří Valoch and Heinz Gappmayr, and the Sufi writer Idries Shah. Their approaches, even to such an elementary concept of blankness, varies considerably, as it is the purpose of this essay to demonstrate.

The research for this essay was commenced in the 1970s. Since then I have come across several more blank books (and recordings), indicating that the idea of blankness is a recurrent and persistent trope in twentieth century art and literature. Newspapers regularly fulminate against the 'emptiness' of modern art, but perhaps this is precisely its strength—to offer a sanctuary, a blind spot, in the face of the profligacy of words and images today. The fact that artists are willing to go to all the trouble of producing an edition of a book that is completely or largely blank testifies to a faith in the ineffable.

> "Get the nothingness back into words. The aim is words with nothing to them: words that point beyond themselves rather than to themselves; transparencies, empty words. Empty words, corresponding to the void in things."—Norman O. Brown, *Love's Body*

Norman O. Brown's chapter on 'Nothingness' at the end of his book *Love's Body* references Tibetan mysticism and European mediaeval scholasticism as promulgating the view that the world is merely a veil that hides the ultimate void. A similar view underlies *The Book of the Book* by the renowned Sufi authority Idries Shah. First published in 1969, it has since gone into at least two further printings. Its popularity attests to the effectiveness of the message that the book conveys, which is basically that of a parable whose illustration is the book itself. The first nine pages relate the seven hundred year old story of a dervish who, on becoming King, needed an instrument with which to teach Truth. The King hears from a stranger the tale of a wise man who attributed all his knowledge to a thick tome which was kept in a place of honour in his room. After the sage's death his students opened the book only to discover one page of writing which says, "When you realise the difference between the container and the content, you will have knowledge". The students, however, failed to understand the meaning of the book. The stranger, on hearing of it, does though, and so does the King, who orders the story to be inscribed into a similar book. This copy is again lost, until a bookseller markets the idea, selling copies of the 'Book of the Book' for two gold pieces. Those people "who preferred mere appearance to inner content" thought they had been deceived; others placed more value on the knowledge gained by purchasing the book. The lesson is completed in the only possible way: the following 128 pages of Shah's *The Book of the Book* are blank. The idea is that a Book of Knowledge need not contain written instructions, indeed need not contain anything, since one of the tenets of Sufism is the attempt to liberate man's ego from material things. Man and all his knowledge are part of the Eternal Whole, from which everything is derived and to which all must return. It is the constant flux, the Void, mere fields of vibrations. The clearest way to perceive this is by observing a blank page—not searching for 'anything', just letting the vibrations create 'everything'.

Shah's book was published in the late 1960s, a period when there was considerable interest in Eastern mysticism. In the art world this was reflected in the interest in Zen Buddhism, particularly by way of the person of the composer John Cage, who later had considerable influence on a number of artists associated with intermedia and Fluxus. Cage's 1952 composition 4'33" can be considered paradigmatic, consisting as it does of silence, or rather, the random ambient sounds produced inside and outside the auditorium during its performance. Apart from a performance by Frank Zappa on a John Cage tribute album issued in 1993, there have not been any recordings of Cage's piece. The British artist Jonty Semper, however, has issued a 6" vinyl recording of the one-minute silence from the funeral of Princess Diana recorded in Hyde Park on 6 September 1997, and a double CD called *Kenotaphion*, which functions as an audio archive of all the recorded silences held at the Cenotaph on November 11th (Armistice Day) in the twentieth century. Silence is a powerful means of commemoration, focussing one's thoughts on absence in a positive way.

At the end of October 2004, sitting in the bar near my studio, I was thinking about Sonic Youth's thirty-second recording of silence, which I'd read about that afternoon in a magazine article. Apparently it had annoyed some purchasers who had downloaded the track from the Internet. Suddenly from out of the babble of voices in the bar came the words "absoluut stilte" [absolute silence].

Early poetics and pictures of nothing

Vasilisk Gnedov, a Russian 'Ego-futurist' poet, published in a book titled *Death to Art* (1913) poem no.15, 'Poem of the End', which consisted of the title printed on a blank page. The poem is described in the book's preface as follows: "'Poem of the End' is actually 'Poem of Nothing', a zero, as it is drawn graphically".

This almost anecdotal use of a blank page to represent nothingness had, of course, already been deployed two centuries earlier in Lawrence Sterne's *Tristram Shandy*. At a certain point in this long, rambling, almost unreadable 'novel', first published in 1759, the narrator conjoins 'Uncle Toby' to draw a portrait of his mistress. The following page is blank, following which the narrator gleefully announces, "Thrice happy book! thou wilt have one page, at least, within thy covers, which Malice will not blacken, and which Ignorance cannot misrepresent". Suffice it to say that elsewhere in the book there are various other graphic elaborations, including copious use of asterisks and a page printed as a black area, antedating by more than two hundred years Endré Tot's *Night Visit to the National Gallery*, published by Beau Geste Press in 1974.

Vasilisk Gnedov's annihilation of art was carried further by Kasimir Malevich who reduced painting to the ineffable. His *Black Square* of 1915 became the symbol, or rather the icon, of the end of painting. Suprematism, as Malevich called his new movement, was designed to convey the feeling of nonobjectivity, a spiritual state that bordered on mysticism. Malevich's *Suprematist Composition: White on White* (1918) depicts a white square at a tilted angle within another white square. Recognising that this indeed represented an end-point in painting, Malevich soon abandoned this approach and reverted to figuration. The idea of white paintings (and the various types of painterly and surface treatment that could be achieved) was later taken up by Robert Ryman in the 1970s, but although Ryman's paintings are not strictly blank (certainly less so than Rauschenberg's 1953 paintings), the idea of the blank canvas had already been taken up by the critic Clement Greenberg as the hypothetical completion and end of modernist painting. Within the formalist terms of Greenberg's aesthetics, the blank canvas was the embodiment of painting's ultimate specificity, its flatness and two-dimensionality. The subject of modernist art, Greenberg famously insisted, is the medium itself. Yet Greenberg seems to have been unwilling to cross the boundary and accept the full consequences of his theory. In 1962 he stated that while a blank canvas could be called a picture, it was "not necessarily a successful one". Perhaps only an artist such as Duchamp could have made a success of it, although the idea of a blank canvas as a 'readymade' would appear to be problematic. The closest that Marcel Duchamp ever got to a blank book was his collaboration with Pierre de Massot who published *The Wonderful Book, réflections on Rrose Sélavy* (Duchamp's alter ego) in Paris in 1924. Prefaced by an introduction by "a woman of no importance" who declares that "Un livre agréable à lire doit toujours être illisible", and with a rear cover bearing a series of puns by Rrose Sélavy, the bulk of the book consists of twelve blank pages headed by the names of the twelve months of the year. Duchamp's famous silence—his avowed abandonment of art in favour of "breathing" and chess—might have been condemned by Joseph Beuys as "overrated", but there is no doubt that he exerted a considerable influence on later generations of artists, including many who are mentioned in this essay.

At any rate, Clement Greenberg's prescriptions did give rise, at least in America, to reactions from artists who were ready to abandon painting in favour of severely minimalist sculpture and conceptual art. Some of these artists almost went so far as to break the ultimate modernist taboo of the blank canvas. Mel Ramsden, a member of the Art & Language group of hard-core conceptualists, made a painting in 1967 which is a stretched canvas, front to the wall, and labelled on the back: "UNTITLED (NONVISUAL ART)". Another piece was entitled *Secret Painting*, also dated 1967–68. Conceived perhaps as an ironic riposte to Malevich (as well as to Greenberg), it consists of a black monochrome canvas placed next to a photostatted text which reads: "the content of this painting is invisible, the character and dimensions of the content are to be kept permanently secret, known only to the artist". 1967 was clearly a fertile year for the minimalist variety of conceptual art. Christine Kozlov exhibited in New York an untitled work consisting of a reel of clear 16mm film, while in London John Latham, known for his book-burning performances ('Skoobs'—books spelt backwards) founded the NOIT chair of nonentity, which focussed on "the least event".

> "The artist must start, like God, with chaos, the void: with blank colour, no forms, textures or details."—Barnett Newman

Around the same time as Clement Greenberg was pondering the issue of blank and monochrome canvasses within the formalist tradition of painting, artists in Europe were pursuing a more metaphysical agenda. Piero Manzoni was making white paintings that sought not an apotheosis of form but an absolute minimum of expressiveness. As he wrote in the magazine *Azimuth* in 1960, "It is not a question of 'painting' blue on blue or white on white (either in the sense of composition or of self expression). It's exactly the opposite: the question as far as I'm concerned is that of rendering a surface completely white (integrally colourless and neutral) far beyond any pictorial phenomenon or any intervention extraneous to the value of the surface. A white that is not a polar landscape, not a material in evolution or a beautiful material, not a sensation or a symbol or anything else: just a white surface that is simply a white surface and nothing else (a colourless surface that is just a colourless surface). Better than that: a surface that simply is: to be (to be complete and become pure)". Not surprisingly, the first monograph to appear on the artist's work—*Piero Manzoni, the life and the works*, (Petersen Press, Glucksburg, Hamburg and Paris, 1962)—consisted of 100 transparent pages, with only the cover being printed, in an edition of sixty copies.

The French painter Yves Klein was another mystical artist who sought to attain the void through monochrome paintings (mostly done in his patented IKB—International Klein Blue) and his famous exhibition *Le Vide* at Galerie Iris Clert in Paris in 1958, where the outside of the window of the gallery was painted blue and the interior, after he had removed all the furniture, white.

Both Manzoni and Klein were members of the Zero group and contributed to the magazine *Nul=0* edited by the Dutch artist Herman de Vries from 1961 until 1964. De Vries then edited *Revue Integration* which appeared from 1965 until 1972. Issue number nine of *Revue Integration* was the most extreme, consisting as it did of twelve black pages by Ad Reinhardt, two gold pages with embossed lines in the form of a cross by Mathias Goeritz and twelve white pages by de vries himself. In 1961 de Vries published 120 copies of what is now recognised as one of the first artist's books: *wit is overdaad* (white is superabundant), which consists of twenty-two white pages, the last of which bears the title in three languages. A year later de Vries published a variant called *wit* (white) consisting this time of two hundred white pages with four white collages and a white introduction by J. C. van Schagen. The first edition was of five numbered and signed copies published by M. J. Israel in Arnhem, and was reprinted by Hansjorg Mayer in 1967 in a numbered edition of 500. A third, revised edition appeared in 1980 from Artists Press, Bern, in the form of a totally blank book with a printed wrapper around the cover bearing the publishing information. As de vries writes elsewhere, "an empty sheet means more than a written one, only meaning is absent. meaning=limitation". Herman de Vries is one of the most uncompromising artists to have emerged from the experimental art scene of the sixties. Trained as a biologist, he gave up his career and family life to go travelling, particularly in India. His art records the random processes and changes engendered through his encounters with the world—gathering dust from the roads, collecting leaves fallen from a tree, allowing nature to go its own way. "To be" is his dictum, which applies not only to himself and others, but also to the randomly generated arrays of words, numbers or newspaper images that constituted his early works. For de Vries, randomness is an "objective creative factor".

Following in the tradition of both the reductive, nature-inspired art of De Vries and the sublime abstraction of Barnett Newman and of American minimalist artists like Brice Marden is the work of the Italian artist Ettore Spalletti. Using grounds and supports varying from stretched canvasses to slabs of marble, Spalletti applies layer upon layer of monochrome pigments to achieve a luminosity that evokes the pure colours and subtle shades of the sky and the sea. One of his publications is a two-volume book titled *Spalletti: Salle des Fêtes / Sala delle Feste*, published in Milan in 1998—one is a thick book consisting of more than a thousand pages of red tissue paper, the other is blue and is an 'ordinary' catalogue. Other publications by Spalletti combine the form of the book and the box—one contains blank sheets of deep blue tissue paper folded in half to form a sheaf of pages with a printed pamphlet in the centre, while another is a white box full of blank sheets of pale grey paper with three small pieces of gold leaf on the top page. Spalletti also uses gold leaf on the edges of some of his paintings, a technique that another Italian artist, Luciano Bartolini, once used for the edges of his otherwise blank book *Come Feticcio* (Like A Fetish). A year before Spalletti's book of red pages, the appropriately named artist Irma Blank published in the same city of Milan a book titled *Ur-buch ovvero Romanzo Blu*, which comprises 1,400 blank blue pages. Suffice to say that the other books for which Blank is known consist of erased texts. The books by both Spalletti and Blank evince a tactile quality that has more recently been exploited by Mark Pawson who published forty-nine copies of a book titled *Pink Paper* in 2004. The intensely bright fluorescent pink sheets of paper that make up the book were repeatedly crumpled up and smoothed out, taking on the character of a fabric rather than paper.

A number of concrete poets, inspired by the graphic use of space (between lines and words) in the work of Stéphane Mallarmé and the 'liberated words' of the Futurists, explored the potential of poetry to expand, or to drastically reduce, the limits of the page and the book. Eugen Gomringer's 1954 poem 'Silencio' arranges the word 'silencio' (silence) in a fourteen-word grid around an empty space. Heinz Gappmayr, many of whose works embody a minimalist aesthetic regarding the use of words, published two books in the late seventies that used the concept of blankness. *Reflex* (first edition 1978, second edition published by Ottenhausen Verlag, Aachen 1983) consisted of forty white leaves and one black leaf in the centre of the book, and *Raum* (first edition UND, Munich 1977, second edition Ottenhausen Verlag, Aachen 1983) simply consisted of forty white leaves.

The Yugoslav concrete poet Jiří Valoch likewise specialises in minimal works. His *Book about Nothing* (Brno, 1970, edition of thirty-three) consists of fifty-four blank leaves and one leaf with the word 'nothing' printed on it, while his *day-and-night book* (Brno, 1971, edition of thirty-three) has only two leaves, one of them white, the other black. Similarly, *Condensed History of Nothing* by the Canadian concrete poets bp Nichol and David Aylwood (published in the Ganglia Press minimimeo series) is reduced to twelve blank pages.

Wally Depew's series of small-format PN2 experiment books, published by the author in Sacramento (California) in the early-1970s, use various low-budget graphic and concrete poetry techniques, including rubber stamp printing, mimeo and photocopy. *Book 21 Punch Book #2* has an array of single random letters punched into the cover so that they penetrate through the following twenty-six otherwise blank pages until all that is visible are some vague depressions in the page. *Book 15 Burial Book* has a dirt streaked cover staple bound over twenty-six slightly grubby blank white pages. On the colophon page it states "This book has been buried for 26 days. After using for 26 days rebury for 26 more days etc".

Blank protests

In 1916 the avant-garde journal *The Little Review*, which was championing the work of James Joyce by publishing sections of his novel *Ulysses*, decided to issue a special issue in protest at the First World War. As its editor Margaret Anderson wrote in her autobiography *My Thirty Years War*, "The only gesture of protest I could think of was to publish an issue of the magazine made up of sixty-four empty pages, stating that since no art was being produced we would make no attempt to publish any. Jane [Heap] drew some cartoons of our occupations—Mason and Hamlin, anarchist meetings, horse-back riding, fudge breakfasts and intellectual combats. These filled the two pages in the centre, and all the other pages were reproachfully blank".

Over the years several other blank books have been published as a way of expressing a social or political protest. These range from the openly racist *Great Achievements of the Negro Race*, published by Sons of Liberty in Hollywood, California, a sixteen-page pamphlet, fourteen of which bear only the title and page number, to *The Official Government Nuclear Survivors Manual—Everything that is known about Effective Procedures in Case of Nuclear Attack*, which was bound in red and gold and contained 192 blank pages and was published in 1982 by Bill Adler Books and distributed by the reputable publishing firm of Farrar, Strauss & Giroux at a price of $4.95. In the same vein, in 1969 a blank book entitled *The Wit and Wisdom of Spiro T. Agnew* (the rabidly anti-liberal Republican politician who served as vice-president of the United States under Nixon from 1969 until 1972, and who was notorious for being neither witty nor wise) was published by the Los Angeles publishers Price, Stern Sloan under the author's name of Victor David Dinnerstein. It includes a biographical checklist and Agnew's high school yearbook picture together with a quotation, but the rest of the pages are blank. Apparently quite successful, it went into at least four printings. Many purchasers of this and similar books, however, might just have wanted a trendy blank book for use as a private journal. In 1980 the British label Stiff Records released an album called *The Wit and Wisdom of Ronald Reagan*, consisting of 40 minutes of silence, but I doubt whether it ever got much airplay. Such recordings were known as 'novelty records', a genre that must also include a record issued in Los Angeles in the early seventies called

The Best of Marcel Marceau. Devoted to the French mime artist, it had forty minutes of total silence and a burst of applause at the end of each side.

In 1997 a thick paperback book titled *Joshua Sofaer, A biography* by Margaret Turner appeared in a select number of London bookshops. The front cover boasts a photograph of a young man crouching naked on the floor and looking up with an intense, serious gaze at the reader, while the blurbs on the back include the statement that this is "a vitally important book for all those who care about the cult of personality". Adrian Rifkin, Professor of Fine Art at the University of Leeds is quoted as saying, "It's a joy… It has an energetic charm that's quite impossible to resist". Inside, apart from a title and a colophon page (including the publication date of 1997), the book is totally blank. Joshua Sofaer's website [www.joshuasofaer.com] reveals that he is a performance artist who regularly appears in clubs and art venues, and also has a career as an art school lecturer. Much of Sofaer's work is about the desire to become famous, particularly through the medium of photography. In an article about the book's launch, Sofaer refers to the 'tradition' of blank books, "I remember another such object being passed round my own class at school. 'Everything that boys know about girls'. As an adolescent, I didn't quite get it from the title and had to be encouraged to have a flick through before realising myself as the target".

In 1998 the Dutch artist Hans Bossmann published a sixteen-page *Newspaper Without News* (Dagblad Zonder Nieuws), which was completely blank. Bossmann's aim was to create an "oasis in the information society", and he pleaded for a day without any news at all, either in the press or on TV. Published in a edition of 250, it was printed, according to the artist, in conventional fashion, only without ink. The absence of art rather than of news is the theme of *Dieter Roth in Greenland*, a book compiled in 2005 by Jan Voss as a persiflage of a profusely illustrated 2004 book celebrating the years that Dieter Roth spent in America. Using the same format and cover typography as the latter and repeating part of the blurb printed on the back jacket flap, its totally blank pages are justified by the fact that Dieter Roth, in all his artistic career, never set foot in Greenland. Similarly tongue-in-cheek is a book by the Italian cartoonist, interior designer and journalist Enzo Apicella published in 1983. Titled *Memorie di uno Sinemorato* (Memoires of an Amnesiac) and with three other author's names on the cover crossed out, its pages are, as one would expect, totally blank.

Do it yourself

Some time in the sixties or early seventies, John Wilcock produced a blank issue of his counter-cultural newspaper *Other Scenes*. Dated June 22–30, it featured on its cover its usual logo and the announcement: "NOTICE. This special issue costs twenty-five cents. Most of it consists of blank pages. Do not waste your money buying it unless (a) you want a collector's item, or (b) you are planning to enter our do-it-yourself newspaper contest. First prize is $250. Details in centrefold". Indeed, the centrefold describes the conditions for participating in the contest, including a declaration that no copyrighted material will be used. The back cover contains an announcement of a new book by Timothy Leary, for which *Other Scenes* readers are also invited to design an advertisement.

Reader participation is also the idea behind a thin, spiral bound book titled *Process*, privately published by the British artist Bill Mitchell. The author's address is given, but there is no indication of date or size of edition. Five of the book's eight leaves contain a plastic bag into which readers are invited to place a different item. The instructions continue: "Each item represents a starting point or extension, and can be developed in any way you choose. The book is a course of action, a method of operation. In the course of any development please write to me, the correspondence will be an integral part and extension of the book". Another of Mitchell's books, *AZONIC 1*, goes from back to front, its thirteen blank leaves held together by a black thread running between the two covers and through small holes punched at different positions on the pages. A similar book, titled *Libro illeggibile N.Y.1*, was once made by the renowned artist and designer Bruno Munari in 1967. Published by the Museum of Modern Art, this 'unreadable' book featured a red thread running through the otherwise blank pages, some of which also had circular diecut holes punched into them.

Daily-Bul in Belgium published another experiment in reader participation in 1968. Titled *Poème collectif* its author is "Robert Filliou et Cie", and is based on a piece first performed in 1964 (and many times since, sometimes by Filliou's long-time collaborator Emmett Williams). The instructions at the front of the book ask readers to fill in the first of the sixteen blank pages with the names of five to seven things they would like to get rid of (such a wedding photograph, the army, rheumatism), and then to hand on the book to another fifteen people, who are instructed not to read the preceding entries before adding their own list of words.

Flux

Robert Filliou was a leading member of the Fluxus group of artists, who pioneered the performance of small Zen-like 'events', many of which involved audience participation. Another of its members was Yoko Ono, whose sound pieces (clearly influenced by John Cage) included such instructions as "Take the sound of the stone aging" or "Take a tape of the sound of the snow falling. This should be done in the evening". Her sales list offered tapes at twenty-five cents per inch, including *SOUNDTAPE* of the snow falling at dawn: a) snow of India, b) snow of Kyo, c) snow of Aos. Naturally, all the tapes were blank.

Fluxus was largely directed by George Maciunas, who produced most of the group's boxed multiples and other publications. His own *Flux Paper Events*, published in book form by Edition Hundertmark in 1976, contained sixteen-pages, each of which has been treated in various ways: from pages four to seven a bigger and bigger piece of the right-hand side has been torn away, the seventh and eighth pages are bound to each other by means of four staples. Apart from the page numbers all the pages are blank (except for a brown stain on one page). There is a reproduction of an old print on the cover, plus the name and author of the book and the publishers colophon on the inside front cover. The top left corner of the book is cut off at a diagonal, and there is a small round hole punched through at the lower right.

Another artist loosely associated with Fluxus, and who took part in some of the group's early manifestations, is Stanley Brouwn. One of his most well-known publications is *1m—1step*, a narrow, one metre tall book published on the occasion of the artist's exhibition in 1976 at the Stedelijk Van Abbemuseum in Eindhoven. The book has sixteen pages, of which only two are printed, one with the words "1 step", followed by a page with a one metre line printed at the edge. The remaining pages are blank. Almost all of Brouwn's post-Fluxus work involves distances counted in steps, illustrated by means of maps and texts.

The work of the American artist James Lee Byars continues in the vein of Yves Klein and Piero Manzoni, but is more performative and sculptural in form. The catalogue published to accompany Byars' exhibition at the Stedelijk Van Abbemuseum in Eindhoven in 1983 is almost cubic in form. Measuring 16.5 by 16.5cm and 15cm thick, it has a total of 1848 pages: 792 central printed catalogue pages, many of them blank, preceded and followed by blank pages.

tabula rasa: erased tablet; human mind at birth viewed as having no innate ideas.

Yet erasure is not the same as originary lack or emptiness. Robert Rauschenberg could not have erased De Kooning's drawing if there had been no drawing there to begin with. In other words, he could not have simply shown a sheet of blank paper and declared "This is an erased De Kooning". It was also crucial, Rauschenberg has said, that it begin as art, which precluded using one of his own drawings. As it was, it took Rauschenberg a month to remove De Kooning's marks. The erased De Kooning dates from 1953 and follows Rauschenberg's series of all-white paintings which he had started while attending the legendary Black Mountain College (where John Cage was one of the tutors). Speaking of the all-white paintings Rauschenberg has said, "I wanted to see how far one can push a truth like that… I came into the artworld absolutely nude with those". Cage has said that Rauschenberg's white paintings inspired his 1952 'silent' composition 4'33".

The American writer and critic Richard Kostelanetz (who coincidentally wrote a book about John Cage) published two totally blank books in 1978 under the imprint RK Editions. One was titled *Tabula Rasa— A Constructivist Novel*, in an edition of twelve copies, and the other, *Inexistencies: Constructivist Fictions*, appeared in an edition of twenty-six copies. Both books bear prefatory quotations by Ulises Carrión from his essay 'The New Art of Making Books' (1975). Kostelanetz developed the idea of Constructivist Fictions from an interest in the work of Moholy-Nagy and Mondrian, composing geometrical sequences that are intended to function as 'visual narratives', employing the form of the book to give them an existence in space and time—"the space of a printed page and the time it takes a reader to turn from one page to the next". If Kostelanetz's stance seems rather self-consciously art historical and self-justifying, it may be that he is only interested in the already established *idea* of blank books. For artists like Manzoni and de vries it was more a question of fulfilling a personal obsession, while Kostelanetz seems to be just carrying out a whim, adding an academic footnote to his adoptions of older art forms, making a wilful noise rather than a respectful silence.

> "The most beautiful and perfect book in the world is a book with only blank pages, in the same way that the most complete language is that which lies beyond all that the words of a man can say."—Ulises Carrión

Anne Lydiat published a book on the deliberately chosen date of 9/9/99, titled *Lost for Words....* Produced in an edition of 100 copies, it has the normal thickness of a hardback book but is totally empty except for an ISBN number blind-embossed on the rear cover. A dustjacket made of blotting paper bears the book's title on the front and a quotation by Maurice Blanchot on the front and rear inside flaps. Lydiat was inspired to make the book while travelling alone in Europe and wondering whether silence could be different in different countries. Blanchot talks of the book that "no longer belongs", which would then be its "consecration". Ann Lydiat consecrated her book by secretly placing it in the philosophy section of libraries nationally and internationally, as an intervention that circumvents the normal system of library acquisition and classification. Belonging and not belonging, lost and found.

Art folds up

> "A blank white sheet of paper with a crease in it—given the title of 'Folded Paper'—has been included in the Thamesdown Borough Council's progressive art gallery in Swindon, Wiltshire. The 18-inches-square piece of paper has been loaned free of charge from a private collection. It was 'created' by artist Sol Lewitt in July 1973."—Undated press cutting.

The British artist Les Coleman is mostly known for his witty drawings, many of which he has published himself in book form. In 1994 he produced, together with Charlie Holmes, *Bookmark*, a long oblong book using the same dimensions as the bookmark issued by the Waterstones chain of bookstores. Its six blank leaves, bound into a glued card cover and adorned with a silk bookmark ribbon, are dedicated to George Maciunas (presumably in homage to his Paper Events). *Bookmark* was issued by Coleman's own In House Publishing in an edition of 200 copies to coincide with the conference on Visual Arts Publishing and Distribution held in Newcastle in March 1994. Ironic self-referentiality is also the trope employed in Coleman's book *GLUE* (In House Publishing, London–Oxford 2002). With the title blind embossed on the cover, the book contains thirty-one numbered pages, all of which are glued together. The key is provided by the contents page which lists the twelve different types of glue used to make the book, from "Coccoina" to "UHU".

Several other artists have produced books in which blankness is combined with a minimal content. The Swedish artist Leif Erikson published two books in the late 1970s that utilise blank pages. *New*

Moves Adada (a Dadaism Handbook) appeared in 1978 under the imprint of Edition Sellem in connection with Lundada, an international *New Dada* exhibition held at Galeria St Petri in Lund, Sweden. The book consists of twenty blue, twenty yellow and twenty green leaves, while stuck to the printed cover is a triangular piece of green plastic grass (echoing perhaps the artificial grass used in Duchamp's *Etants Donnés*, or his earlier *Prière de Toucher*, the foam-rubber breast attached to the cover of the catalogue *Le Surrealisme en 1947*). The second book is called *The Waste Paper Act*, published the same year by Erikson's own imprint Wedgewood & Cheese, whose motto is "The totality does not get more total by its parts; i.e. only the unspoken is true!" True to his word, and to the book's title, forty-two of the forty-six leaves are blank—waste paper indeed! The eight printed pages contain a "List of Works" (brief descriptions of Erikson's projects and editions since 1976), a blank page headed "Literature", an Index (referring to the List of Works) and a ruled page headed "Note". Erikson works in an extremely capricious manner, challenging copyright laws and producing multiples that make use of a variety of objects and printed materials. In 1978 he took part in The Disposable University held at Balderup on the west coast of Sweden, where two main issues were dealt with: 1. The inability to formulate a proper and logical model of art conception, and 2. The silence of contemporary art. It appeared that in order to 'recover art' it was necessary to make a *tabula rasa*, to enact the wasting of paper and perhaps to start again with new moves like the use of pure colour.

The Canadian poet Childe Roland's book *un fleuve saint laurent* consists of two blank fly-leaves, forty-eight blank leaves incised with six wavy lines, and a silkscreened glassine wrap containing the publishing information ("les enterprises childe roland ottawa 74") and a short text referring to hieroglyphics and the notion that the Saint Lawrence river is a mixture of water and ice. Each time the book is opened a snow of tiny paper fragments floats down from the incisions.

Cuts are combined with colour in Francisco Pino's *Terron, Cantico*, published in Valladolid, Spain, in 1974. The book itself is a kinetic object comprising sequences of brown, beige, red, green, white and blue pages from which three-quarters of a rectangle have been cut, in such a way that a brown quadrant is continuously visible. A band around the cover denotes the book as "poesia experimental", and the two quotations on a page at the end (by St John of the Apocalypse and the Lettriste poet Isidore Isou), together with a list of "indices variables", suggest that the book is a visual meditation on, or sung celebration of, the earth (*terra*).

Another book with coloured pages is *Kelly 1:1* by the Dutch designers' collective Experimental Jetset and published in an edition of 250 copies in 2003. The cover describes it as a "cover version" (or "reinterpretation") of Elsworth Kelly's 1966 minimalist painting *Blue, Green, Yellow, Orange, Red*. The first thirty leaves are printed blue on the facing side, the next thirty green, then yellow, orange and red. Collated, the printed sheets form the cover version of the painting which measures six by one and a half metres. Two years earlier, Kristjan Gudmundsson applied the same principle in his book *200 Pages on Barnett Newman* which reproduces, in page form, Newman's famous painting *Who's afraid of red, yellow and blue*, which had been vandalised while hanging in Amsterdam's Stedelijk Museum. The restorer of this priceless painting apparently used ordinary house paint, so perhaps Gudmundsson's version would have been just as acceptable as a replacement. Other books by Kristjan Gudmundsson, many of them privately printed by the artist himself, are close to being blank in that they consists almost solely of page after page of repeated lines or dots. The two-volume *Once Around the Sun*, for example, represents in dots the number of seconds it takes for the earth to orbit the sun.

Sigurdur Gudmundsson's *Journey Book*, published to accompany an exhibition of the artist's photoworks at the Centre Georges Pompidou in Paris in 1977, uses blank pages as a reference to indefinite time and space. The first twenty-four leaves are blank, then there is a photograph of the artist standing dressed in a raincoat, his back to the camera and turning his head to face the reader, which is followed by fourteen blank leaves. Gudmundsson momentarily pauses in his journey through life, the past and the future a *tabula rasa*.

The artist Sarkis published a book in 1976 titled *Blackout Leica Museum* (published by the Berliner Künstlerprogramm DAAD and Galerie Folker-Skulima). The first page (p.4) shows a colour photograph of the first Leica camera made in 1913. The next printed page (p.121) has another colour photograph, a view of Grunewald taken by the artist on 21/7/76. In between are sixty blank, unnumbered leaves with a die-cut hole framing the front and back photographs. At the end of the book are four pages of notes in which Sarkis gives the background to the work and a contents page listing the complete Leica models from 1913 to 1973, a total of sixty, that is, so we are led to surmise, one every two pages. The missing photographs, the blank pages, testify to the "blackout". Sarkis identifies the camera with death, noting that the first Leica camera was developed as a "Kriegsgerät"—a piece of war equipment—and mentions its resemblance to a pistol (both in form as well as metaphorically, as in the notion of 'shooting'). He further remarks that people who collect weapons are very much like people who have a camera collection. *Blackout Leica Museum* is a work of denial, of voluntary exile from the state/status of objects. The museum as mausoleum. Sarkis wants his work to be a closed, hermetic system, a blackout "dessen Strategie keine Öffnung mehr hat" (whose strategy has no opening). *Blackout* is also the title of another book by Sarkis, published in an edition of 102 copies by Ecart in Geneva in 1975. Each of its 102 black pages is printed (in a dark colour approaching black) with the names of colours used by the military of various countries. Blackout curtains were, of course, the means used to hide cities from enemy bombers during the Second World War. In 1993 Sarkis returned to the theme of the denial of objects by publishing forty-eight copies of *L'Atelier* (Editions Ste Opportune & Sarkis, Paris/Brussels), a hardbound, slipcased book of 800 blank pages and one double-page coloured photograph showing the interior of the artist's studio. As though to acknowledge the inadequacy of language to describe the objects produced by an artist and the context in which this occurs, Sarkis has no other recourse than to depend on the indexicality of the photograph. All the rest is silence.

Allen Ruppersberg's *Greetings from L.A.* is subtitled "A Novel" and its back cover carries a strident blurb written in the style of the popular paperbacks that feature in much of Ruppersberg's artistic work. However, most of the book's 240 consecutively numbered pages are blank. Besides the title page and a quotation from the 1971 *World Almanac* on the following page, there is text to be found only on pages 35–38, 100–103 and 180–181. This text consists of fragments from a narrative in which the names of cars and Los Angeles streets feature prominently. Ruppersberg's book presents a parable about Los Angeles—its vacuity and banality, its superficiality, its endless desert of highways, and its empty characters and conversations. Under its misleading cover, the book is virtually empty and is further depersonalised by its having no information as to name, place or date of publication.

Existing books can also be erased in order to produce a new volume. Manuel Raeder's *Agenda 2005 Brand New Second Hand*, published by Revolver, Archiv für aktuelle Kunst in Frankfurt, uses reproductions of pages from old diaries contributed by twelve different people. White rectangles bearing 2005's month, date and day cover all the existing entries, thereby making these diaries reusable again. Thirty years earlier, Marcel Broodthaers published (in an edition of forty-four copies) a blanked out version of Charles Baudelaire's essay on Belgium, *Pauvre Belgique*, that the poet had written after living there for two years from 1864, but which was only published posthumously in the 1950s. Adopting the same title, Broodthaers' book negated Baudelaire's negative view of Belgium (and thus, according to the laws of algebra, turning it into a positive opinion of the artist's native country) by reproducing the exact page numbers, headings and layout from the Pléiade edition of Baudelaire's essay, but omitting the text entirely. Another book that Broodthaers 'wiped out' was the first edition of Stéphane Mallarmé's poem *Un coup de des...*, published in 1914 by Gallimard. In Broodthaers' version, published in 1969 as *Un coup de des jamais n'abolira le hasard (Image)*, all the words of the original poem are replaced by black blocks that nevertheless conform to the original radical layout. Words are reduced to blank images in space.

On a more whimsical note is a small sixteen-page book by (Roland) Topor, which is a hand crossed-out version of someone else's book. Every word, including the title on the cover, has been rendered illegible. Only a wrapper around the cover reveals Topor's name, the title *Souvenir* and the publisher: Uitgeverij De Harmonie in Amsterdam. Printed text can also be rendered almost illegible by printing it in white on white paper, which is the strategy employed in an issue of *Perfect Magazine*, curated by Mathieu Copeland and published in 2003 in Lagny-sur-Marne, France, featuring contributions from a plethora of well-known artists such as Gilbert & George, Art and Language, Daniel Buren, Christian Boltanski and Yoko Ono. The entire 128-page magazine is printed in glossy white ink on white paper, which makes it virtually unreadable. Only by turning the pages to the light at a certain angle is it possible to make out the text, photographs and drawings.

In itself any book is an hermetic system—it is bound by covers and its pages are of a finite size and number. Jorge Luis Borges, in one of his intriguing tales, imagines a "book of sand" whose pages are so thin that, like points on a line, their number is infinite. Just as there are an almost infinite number of books in Borges' equally fascinating story 'The Library of Babel', so too there seem to be countless blank books. Since beginning to research the subject in the mid-seventies, I have come across, or heard about, literally dozens. Type in the keyword 'blank books' into the Google search engine and you'll get hundreds of thousands of listings. But almost all of these refer to 'dummy books', and these are a long way from the perfection of the blank book as eulogised by Stéphane Mallarmé, Herman de Vries or Ulises Carrión. Blankness is as much a state of mind as it is a material condition, and as such it can be deceptive, hallucinatory, intentional, poetic or spiritual. It can be legible or illegible, present or absent, perfect or imperfect. But it is never empty. As John Cage so eloquently expressed it in 1959 in his 'Lecture on Nothing', "I have nothing to say and I am saying it and that is poetry as I need it".

Bibliography

Enzo Apicella *Memorie di uno Sinemorato*, 1983; Hans Bossmann *Newspaper Without News*, 1998; Stanley Brouwn *1m—1step*, 1976; James Lee Byars *catalogue (cube book)*, 1983; Les Coleman & Charlie Holmes *Bookmark*, 1994; Herman de Vries *wit*, 1962; Victor David Dinnerstein *The Wit and Wisdom of Spiro T. Agnew*, 1969; Leif Erikson *The Waste Paper Act*, 1978 Robert Filliou et Cie *Poème collectif*, 1968; Heinz Gappmayr *Reflex*, 1978; Vasilisk Gnedov *Poem of the End*, 1913; Sigurdur Gudmundsson *Journey Book*, 1977; Richard Kostelanetz *Tabula Rasa—A Constructivist Novel*, 1978; Anne Lydiat *Lost for Words...*, 1999; *Piero Manzoni, the life and the works*, 1962; *The Official Government Nuclear Survivors Manual—Everything that is known about Effective Procedures in Case of Nuclear Attack*, 1982; Allen Ruppersberg *Greetings from L.A.*, n.d. Sarkis *L'Atelier*, 1993; Idries Shah *The Book of the Book*, 1969; Margaret Turner *Joshua Sofaer, A biography*, 1997; Jiří Valoch *Book about Nothing*, 1970; Jan Voss *Dieter Roth in Greenland*, 2005; John Wilcock *Other Scenes*, n.d.

This essay was originally published by RGAP (Research Group for Artists Publications) Cromford, Derbys, 2005.

15

Poems, publications, performance, and photography

Quotations from Michael Gibbs' notebooks and other papers.
Photographs pp.112–113 Rod Summers; p.115 Raul Marroquin; pp.146–147 Hans Pattist; p.155 G. de Rooij; miscellaneous others John Liggins.

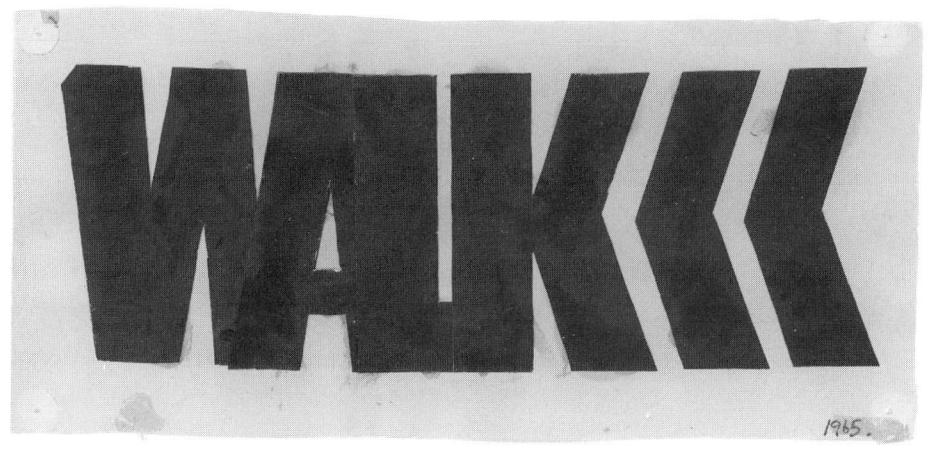

Walk
Collage, 1965.

Sun Prayer
"My first concrete poem done on the typewriter...", 1965.

```
11111111111111111111111111111111111111111111111111111111111111
11111111111111111111111111111111111111111111111111111111111111
11111111111111111111111111111111111111111111111111111111111111
11111111111111111111111111111111111111111111111111111111111111
11111111111111111111111111111111111111111111111111111111111111
111111111111111111111111111iiiiiiiiiii11111111111111111111111111
111111111111111111111111111iiiiiiiiiii11111111111111111111111111
111111111111111111111111111iiiiiiiiiii11111111111111111111111111
111111111111111111111111111iiiiiiiiiii11111111111111111111111111
111111111111111111111111111iiiiiiiiiii11111111111111111111111111
11111111111111111111111111111111111111111111111111111111111111
11111111111111111111111111111111111111111111111111111111111111
1111111111111111111iiiiiiiiiiiiiiiiiiii11111111111111111111111111
1111111111111111111iiiiiiiiiiiiiiiiiiii11111111111111111111111111
1111111111111111111iiiiiiiiiiiiiiiiiiii11111111111111111111111111
111111111111111111111111111iiiiiiiiiii11111111111111111111111111
111111111111111111111111111iiiiiiiiiii11111111111111111111111111
111111111111111111111111111iiiiiiiiiii11111111111111111111111111
111111111111111111111111111iiiiiiiiiii11111111111111111111111111
111111111111111111111111111iiiiiiiiiii11111111111111111111111111
111111111111111111111111111iiiiiiiiiii11111111111111111111111111
111111111111111111111111111iiiiiiiiiii11111111111111111111111111
111111111111111111111111111iiiiiiiiiii11111111111111111111111111
111111111111111111111111111iiiiiiiiiii11111111111111111111111111
111111111111111111111111111iiiiiiiiiii11111111111111111111111111
11111111111111111111111111111111111111111111111111111111111111
1111111111111111111iiiiiiiiiiiiiiiiiiii11111111111111111111111111
1111111111111111111iiiiiiiiiiiiiiiiiiii11111111111111111111111111
1111111111111111111iiiiiiiiiiiiiiiiiiii11111111111111111111111111
11111111111111111111111111111111111111111111111111111111111111
11111111111111111111111111111111111111111111111111111111111111
11111111111111111111111111111111111111111111111111111111111111
11111111111111111111111111111111111111111111111111111111111111
```

Typewriter poem
1968.

potato / mirror
Typewriter, 1968.

ᛉᛉ.... NO

ᚠᚱᚱ... ALL.

NO / ALL (KonKrunes Series)
Ink, 1968.

```
art   slab
rat   salb
tar   bals
rab   last
sal   tarb
sat   bral
sar   balt
tas   larb
bat   slar
tab   rals
sab   lart
las   bart
bal   sart
lat   bars
ral   bast
tal   sarb
ras   talb
lar   stab
bar   slat
bas   ralt
```

art slab
Typewriter, 1969.

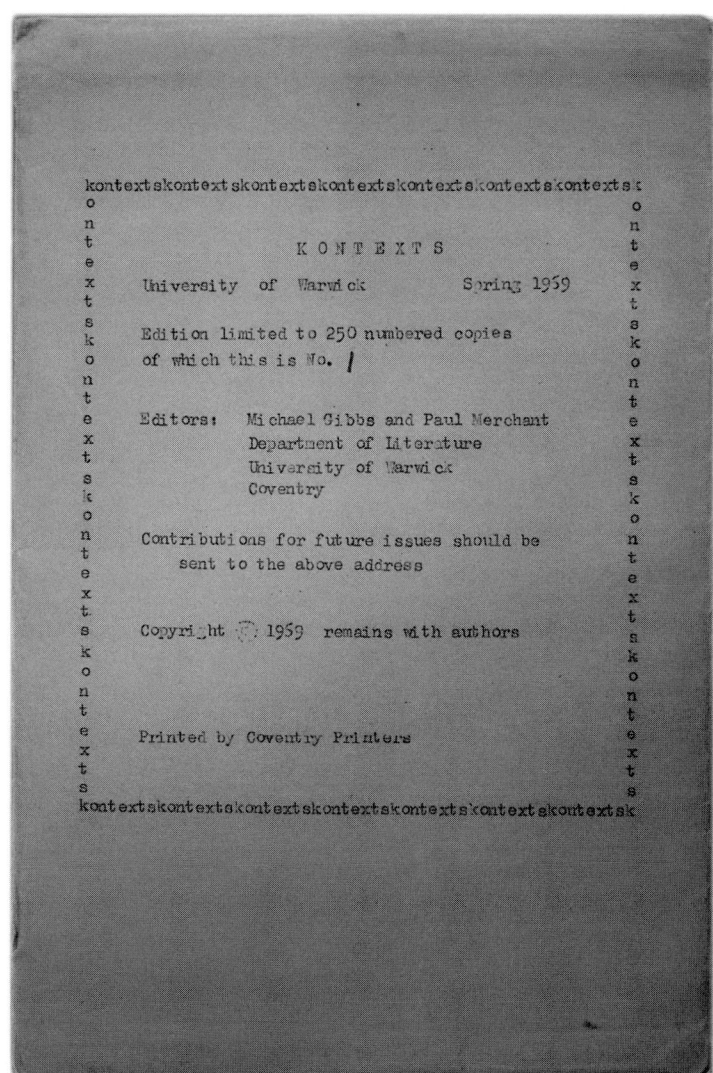

Kontexts 1
"I arranged for John Sharkey to come to the University to give a lecture on concrete poetry, and it seemed that there was some interest in the subject from my fellow students. Paul Merchant, the young lecturer who was taking us for the Periods and Themes poetry course, expressed a particular interest, and the spring of 1969 we co-produced the first issue of *Kontexts*, which consisted of a buff envelope containing eight poem-cards printed on yellow, blue and green card. Besides two works each by myself and Paul, the other contributors were fellow-students: Andrew Belsey, Alan Shutt, Terence McCarthy and Wendy Opie. The edition was of 250 copies, and the costs were divided between myself and Paul."

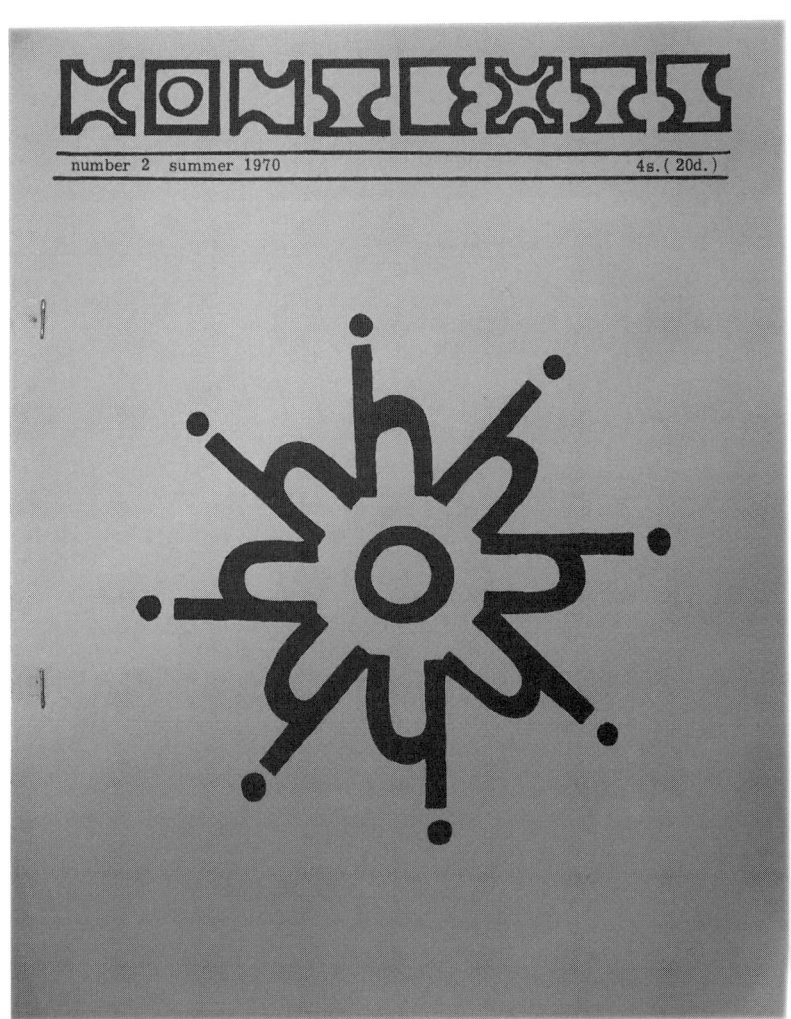

Kontexts 2

"The magazine was printed in at least 3 places: a commercial printer for the cover, a page by Houedard, and a fold out page by Richard Chadwick, the campus printer for some other pages, and the English department for mimeo pages. It was, as was to become usual, decidedly a low budget operation. Besides those I've already mentioned, I had contributions from Cavan McCarthy (editor of the concrete mag *Tlaloc*), Bob Cobbing, Andrew Lloyd, Nicholas Mann (a lecturer in the French dept. at Warwick), Peter Mayer, Gerald Rocher, Paul de Vree (the Belgian editor of *De Tafelronde*, which like *Tlaloc* had just published my poems), Nicholas Zurbrugg, Alan Ridell, myself, and Jenny Rouse (with a piece of cut-up prose). There was a short review section which publicised some other British concrete poetry presses. The edition was 250 copies, and Jenny and I did all the collating and stapling at home. The living room table was piled with stacks of pages and one day we returned to find them spilt all over the floor having been knocked over by the cats. That explains why some copies have paw-prints on them." Summer 1970.

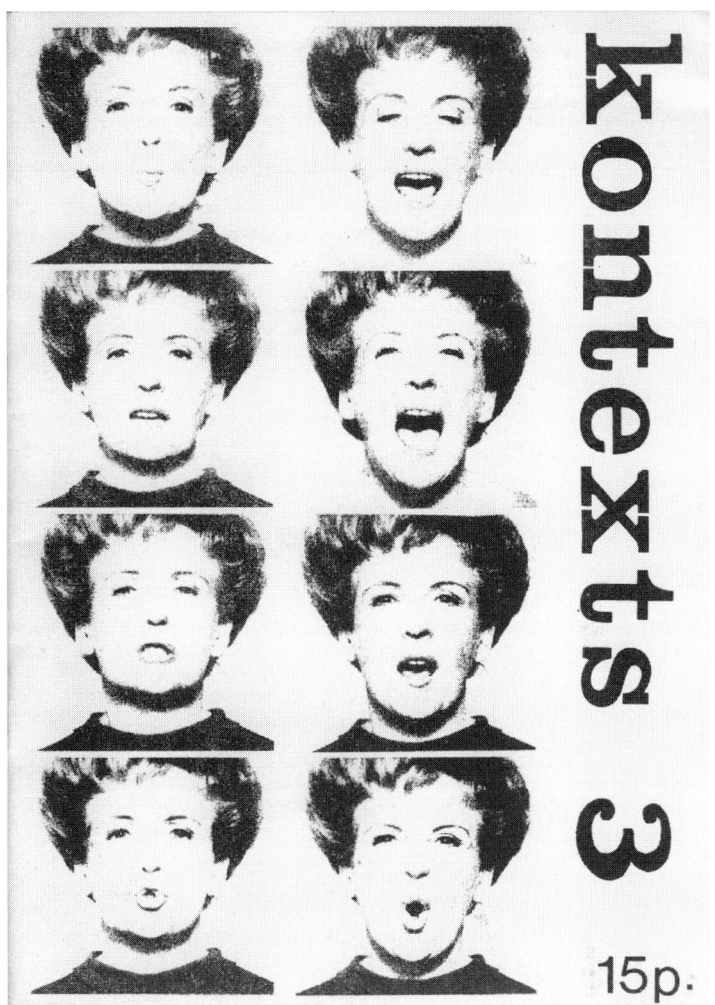

Kontexts 3

"Since the publication of issues 1 and 2 I had established several new connections with visual poets in other countries: Sarenco's group in Brescia, Italy, Todorović's Signalist Poets in Yugoslavia, and Edgardo Antonio Vigo in Argentina. *Kontexts* 3 contained 10 pages of 'Notes form the Concrete Jungle', listing publications from these and other concrete/visual poets, and contributions from 16 poets, including some who had contributed to the previous issue. Bob Cobbing contributed a found sound poem for the cover and G-J. de Rook a piece called 'The poet is an alchemist', which necessitated cutting out 200 squares of silver foil and typing each one individually with the word 'gold' before gluing to the pages. Some of the printing was in offset, but most of it had to be done by stencil, which I did myself using (unofficially) the duplicator in the office of the secretary for English Studies. It was my first attempt at duplicating, and I had made the mistake of using an IBM Executive for cutting the stencils which made rather too wide letters, so that in the printing many of the sheets stuck to the stencil drum and had to be prised off by hand. The whole edition was supposed to be 200, but because of spoilage there were probably no more than 150 good copies." Summer 1971.

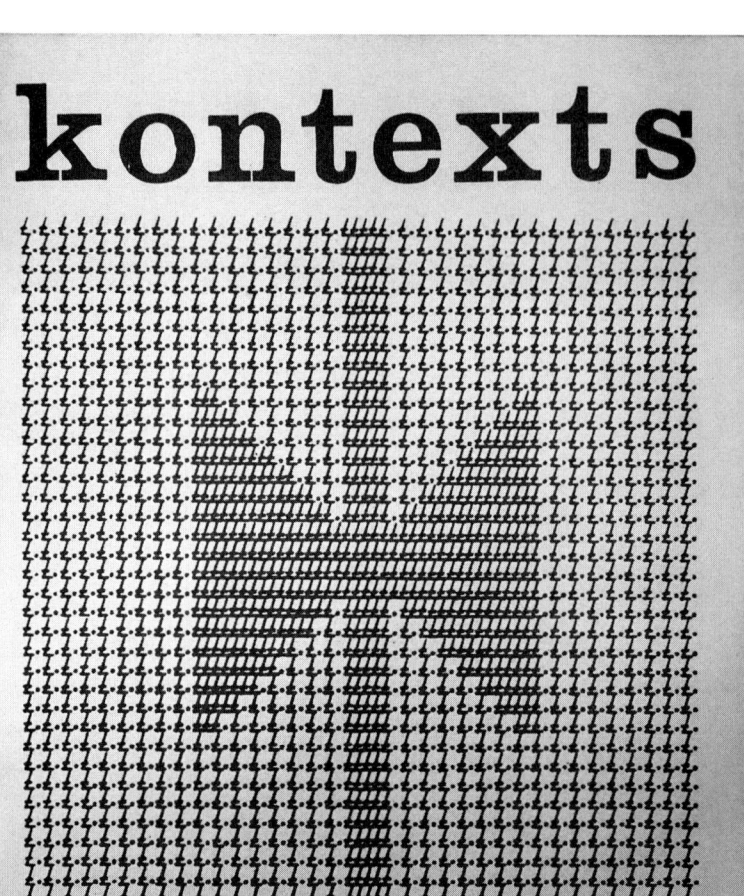

Kontexts 4 "U.S. Edition"
Edition of 250 copies, winter 1972/73.
"*Kontexts* 4 (dated winter 72/3) appeared as a special U.S. issue, featuring Richard Kostelanetz, Dan Graham, Wally Depew & others. Again, it was a mixture of offset and stencil printing, the latter being done at Beau Geste, the former by a small commercial printer in Exeter (who, as far as I recall, never sent a bill for the work!). *Kontexts* 5 came out a few months later, produced in yet another format, this time oblong A5 with, for the first time perfect binding (in other words, hand-gluing, a technique I'd learned from Felipe [Ehrenberg]). All the printing, again a combination of offset and mimeo, was done at Beau Geste [Press]. It was quite an international issue, including work from Eastern Europe, USA, etc., as well as a fairly extensive reviews section. By this time I'd accumulated a substantial collection of books, pamphlets and magazines of visual poetry sent to *Kontexts* for review or as exchange, and I was engaged in a wide correspondence soliciting new material and keeping in touch with visual poets all over the world."

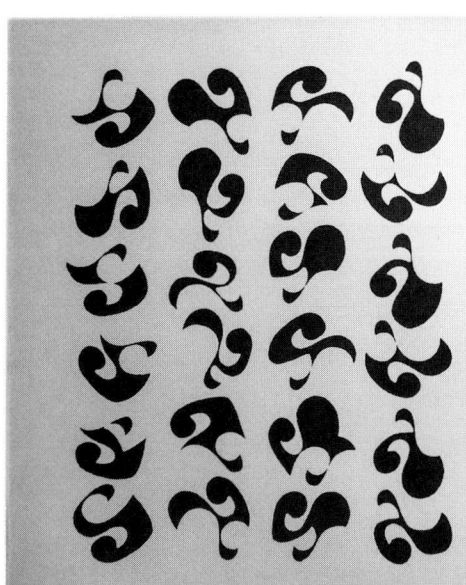

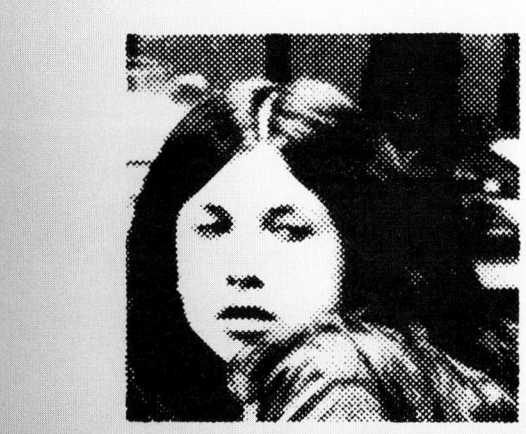

Kontexts 5
Contributions by four East European poets: Karel Adamus, Toth Gabor, J. H. Kocman, Jiří Valoch; also Michael Gibbs, Peter Finch, Bob Cobbing, Jochen Gerz, Ulisses Carion etc.; edition of 250 copies, 1973.

C.I.A. - CREATIVE INDEX ARTISTS
C.I.A. - CENTRAL INFORMATION ARTISTS
C.I.A. - CONFIDENTIAL INTERPERSONAL ARTISTS
C.I.A. - COMMON INTEREST ARTISTS
C.I.A. - CAPITALIST IMAGE ARTISTS
C.I.A. - CATALOGUE IDOLIZATION ARTISTS
C.I.A. - CIVIC INVOLVEMENT ARTISTS
C.I.A. - CLASSICAL INDOCTRINATED ARTISTS
C.I.A. - CLOSED INQUEST ARTISTS
C.I.A. - COLLABORATIVE INCESTUOUS ARTISTS
C.I.A. - CONFORMIST INTELLECTUAL ARTISTS
C.I.A. - COMMERCIAL INDUSTRIAL ARTISTS
C.I.A. - CYBERNETIC INNOVATION ARTISTS
C.I.A. - COSMIC ILLUSION ARTISTS
C.I.A. - CONTROLLED IDENTITY ARTISTS
C.I.A. - CONTEMPORARY INCIDENT ARTISTS
C.I.A. - CEREMONIAL ICONOGRAPHY ARTISTS
C.I.A. - COLLECTIVE IDEA ARTISTS
C.I.A. - COMMUNICATION IMITATION ARTISTS
C.I.A. - CLASSIFICATION INVESTIGATION ARTISTS
C.I.A. - CONCRETE IMAGE ARTISTS
C.I.A. - CHANCE INVENTION ARTISTS
C.I.A. - COMMUNAL INFLUENCE ARTISTS
C.I.A. - COGNITIVE INDETERMINATE ARTISTS
C.I.A. - CONTINUOUS INSTANT ARTISTS
C.I.A. - CONCEPTUAL IDEALIST ARTISTS

Michael Gibbs C.I.A.   KONTEXTS Publications 1972

C.I.A. (Corruption in Art)
"Everyone at Beau Geste, including Felipe's kids Yael and Mathias, was busy making their own little books with the mimeo machines, so I made one too—a 16-page poem sequence entitled *Lifeline*, small oblong format, in an edition of 100 copies. I also produced an A3 poster poem (in offset) called *C.I.A. (Corruption in Art)*, and made plans for a series of 'supply and demand editions' which were to be A3 posters photocopied only when someone ordered one." Kontexts Publications, Exeter, 1972.

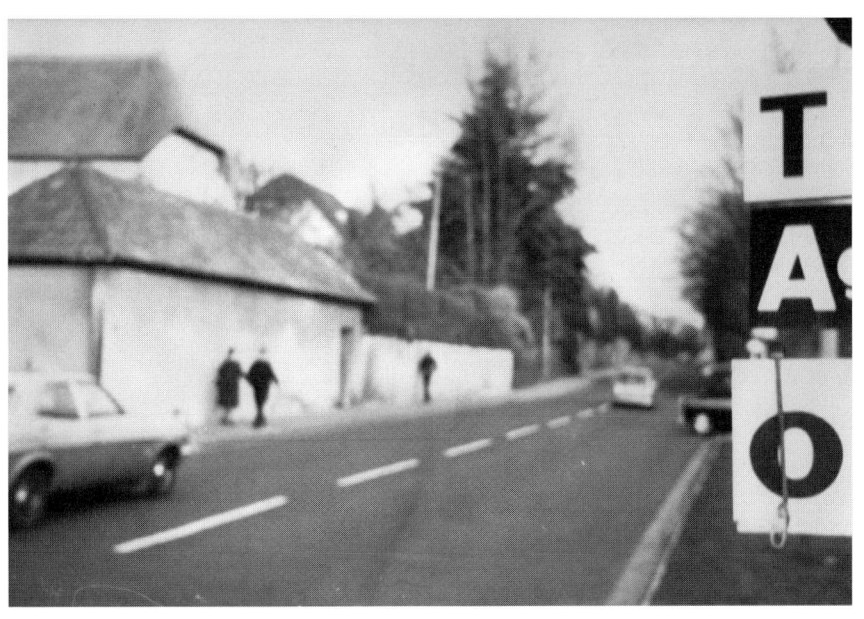

Found TAO Poem
Photograph, 1972.

```
different                          the same
different                          the same
different                          the  ame
different                          the same
different                          the same
different                          the same
different                          5he same
differen                           the same
different                          the same
different                          the same
differeent                         the same
diffœrent                          the same
different                          the same
different                          the same
duifferent                         the same
fdifferen                          the same
different                          the same
different                          the same
differeny                          the same
different                          the s me
different                          the sam
different                          the same
different                          the sam
different                          the same
eifferent                          the same
different                          the same
different                          the same
different                          the same
different                          the same
different                          the same
different                          the same
different                          the same
different                          the same
diifferent                            the same
different                          the same
different                          the same
d ffferent                         the same
different                          the sam
different                          the same
different                          the same
different                          the same
differen6                             the same
different                          the same
dufferent                          the same
different                          the same
different                          the sam
d ifferent                         the same
different                          the same
different                          the same
different                          thr same
differ t                           the same
```

Operational Text
"Instructions: type as fast as possible; do not correct any mistakes that are made."
1973.

<u>causality</u> — Z because of Y because of X because of W because of V because of U because of T because of S because of R because of Q because of P because of O because of N because of M because of L because of K because of J because of I because of H because of G because of F because of E because of D because of C because of B because of A

Alpha – Aleph / Alphabet
Beginnings /
Codes to be
Deciphered /
Experiments in language-events /
Formulas /
Games to break
Habits & Hierarchies of syntax
Imposed / Implanted onto the way we think
Jamming the mental circuits /
Korzybski (Alfred):
Language as a
Map ("A map is not the territory it represents, but, if correct, it has a similar structure to the territory")
New linguistic structures
Open new territories & new
Perceptions /
Questioning the
Reliability of
Signs /
Text as Test /
Uni –
Verse /
Word
X - tensions towards
Yet more
Zones of meaning

1974/1976.

Language Art / Causality
1974/1976.

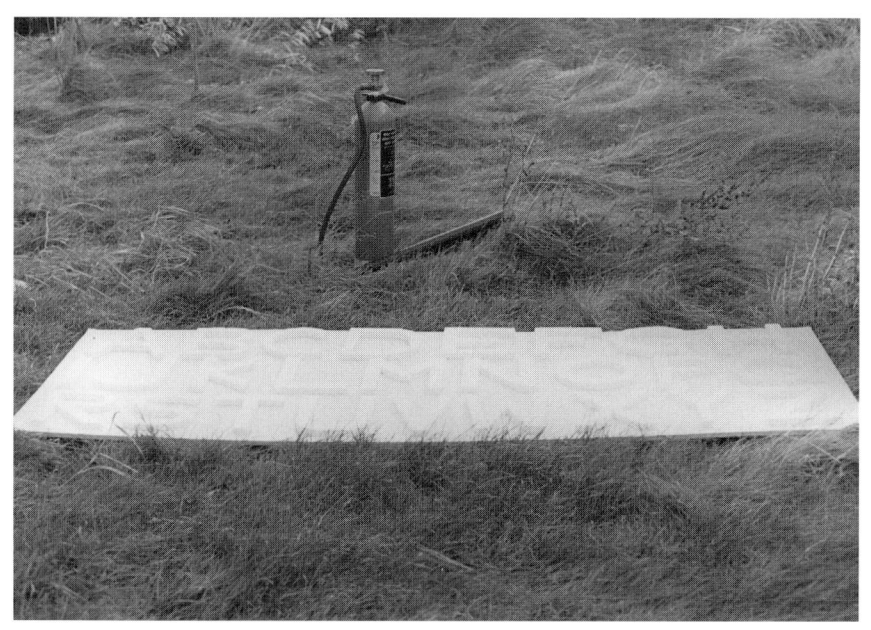

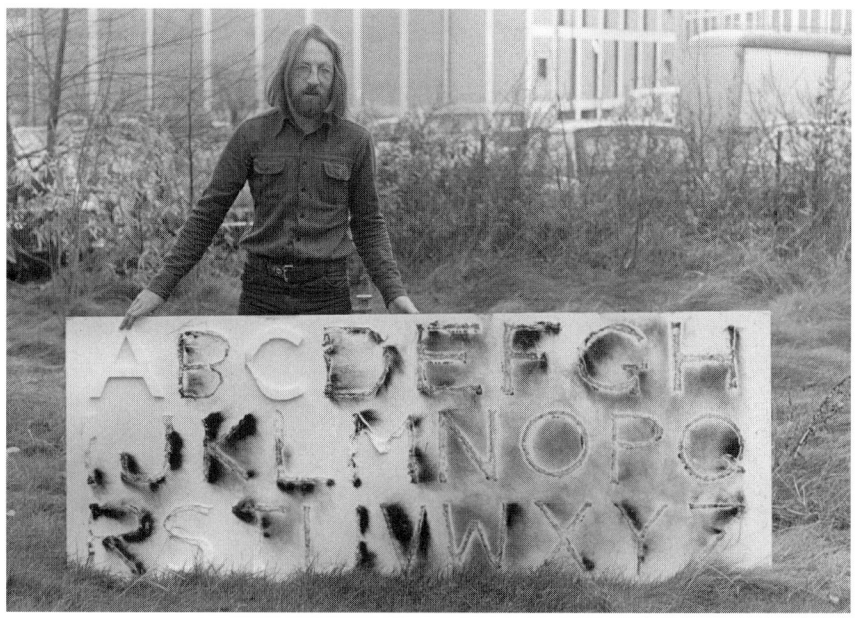

Extinction
Performance, Jan van Eyck Academie, Maastricht, November 1974.

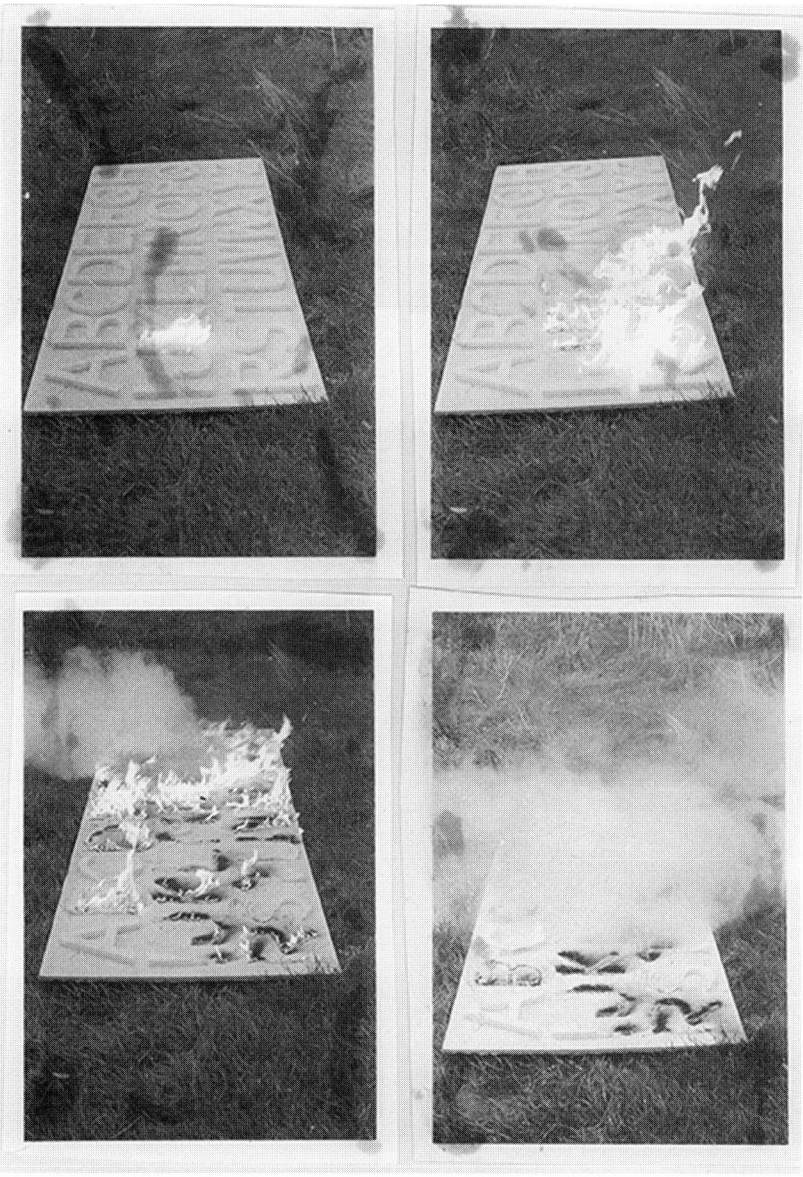

"The workshop at the Jan van Eyck developed into a project for a book, called 'Scriptimages', to which each of us contributed our own work, as well as photographs of graffiti from the walls of the caves and tunnels under the 'mountain' (in Dutch terms!) of St Pietersberg, Maastricht... I worked hard on laying out of the book and preparing the plates for printing, and it finally appeared in February 1975. Part of my contribution was two photographs of a performance piece called 'Extinction', which involved setting fire to an alphabet of large letters cut out of polystyrene and then putting out the blaze with a fire extinguisher, This was done in the garden of the Jan van Eyck and recorded on video by Raul Marroquin."

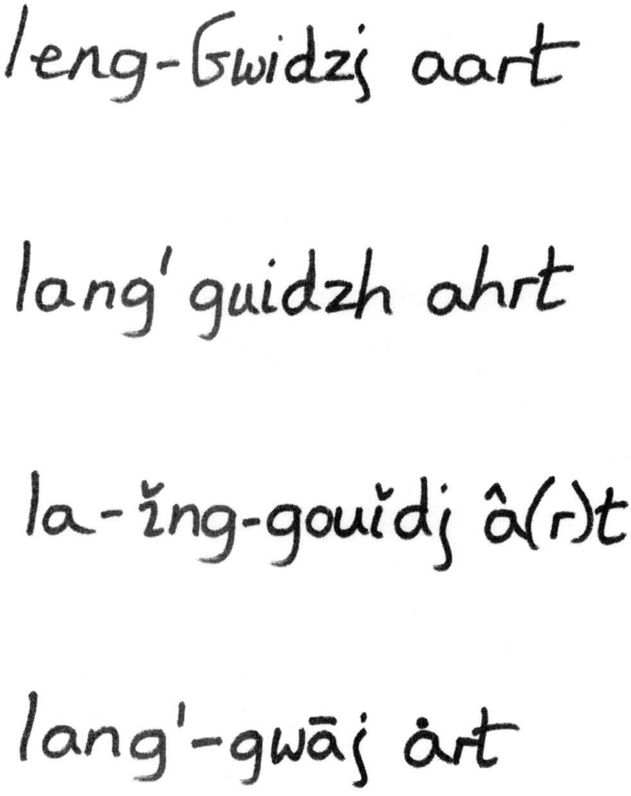

leng-Gwidzj aart

lang' guidzh ahrt

la-ĭng-gouĭdj â(r)t

lang'-gwāj årt

Language Art
"Visual art in any form/media/inter-media, in which the principle idea is related to linguistic (and para-/meta-linguistic) expression and invention in terms of writing, speech, words, letters, syntax etc. (i.e. language systems). My own particular contribution in this new genre was initially 'concrete' and visual poetry, but more recently I have been concerned with exploring the basic elements of language in terms of minimal verbo-visual structures—this led me to a number of works which use the visual possibilities of one of the most basic linguistic structures: the alphabet.'
Ink on paper, 1974.

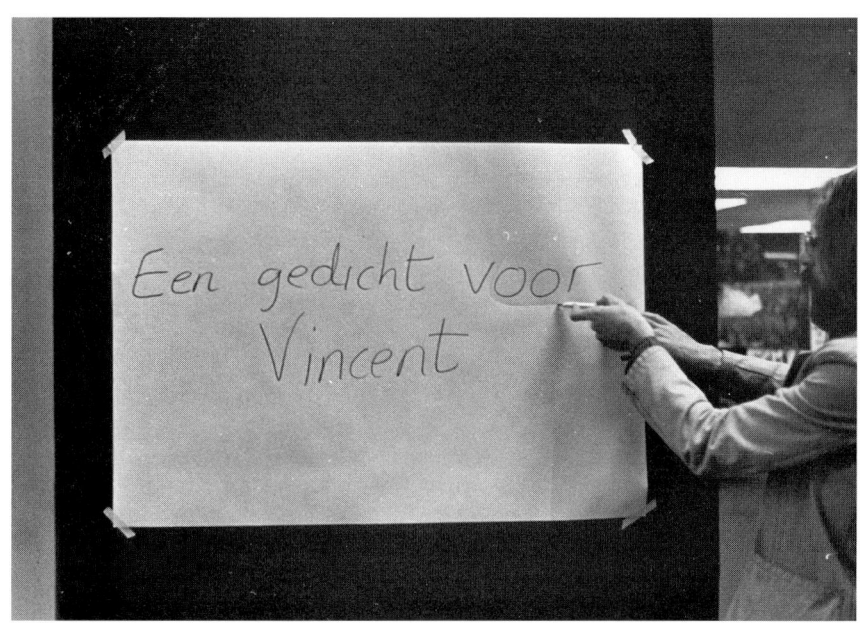

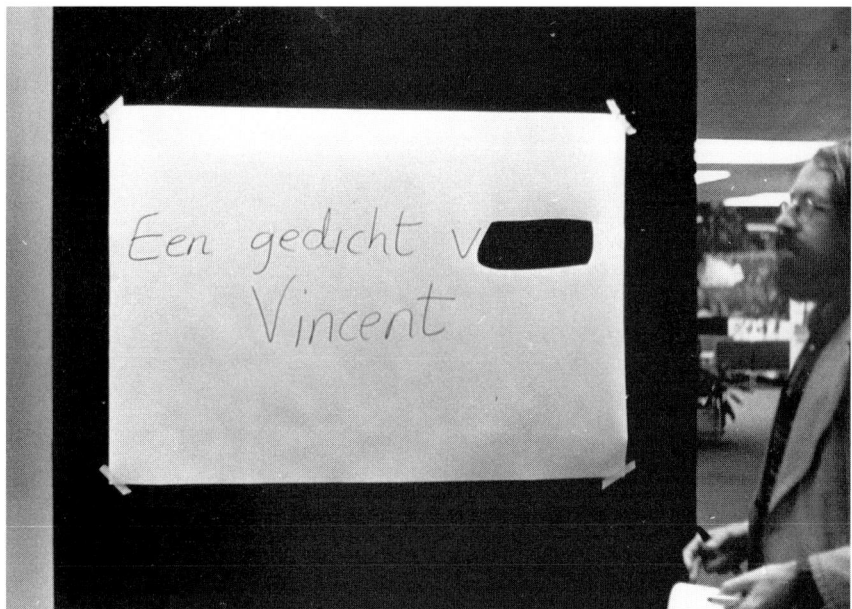

Een gedicht voor Vincent (A poem for Vincent)
Performance, Van Gogh Museum, Amsterdam, 15 November 1975.

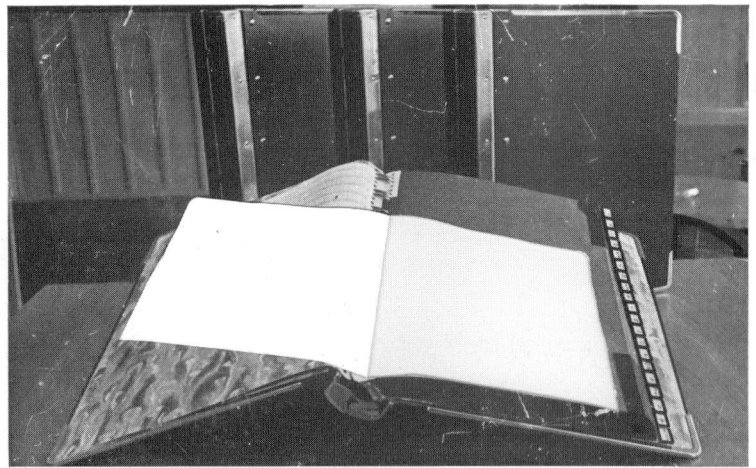

The Book
Amended photograph printed from a copper plate found in an Amsterdam junkshop, 1975.

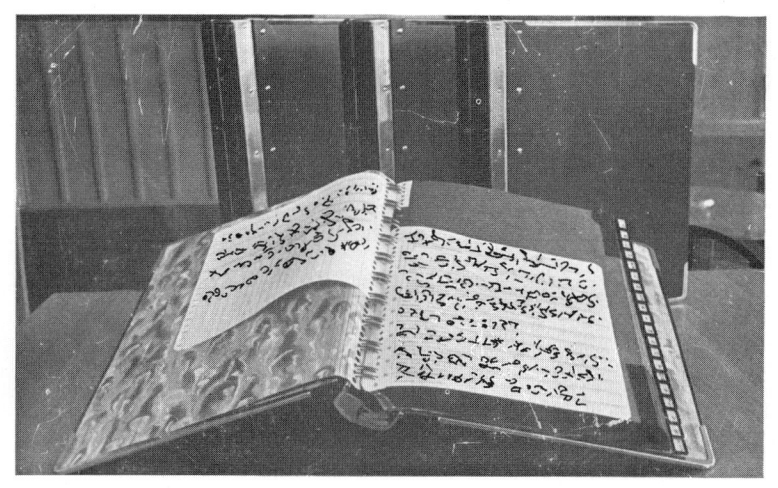

Secrets of the Book

→

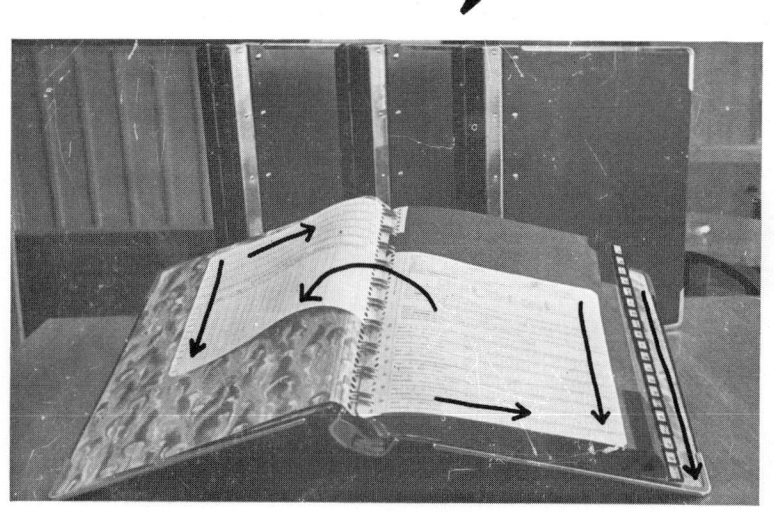

Directions of The Book

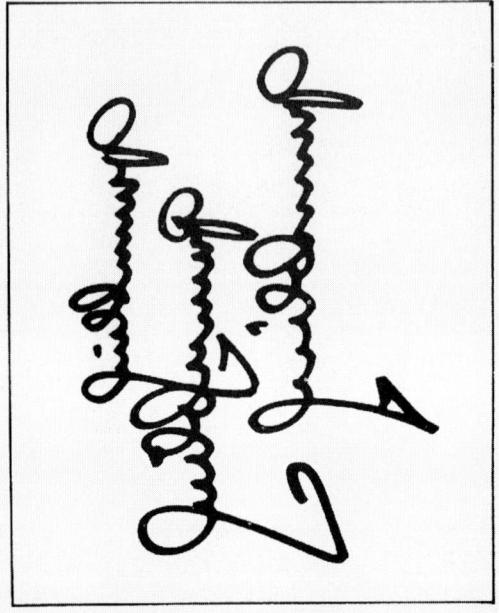

Kontexts 6 & 7 "A review of visual / experimental poetry and language art"
"In the early part of 1975 I made occasional trips to Amsterdam, staying with Tony and Plym... I had a lot of contact with Ulises [Carrión] and the Icelanders and with John Liggins whom i'd met at the Jan van Eyck [Academie] where he was printing cards and booklets of his own work. The In Out Centre had closed and Ulises was planning to open a shop for artists' books. I was able to supply Ulises with a lot of addresses of concrete/ visual poetry publishers. Ulises had written an essay called 'The New Art of making Books', which I decided to publish in the next issue of *Kontexts* (issue 6/7). The Jan van Eyck agreed to let me print this issue of *Kontexts* using their facilities, which saved an enormous amount of money as I only had to pay the costs of paper and prints. It turned out to be the best produced issue of the magazine so far, the first to be printed entirely in offset. As soon as the magazine was printed I packed a rucksack full of copies and took the train and boat to London to attend the Sound Poetry Festival which was being held at the Poetry Society."

kontexts

an occasional review of visual poetries and language arts – issue no. 8 spring 1976   price f3.50 / £0.50 / $1.25

poetry in action

The opening of the exhibition Internationale Visuele Poëzie at 't Hoogt in Utrecht last July was celebrated with a programme of performances by some of the poets & artists represented in the show. In various ways they showed how their visual experimentation with poetry and language could be extended & realised through actions and events. Most of the pieces were short, simple presentations of a particular idea, such as Pieter Mol's literal interpretation of the dutch phrase "eens flink met mezelf de vloer aanvegen" ("wiping the floor with myself"). Peter followed this with a piece in which he walked across the stage announcing "I am mak-ing his-tor-y", pacing each syllable, and then returning, with the words "Beh-ind me is his-tor-y". Sigurdur Gudmundsson's "Animal Opera" was, like his earlier versions of Little Red Riding Hood and Aladdin, a minimal stripped-down concept: the Opera consisted of an arm appearing from behind the backdrop holding a piece of sheep's wool and the sound of Sigi saying "baaaa". On appearing for the second time the arm is holding a horseshoe with the sound of a neigh from Sigi. John Liggins (photos page 1) also aided the visual element of the show by demonstrating each one somewhat with the air at a school physics teacher practising alchemy. Michael Gibbs's installation piece "Conversations" in which books conducted imaginary discussions among their authors, was followed by three "Body Poem" actions – the last of these was the literalisation of its title, "These Letters are my Flesh & my Blood".
Among the other performers at this first programme of visual poetry in action were Robert Joseph, Pier van Dijk, U.G. Stikker, Ulises Carrion, and Mark Insingel.
In November, when the same exhibition opened at the Van Gogh Museum in Amsterdam, another series of performances marked the occasion. This time, Vincent van Gogh's presence rather dominated the proceedings, as three of the performances paid homage to him: Robert Joseph and Pier van Dijk ate potatoes under the famous "The Potato Eaters" painting, Ulises Carrion read out all the Van Goghs from the Amsterdam telephone directory, and Michael Gibbs wrote "Een Gedicht vóór Vincent" (oor = ear).
On the same day another smaller exhibition of dutch visual poetry opened at Amsterdam's Kunsthistorisches Instituut, and again there were performances. Altogether an active day for visual poetry!

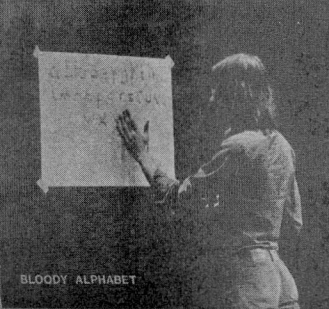
BLOODY ALPHABET

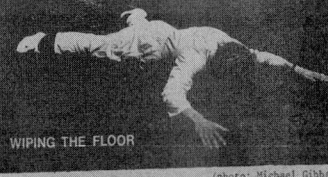
WIPING THE FLOOR
(photo: Michael Gibbs)

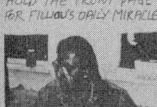
STOP PRESS
HOLD THE FRONT PAGE FOR FILLIOU'S DAILY MIRACLE!

A MESSAGE FROM ROBERT FILLIOU TO GEORGE BRECHT

dear george today the daily miracle is) was telling Rod Summers, here in Maastricht, about daily miracle, and he said " it would be a great title for a newspaper" and I said " yes. and I'd be a newspaper editor and when people would come in, I'd ask : " what's the daily miracle?", and just at that moment Raul' Marsupini came in And I told the story to Michael Gibbs, and he said " next issue of Kontexts will be a newspaper and please tell me the story."
Maastricht, March 26, '76

kontents

pages 8-11
THE NEW REFORMERS:
WILLIAM BURROUGHS &
BRION GYSIN IN GENEVA
interview * video
portrait * pages from
THE THIRD MIND

pages 2-3
VOCABULARY by
Jackson Mac Low

pages 4-5
POESIE SONORE by
Henri Chopin

page 7
VERBOTECTURE by
Arrigo Lora-Totino

page 12
MOLLTOR

feature pages by
Mirtha Dermisache and
Richard Hartwell

NEWS AND REVIEWS
books/exhibitions
records/video

kontexts

editor: michael gibbs
contributing
editor: ulises carrion
design: michael gibbs

printed at the jan van
eyck academy, maastricht
in an edition of 500
copies.

editorial content © 1976
KONTEXTS publications.
contributors retain
copyright.

ADDRESS for all
correspondance:

KONTEXTS Publications
c/o Other Books & So
Herengracht 227
Amsterdam
Netherlands.

Kontexts 8 "An occasional review or visual poetries and language arts"
Contributions by Jackson Mac Low; Henri Chopin; Arrigo Lora-Totino, John Liggins et al;.
Ulises Carrión is contributing editor and Other Books & So the editorial address; edition of 500 copies, spring 1976.

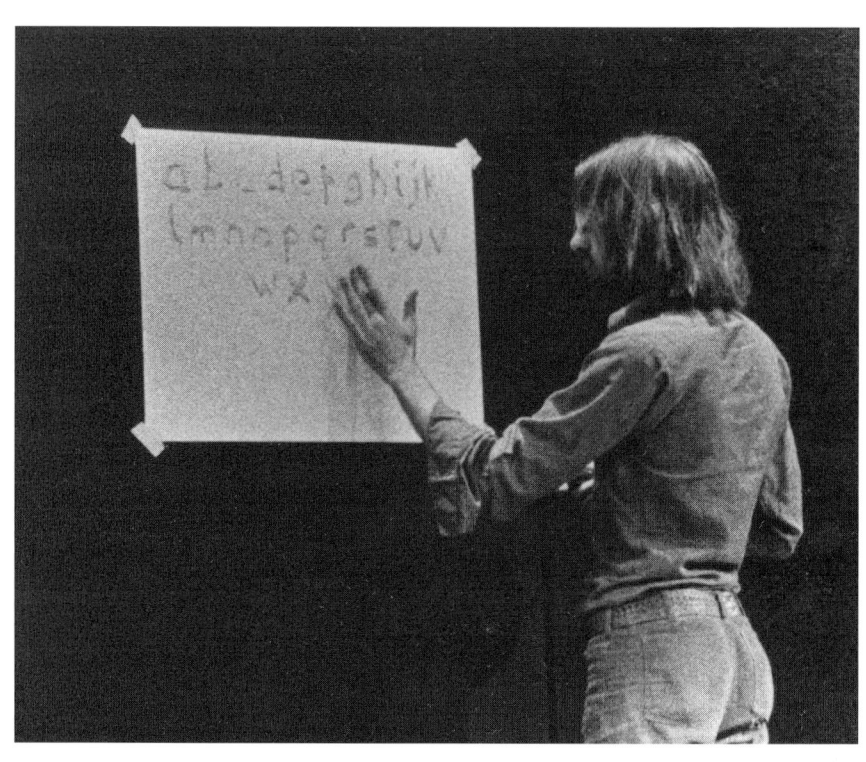

These Letters Are My Flesh and My Blood
Performance, 't Hoogt, Utrecht, 1976.

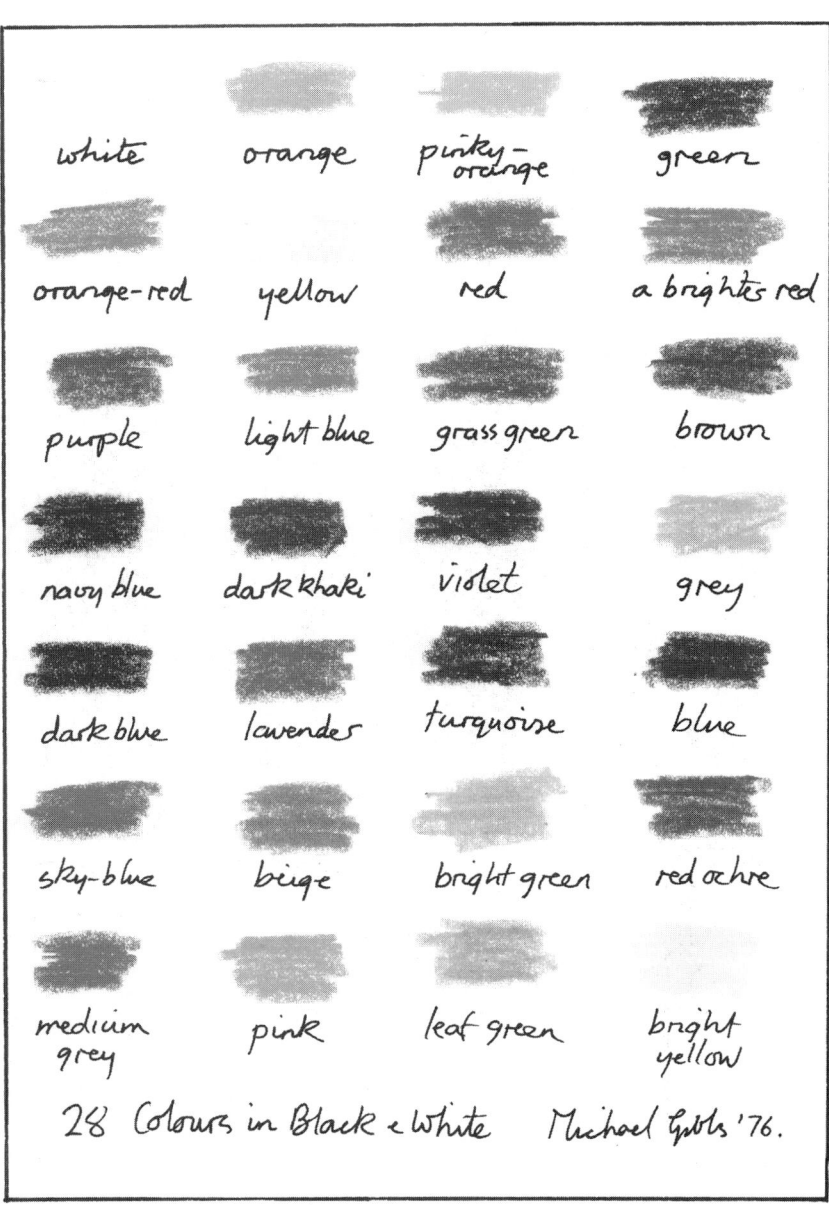

28 Colours in Black & White
Ink and coloured crayon, 1976.

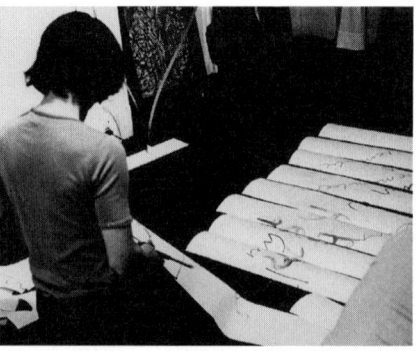
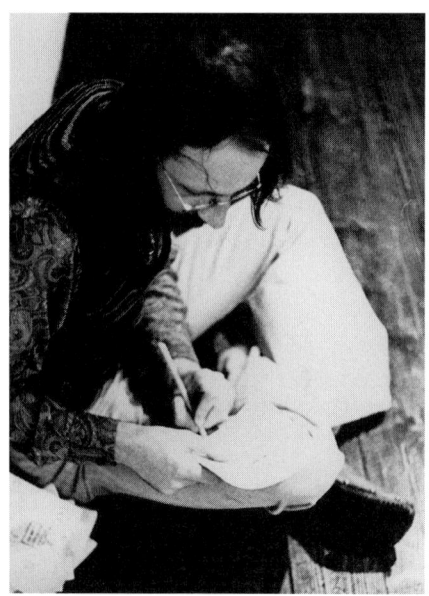
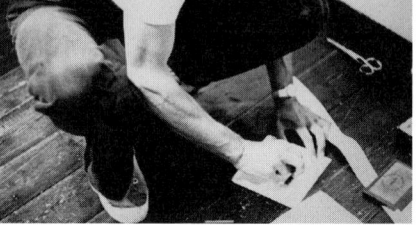
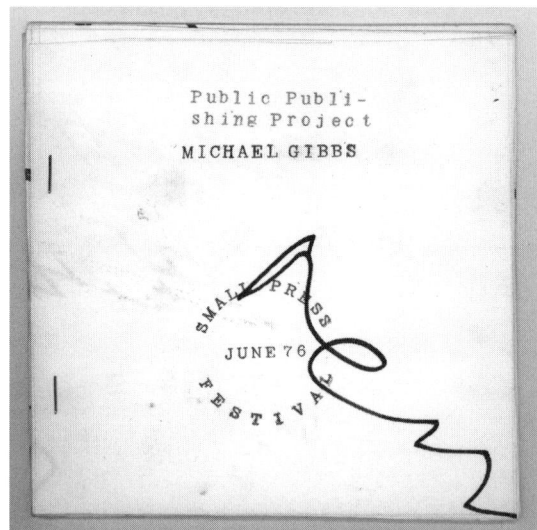

Public Publishing Project
"A 24-page book in an edition of 14 original copies produced in about one hour.
1. Writing, 2. Cutting, 3. Cutting, 4. Collating, 5. Binding, 6. Titling, 7. Signing."
Galerie Kontakt, Antwerp, 12 June 1976.

Newspaper Art / Art Newspapers
Announcement for the exhibition at Other Books and So, organised by Michael Gibbs, 1976.

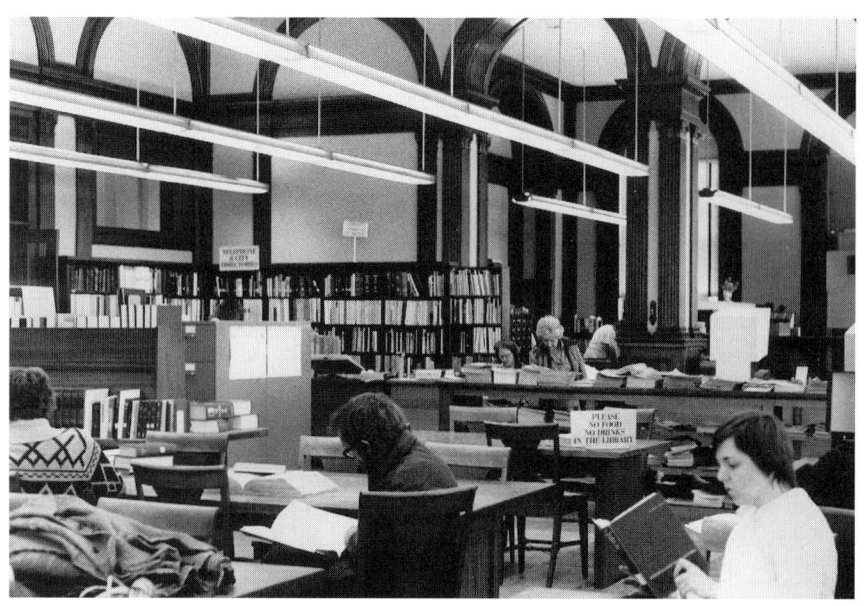

Proposal for 'Event for Large Public Library'
"At 11.30 a.m. a card will be distributed to every seat in the library... it is hoped that the event may be tape recorded, with the aid of several microphones discreetly placed around the library." 1977.

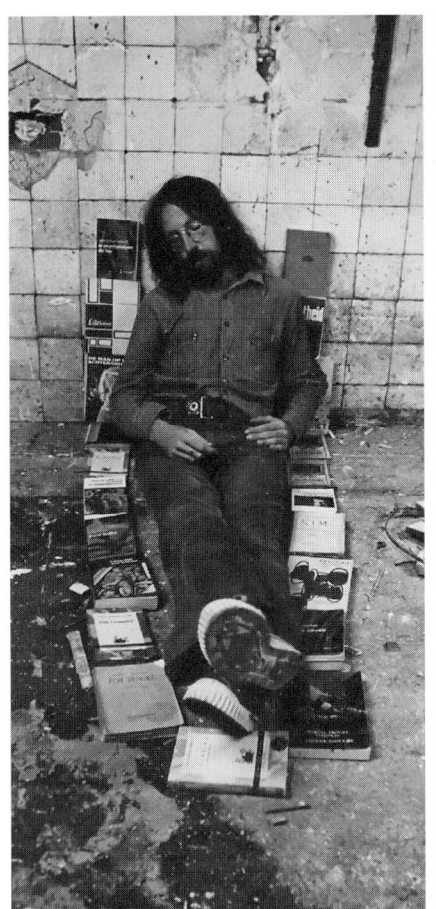 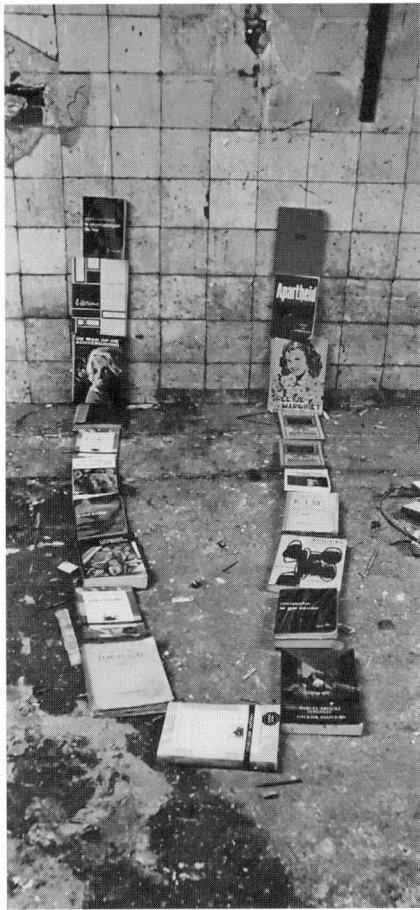

Un Poème Symboliste
Photographs, 1977.

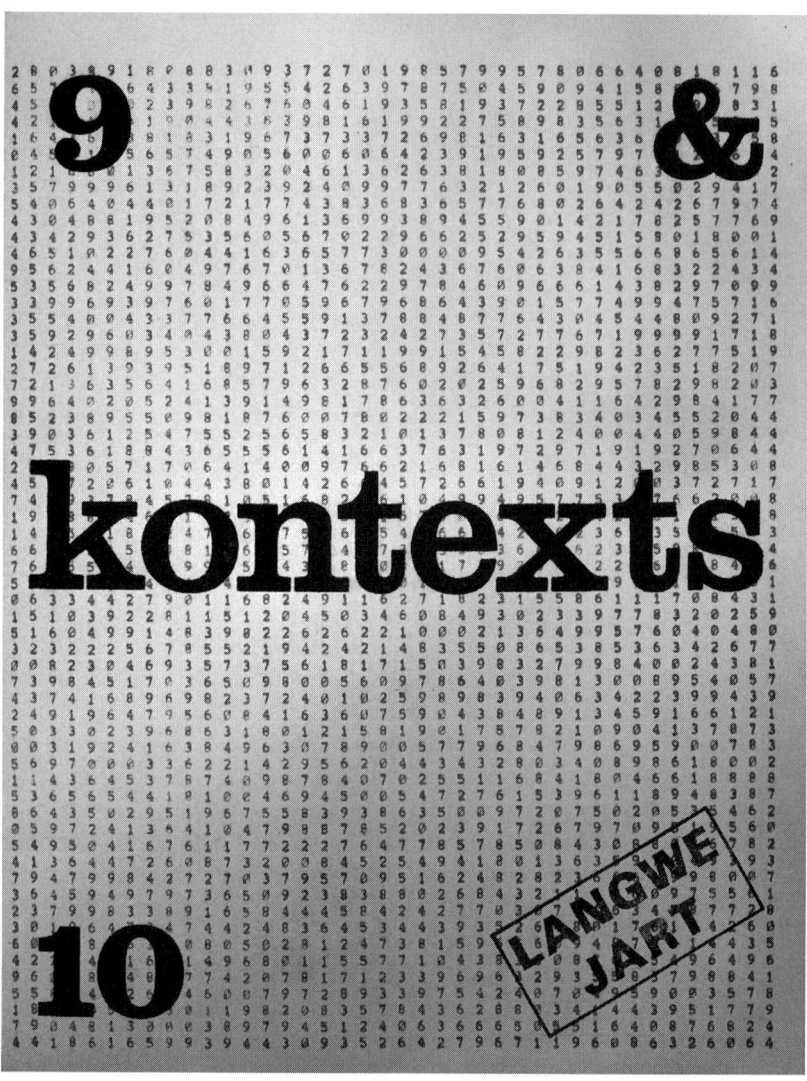

Kontexts 9 & 10 "Langwe Jart"
Contributions by Dick Higgins, Ivan Nahem, Richard Hayman, Jean-Jacques Cory, Fred Truck, Tony Rickaby, bp Nichol, Scott Helmes, Peter Mayer, Stephen Williams, A. C. Carvalho, Bill Bissett, Wilson Stapleton, Carl Clark, Muriel Osesen, Jose-Luis Castillejo, Ulises Carrión, Tom Winter, Robin Crozier, Ladislav Novak, John Christie, Nicholas Zurbrugg, Michael Druks, John Liggins, Endre Tot, and Michael Gibbs; "*Kontexts* 9/10 was printed using the colour stencil facilities at the Paradiso". Edition of 500 copies, winter 1976/77.

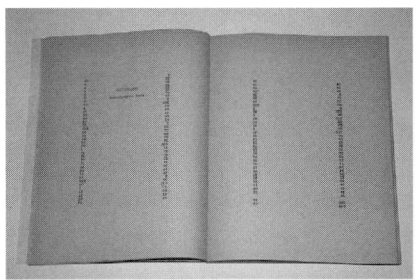
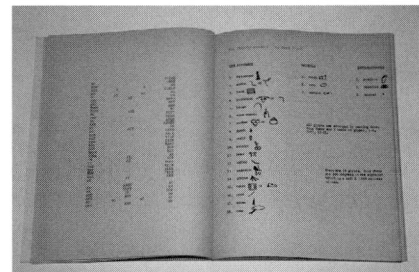
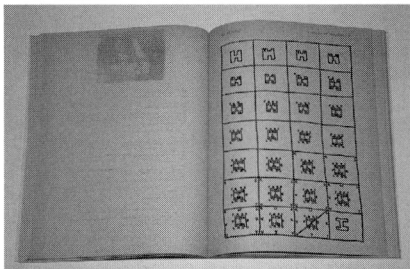
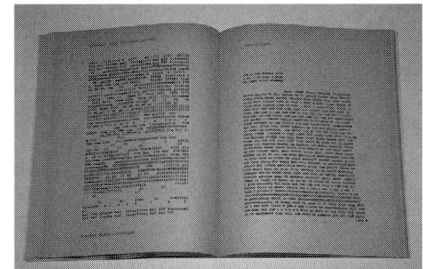
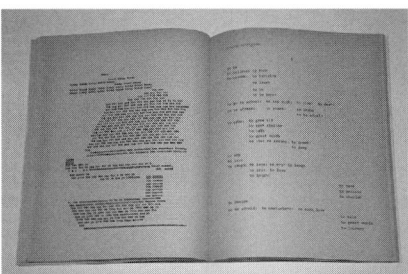
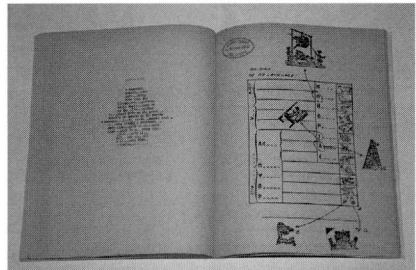
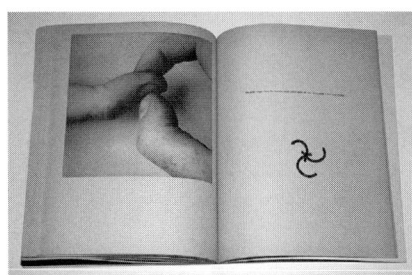
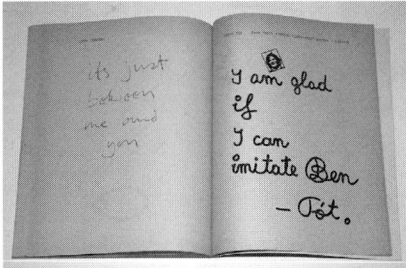

"…initially devoted to 'concrete' poetry (hence the title, from the german 'konkrete'), it very soon became involved with visual poetry, and more recently, as particularly exemplified in this [final] issue, the development of a more conceptual, rather than purely visual (or 'retinal') approach to language experimentation, together with related processes in the fields of photography, video, performance and music."

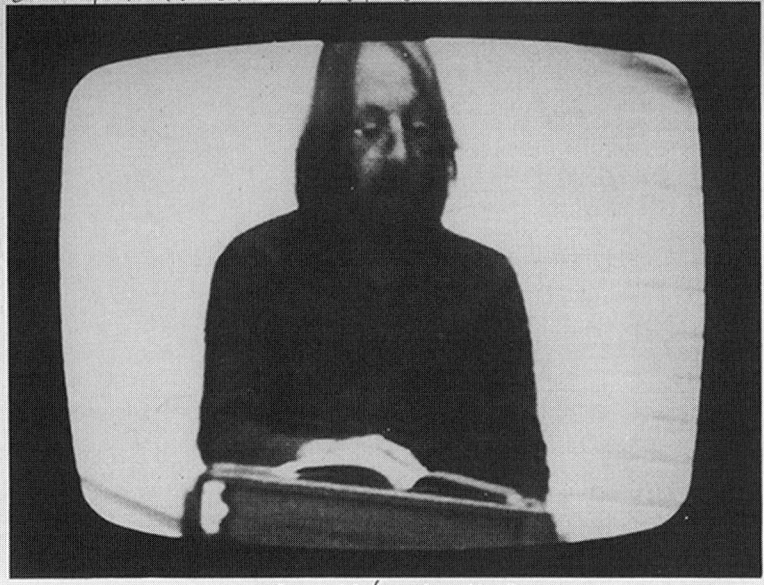

Open Page / Closed Mind
Performance, Toronto, 1977.

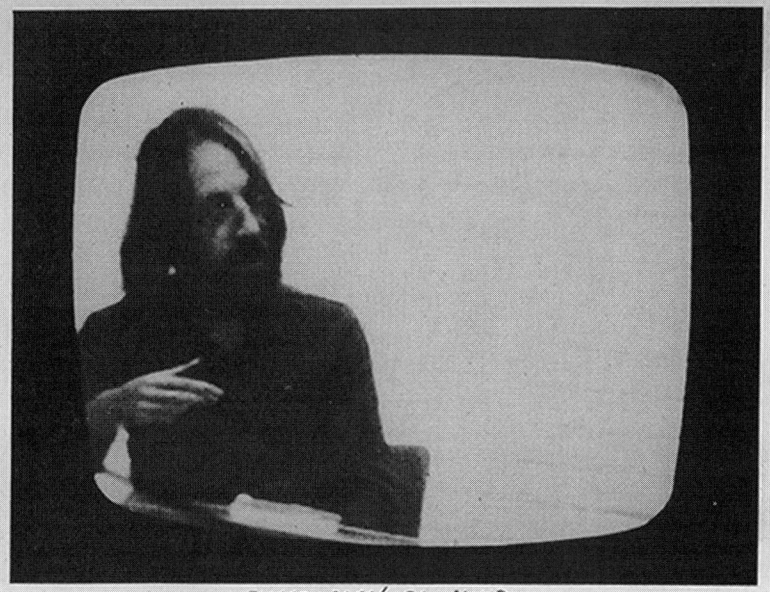

Closed Page / Open Mind
Performance, Toronto, 1977.

GALERIE WAALKENS, HOOFDWEG 39, FINSTERWOLDE,
tel. (05971)-1426.

MICHAEL GIBBS: 8 OKTOBER t/m 5 NOVEMBER 1977

PROPAGATION PIECE part/deel 2: *DISPLAY OF PRODUCE.*

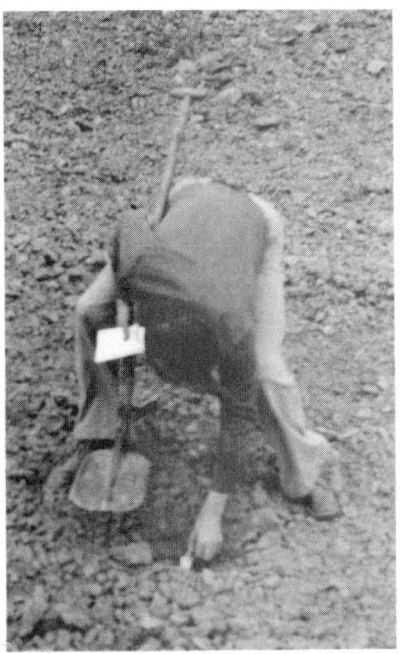 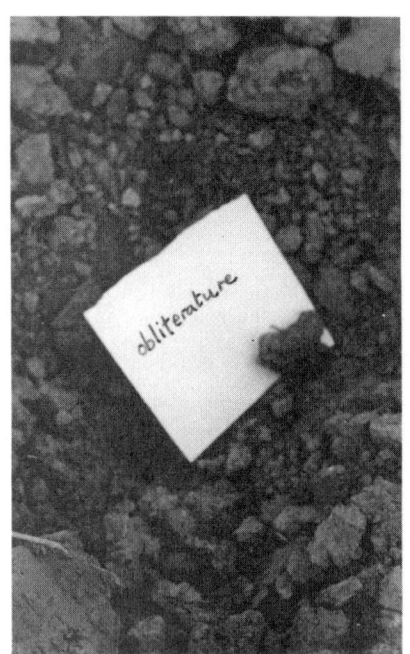

photos of Propagation Piece part 1 (4 June 1977)

Propagation Piece
"Each 'seed' was an idea typed onto a piece of paper—after planting these ideas I would come back three months later and make a display of the ideas which had germinated and grown into products." 1977.

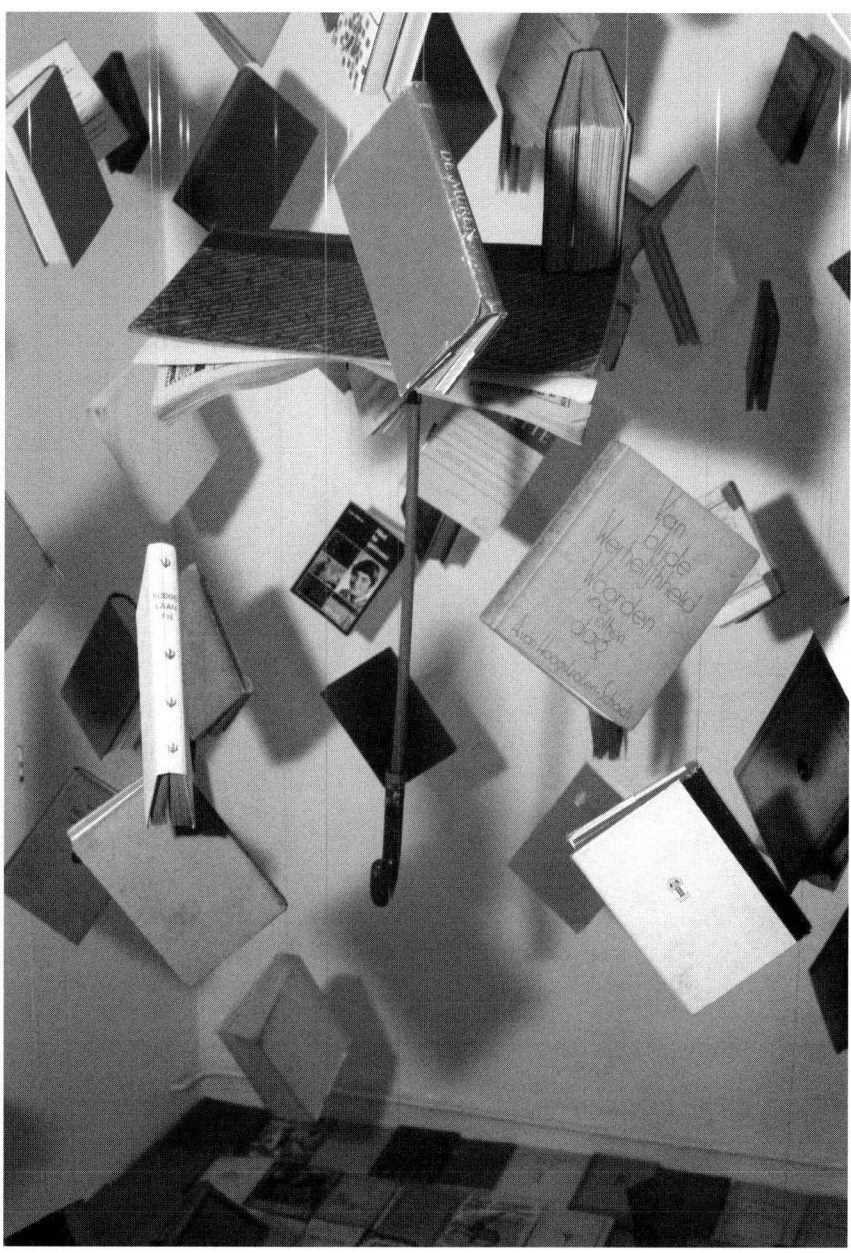

Rain & Umbrella
"I was due to have an exhibition at Lóa Gallery in Haarlem, for which I decided to make an installation with a 'rain' of books hanging from nylon wires, the floor covered with books, and 'book-hats, book-shoes and a book-umbrella' for spectators to wear when entering the piece. It meant accumulating hundreds of second-hand books, many of which I acquired from a shop in the Damstraat for 50 cents each."
Installation, Galerie Lóa, Haarlem, December 1977.

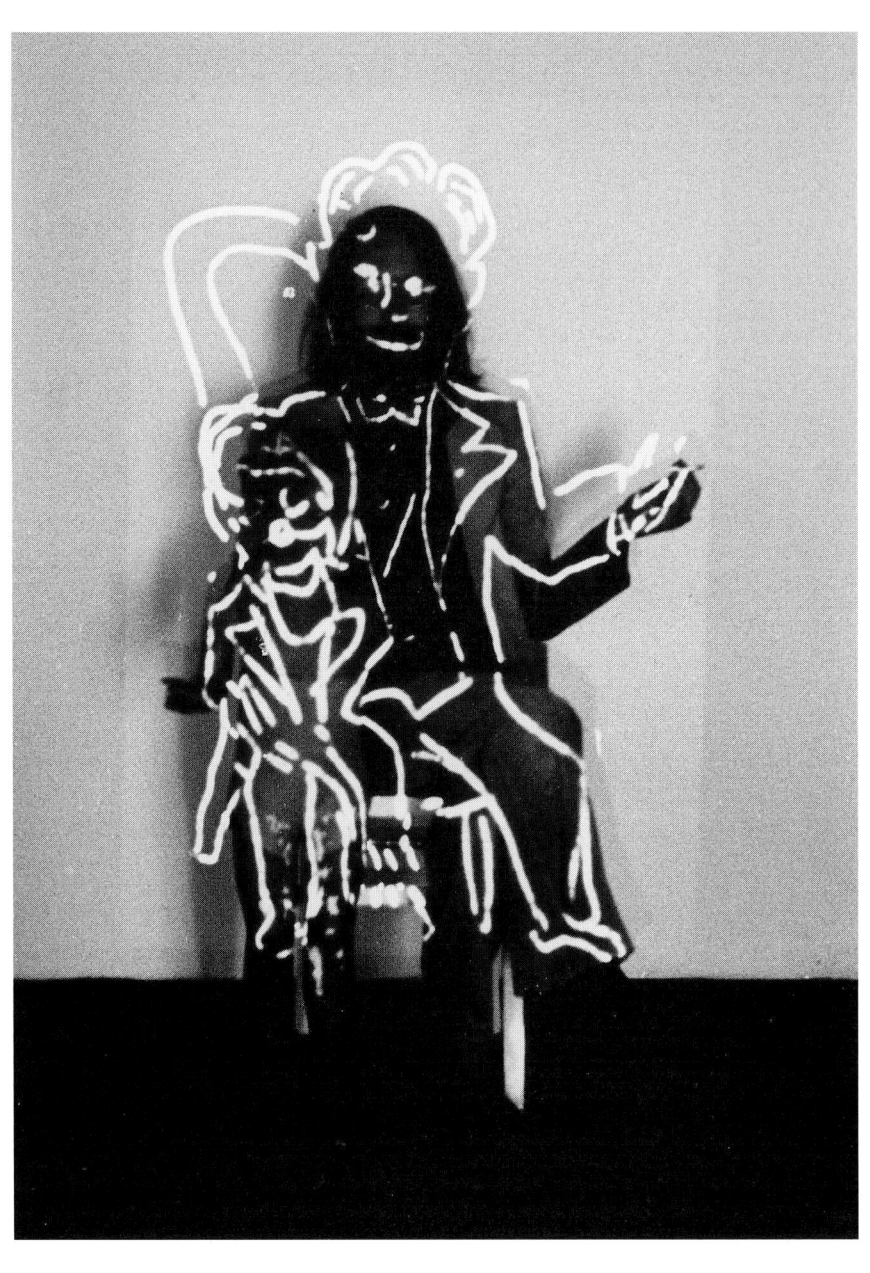

The Art of Ventriloquism
Performance, Gallery A+, Amsterdam, 2 September 1978.

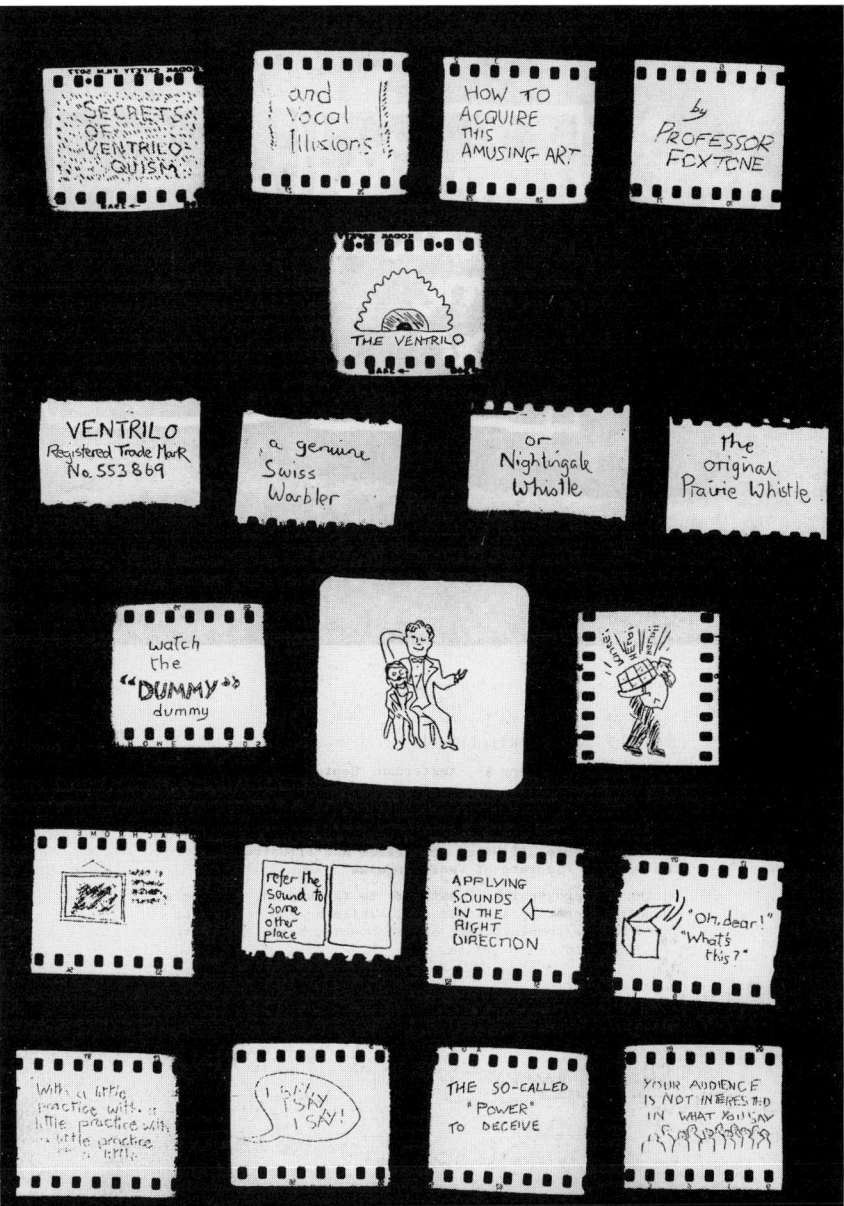

"36 hand-etched slides were projected. The slides were all based on phrases and illustrations from the booklet *Secrets of Vetriloquism*. During the projections I sat next to the screen, holding a standing puppet of a little girl, while a tape played the sound of the complete text of the booklet being read with the 'Ventrilo' in my mouth."

TOME TONES

use this book as a sound-producing instrument

e.g.
turn the pages
flip the pages
rustle the pages
slam the book shut
blow (using edge of pages as reed)

Michael Gibbs 1978

Tome Tones
A4 instruction sheet, edition of 10, 1978.

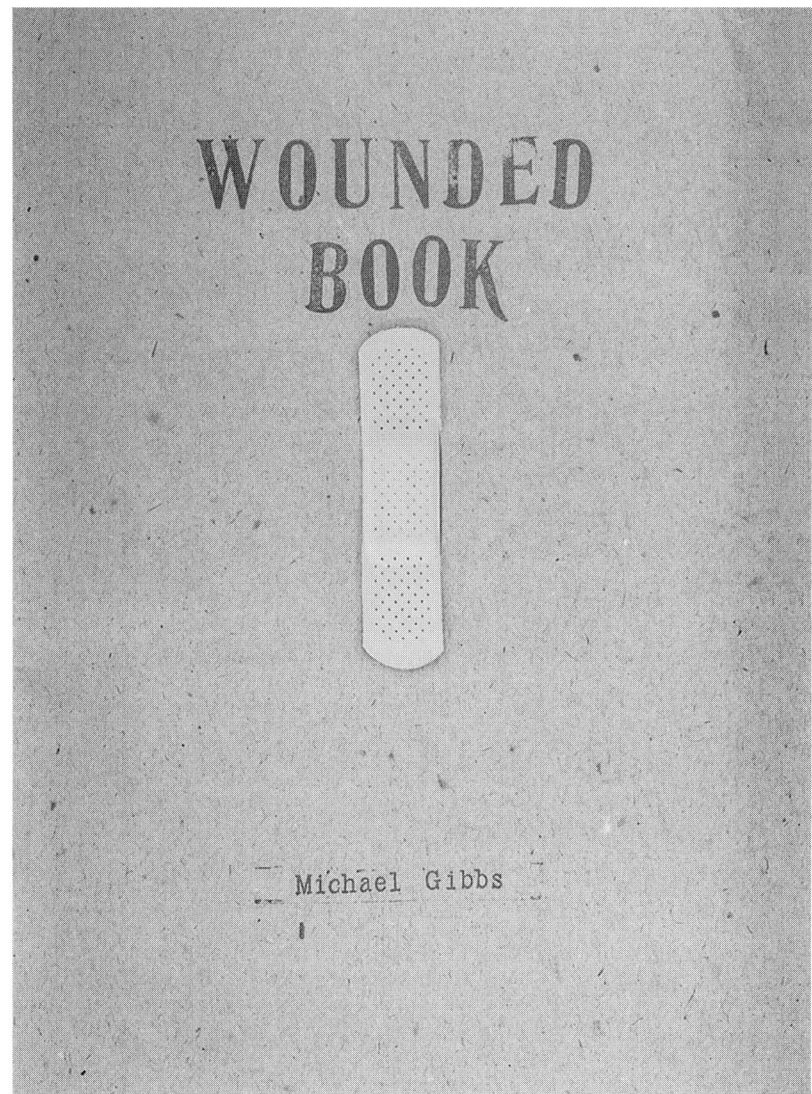

Wounded Book
A plaster on the front covers a small blood red incision cut through the entire book.
Handmade, edition of 100 copies, 1979.

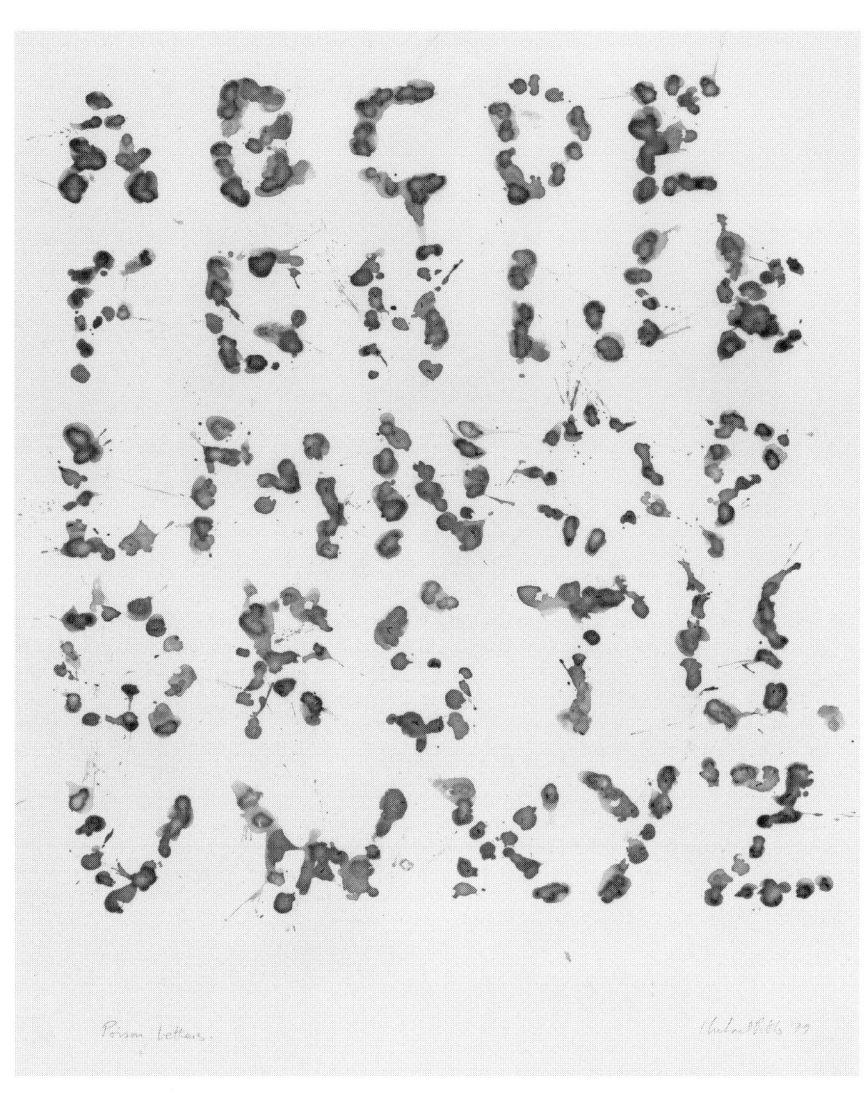

Poison Letters
[Unknown] poison on paper, 1979.

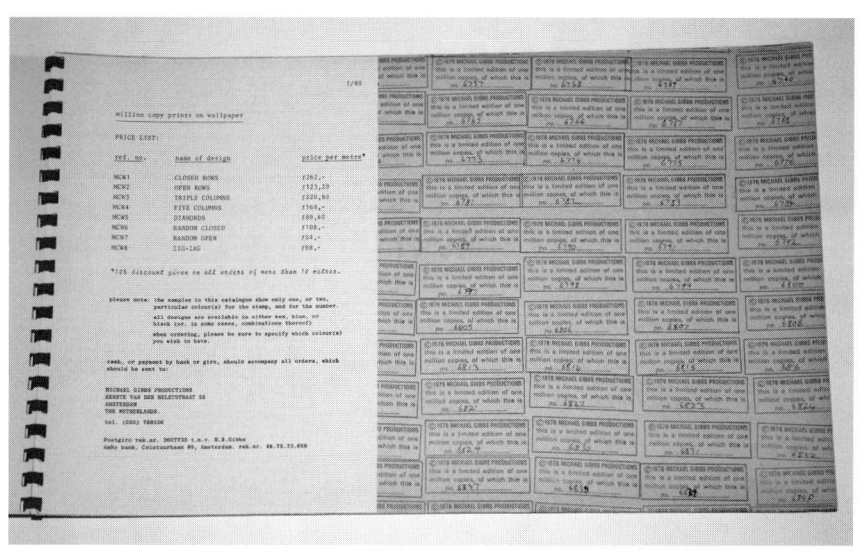

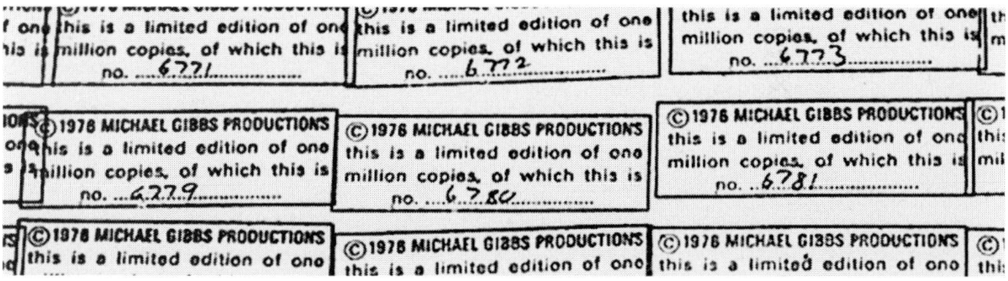

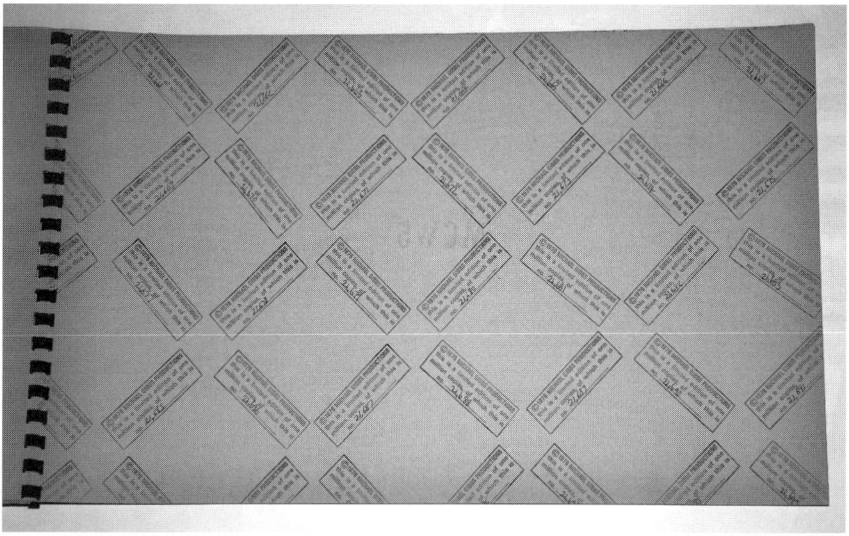

Exclusive Decor for the Modern Art Collector's Home
Sample catalogue of the 'one million copies' rubber stamp wallpaper designs, 1979/80.

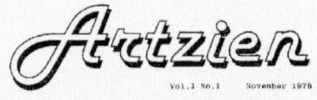

reviews on
REINDEER WERK
PNINA REICHMAN
PIETER MOL

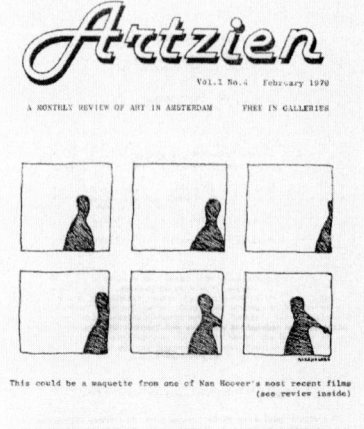

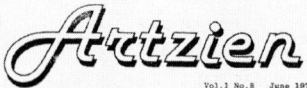

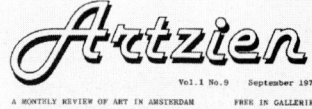

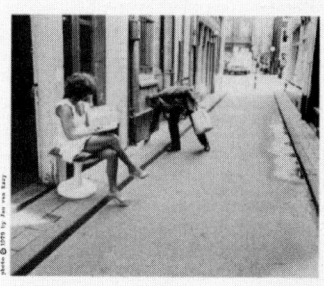

Artzien, 28 issues, Amsterdam, 1978–83.
"ARTZIEN was conceived and has come into being largely as a result of the shocking realisation that Amsterdam has no regular journal devoted to art criticism and reviews of current exhibitions. The art magazines that do exist—*Museum Journal*, *Kunstbeeld*, *Kunstschrift*, and the Rijksmuseum's glossy new magazine for antique collectors—concentrate on museum shows within an art historical context and on established artists. There are over 70 art galleries in Amsterdam, and at least 12 of them are showing interesting and innovative work, which deserves to be noticed while it is happening. Many art events, such as performances and film and video showings, happen only once and can be easily forgotten unless a permanent written record is available. It is hoped that ARTZIEN will provide a platform, not only for coverage of current exhibitions and events, but also for criticism and debate. We want to reform, as well as inform, to promote a pluralistic attitude to art, to provoke a response.

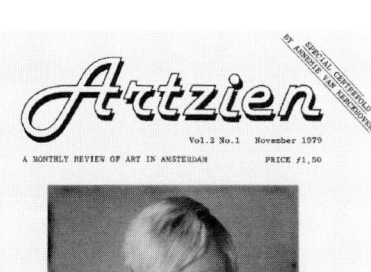
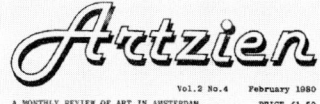

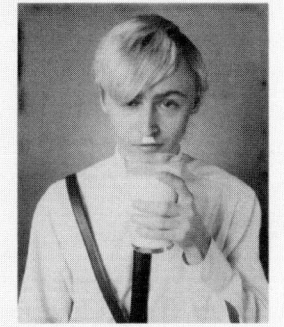

"NAZI MILK" - one of GENERAL IDEA's potent cultural cocktails

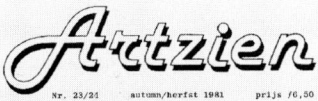
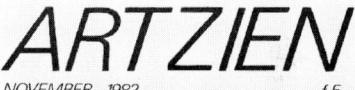

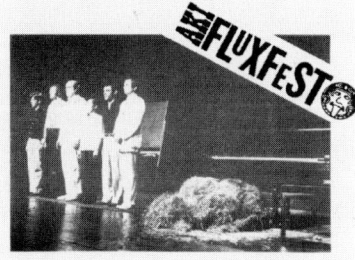
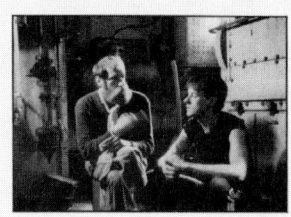
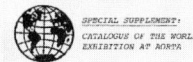

FLUXFEST IN ENSCHEDE ++++ ALTERNATIEVE CIRCUIT ++++
TOM PUCKEY ++++ DIRK LARSEN ++++ PHILIP PETERS ++++
SCHUMANN ++++ GUDMUNDSSON ++++ JAMES LEE BYARS ++++

    To achieve all this, ARTZIEN has to survive, and grow. For that we need writers and cash. Space and deadline permitting, all reviews and articles received will be published, in their original language: either english or dutch. For the moment we are only interested in reviews of exhibitions and events in Amsterdam, although general articles concerning art issues will also be considered. If the magazine expands, we'll expand the coverage. To help us financially (and to make sure you receive the magazine regularly) you are urged to subscribe—please use the enclosed form. Paid advertisements would also be very welcome: our rates are quite reasonable.
    Lastly, a brief apology for the thinness and the cheap quality of the printing of this first issue. It was put together on a loose shoestring, but it was felt to be needed. And anyway, it's just the beginning. And it's free."
—The Editor, 'Introduction', *Artzien*, vol.1 no.1, November 1978.

performance   "THE NAME OF THE GAME"   Michael Gibbs   1979

* the piece begins with the projection of a series of 40 slides, every 5 seconds, each slide showing a single word.

* the lights are turned on.
  in the performance area a large sheet of glass, ± 2 metres by 1,50 metres, is standing on trestles. the top of the glass is covered with blank sheets of typing paper laid edge to edge.

* at the rear of the area is a pile of around 50 bricks. i throw some of the bricks (for a distance of 3-4 metres). a child comes forward and builds the thrown bricks into walls.

* the lights go out and a stereo tape of my voice speaking the six texts begins to issue from the other end of the room (behind the spectators).

* between each of the six texts there is a period of ± 5 minutes (with lights on) during which I throw more bricks, and the child continues building walls.

* the piece ends with the reading of the sixth text.

approx. duration: 35 minutes.

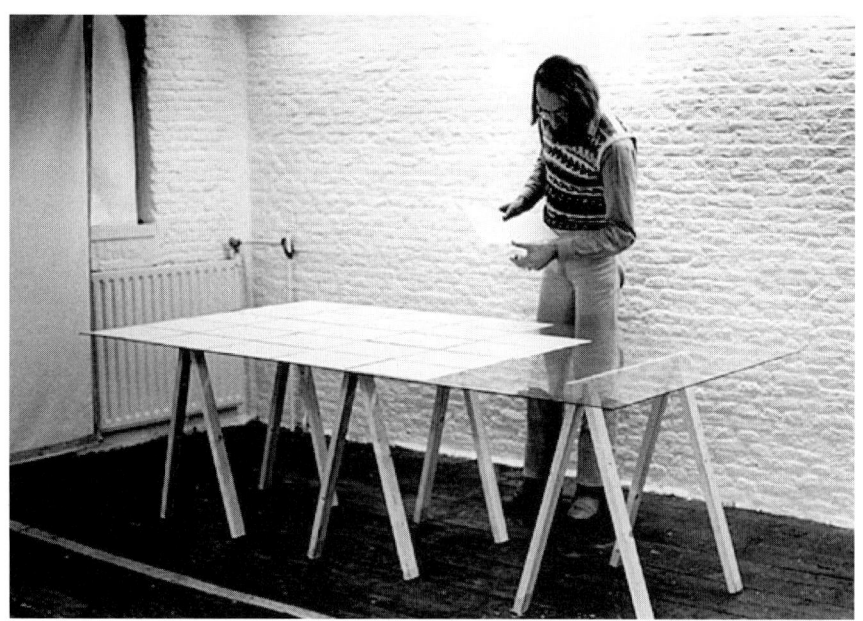

The Name of the Game
Performance, de Appel, Amsterdam, 9 January 1980.

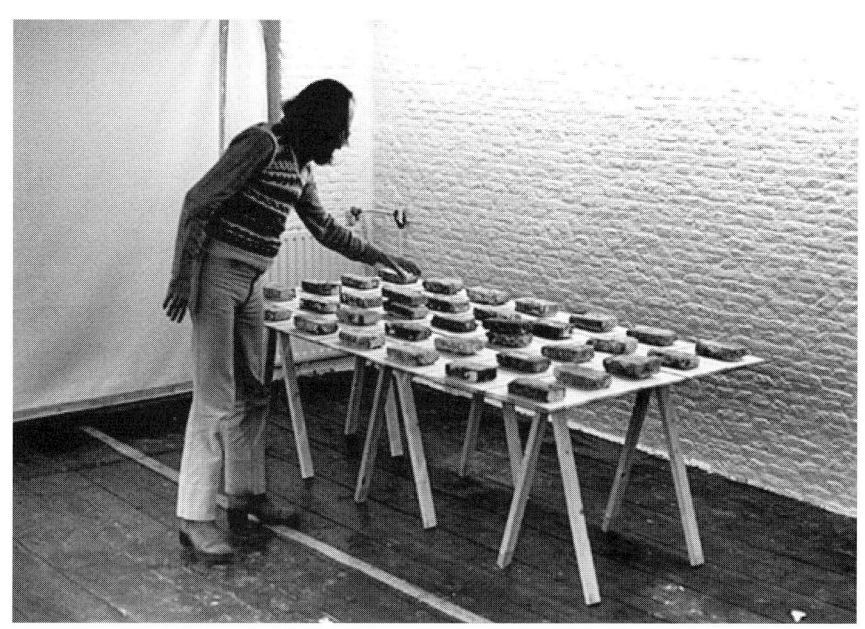

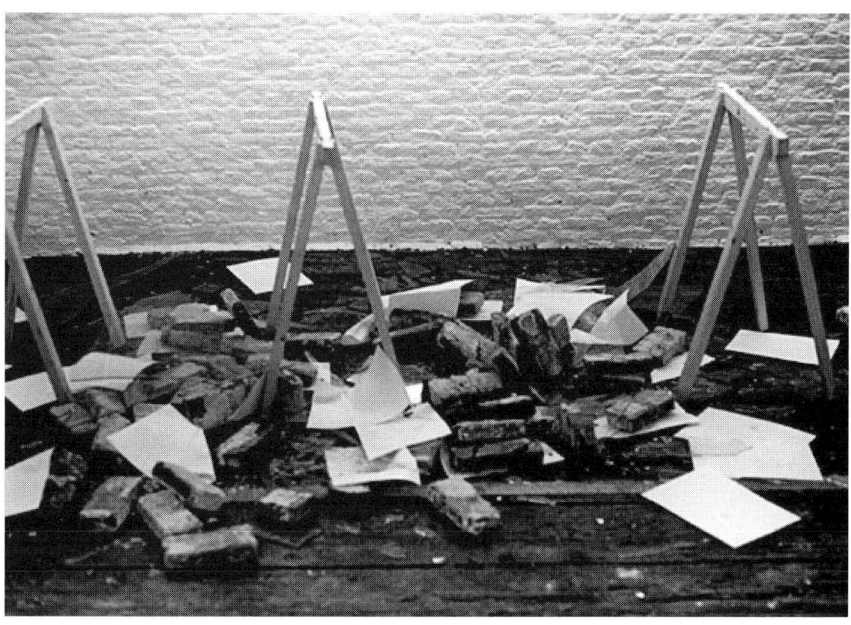

ALL / WORDS / ARE / MIND / THERE / BY / ARTISTS / MORE / MORE / RESEARCHING / THE / CONSIDERABLY / SPECTATORS / CONTENT / ENGINEERS / THAN / DISAPPOINTED / IN / MORE / FREQUENT / ALWAYS / RISKS / FACT / INCLUDED / WERE / REVIEWS / MAKE / COULD / PAPER / ART / TRANSMITTERS / REAL / EARLY / THAN / WITHOUT / THE / PARTICIPATING / ONE / NINETEEN / EQUAL

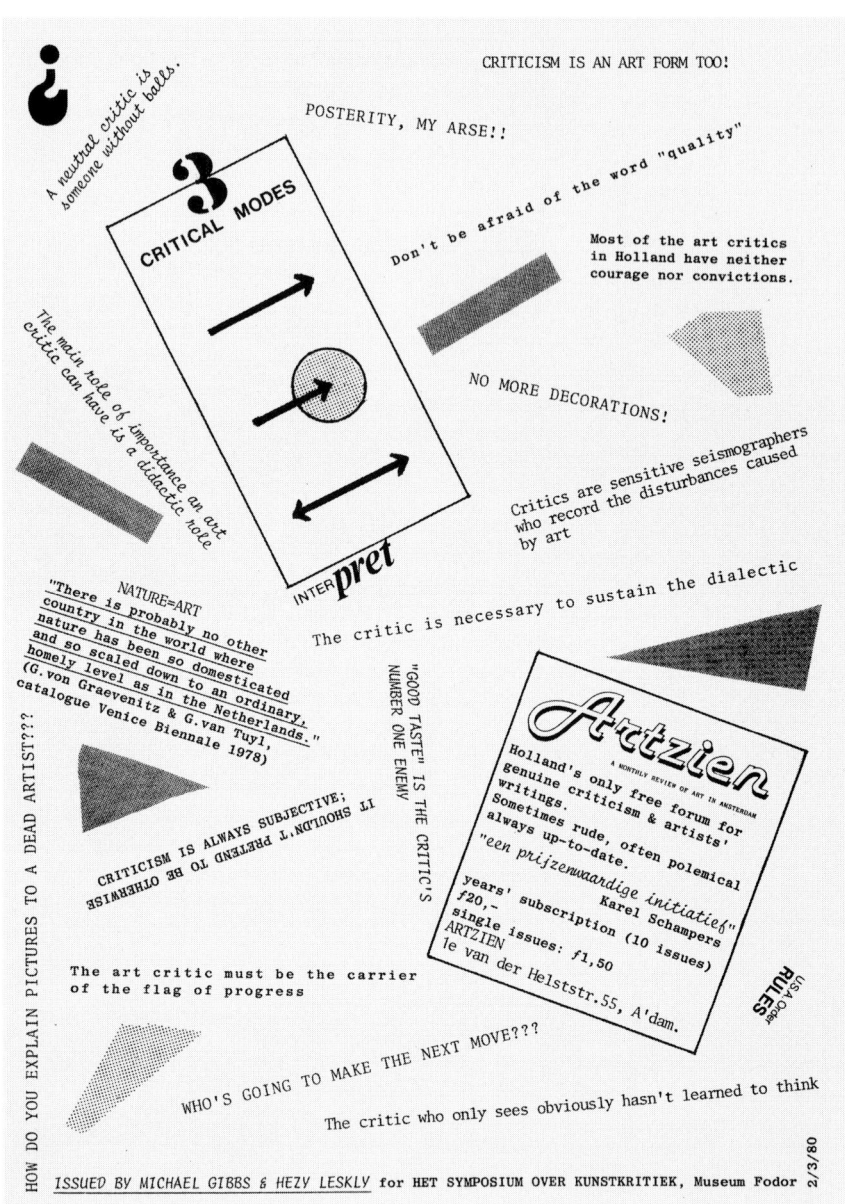

Artzien
Polemical flyer for symposium on art criticism, Museum Fodor, Amsterdam, 2 March 1980.

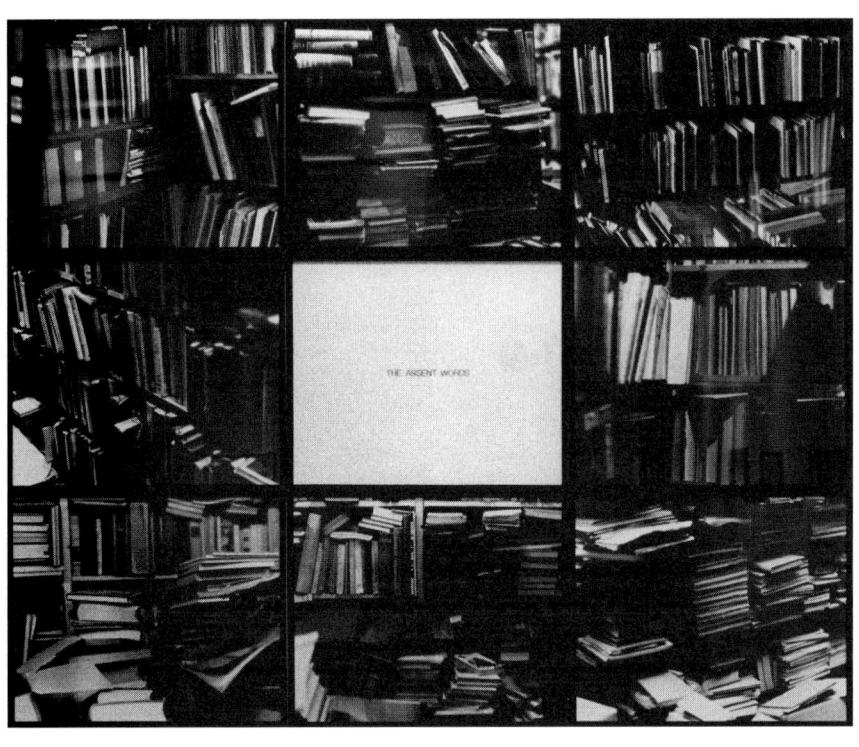

The Absent Words
Framed photographs and text, 1980.

QUANT AU LIVRE
───────────

1   I rejoice if the passing wind half opens and unintentionally animates aspects of the book's exterior

2   spread out amidst the clump, I shall abandon it, and the flowering words, to their silence

3   the miniature tomb, indeed, of the soul

4   a wing about to unfold

5   the shadow scattered in black characters.....like a wreckage of mystery

6   capable of infinity almost to the point of sanctifying a language

7   a special place, the page and the height

8   the incessant coming & going

9   the unbearable column

10 an array of flourishes

11a everywhere at once, nowhere
 b
 c
 d
 e

Stéphane Mallarmé 1895

Michael Gibbs 1979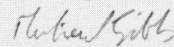

Quant au Livre
"One of my biggest inspirations has been Stéphane Mallarmé, in particular his unfinished project 'Le Livre' which was a plan for presenting an inter-/multimedia fusion of theatre, song, dance, and poetry… it is now my main concern to take the book out of its covers and onto the stage."
A4 sheet, 1979.

Uxkax	Uxrih	Uybul	Uyjec	Uypre	Uzbar
Uxkeb	Uxroj	Uycag	Uyjih	Uypug	Uzbes
Uxkig	Uxrup	Uycek	Uyjoj	Uyrat	Uzblo
Uxkoh	Uxsaf	Uycip	Uyjur	Uyrey	Uzbob
Uxkro	Uxsej	Uycor	Uykaw	Uyrid	Uzcaf
Uxlac	Uxsin	Uycuz	Uykez	Uyroz	Uzcej
Uxleg	Uxsop	Uydak	Uykif	Uyryf	Uzcin
Uxlil	Uxsuz	Uydiv	Uykog	Uysad	Uzcop
Uxlom	Uxtad	Uydle	Uykup	Uyseh	Uzcuy
Uxluv	Uxteh	Uydow	Uylab	Uysim	Uzdaj
Uxmaj	Uxtim	Uydud	Uylef	Uyson	Uzdev
Uxmem	Uxton	Uyebo	Uylik	Uysyz	Uzdir
Uxmit	Uxtyz	Uyege	Uylol	Uytac	Uzdos
Uxmos	Uxvap	Uyeks	Uylut	Uyteg	Uzebe
Uxmuc	Uxvet	Uyemb	Uymah	Uytil	Uzego
Uxnag	Uxvoz	Uyept	Uymel	Uytom	Uzekt
Uxnek	Uxvuh	Uyfav	Uymis	Uytuv	Uzemp
Uxnip	Uxvyn	Uyfex	Uymot	Uyvan	Uzeph
Uxnor	Uxwak	Uyfib	Uymub	Uyvev	Uzfas
Uxnux	Uxwen	Uyfof	Uynaf	Uyvox	Uzfew
Uxock	Uxwiv	Uyfum	Uynej	Uyvuj	Uzfiz
Uxogn	Uxwow	Uygal	Uynin	Uyvye	Uzfoc
Uxole	Uxwud	Uygep	Uynop	Uywaj	Uzgak
Uxops	Uxzas	Uygit	Uynuy	Uywem	Uzgen
Uxowf	Uxzew	Uygov	Uyoce	Uywir	Uzgiv
Uxpan	Uxziz	Uyguf	Uyogo	Uywos	Uzgow
Uxpes	Uxzoc	Uyhax	Uyolf	Uywuc	Uzgud
Uxpox	Uxzul	Uyheb	Uyonz	Uyzar	Uzhof
Uxpuj	Uybas	Uyhic	Uyowd	Uyzes	Uzhup
Uxpye	Uybew	Uyhod	Uypam	Uyzob	Uzjax
Uxraw	Uybiz	Uyhus	Uypix	Uyzuk	Uzjeb
Uxrez	Uyboc	Uyjay	Uypoy	Uyzym	Uzjig

1919

Some Sounds
A page from *The Timber Trades Journal Zebra Code* (London: William Rider & Son Ltd, 1919), of five-letter combinations used in telegraphy for types of wood and their measurement. Published *Artzien*, 'Sound Projects', September 1980.

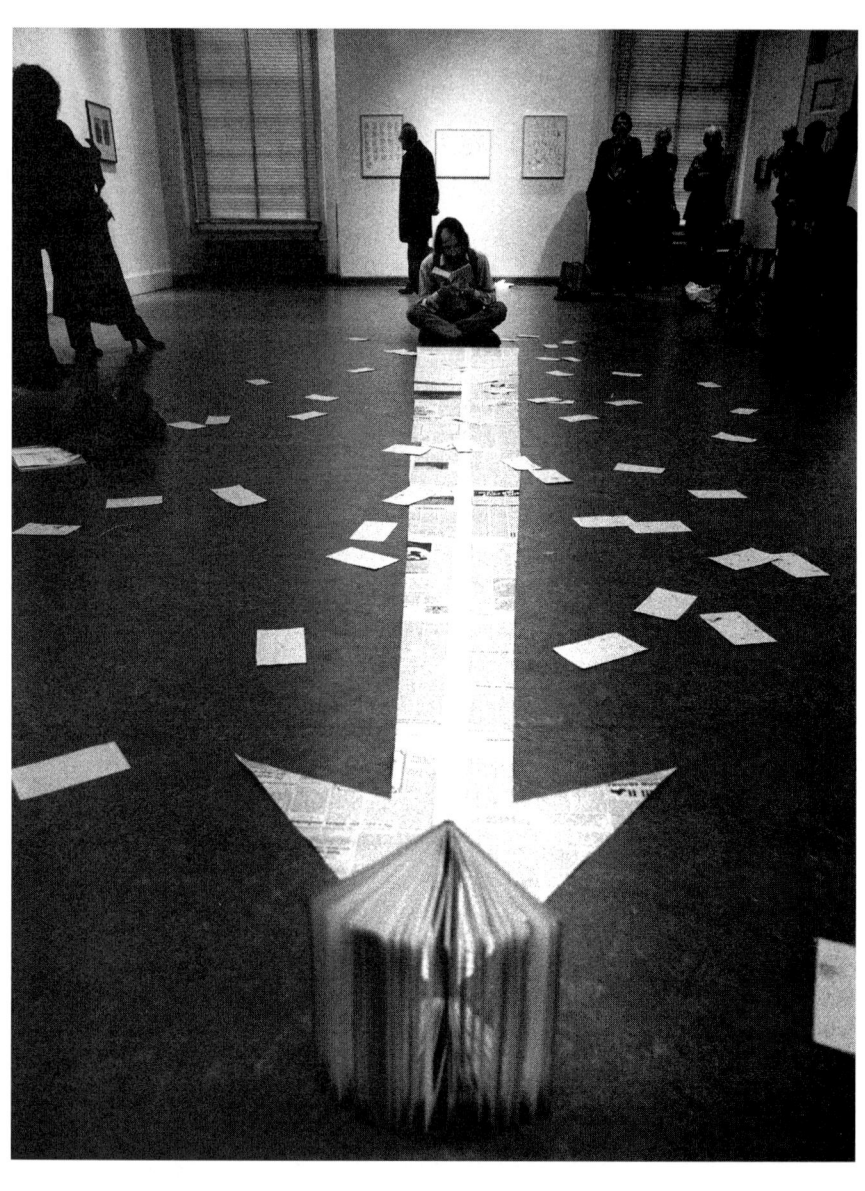

The Absent Words
Performance, Stedelijk Museum, Schiedam, 1 November 1980.

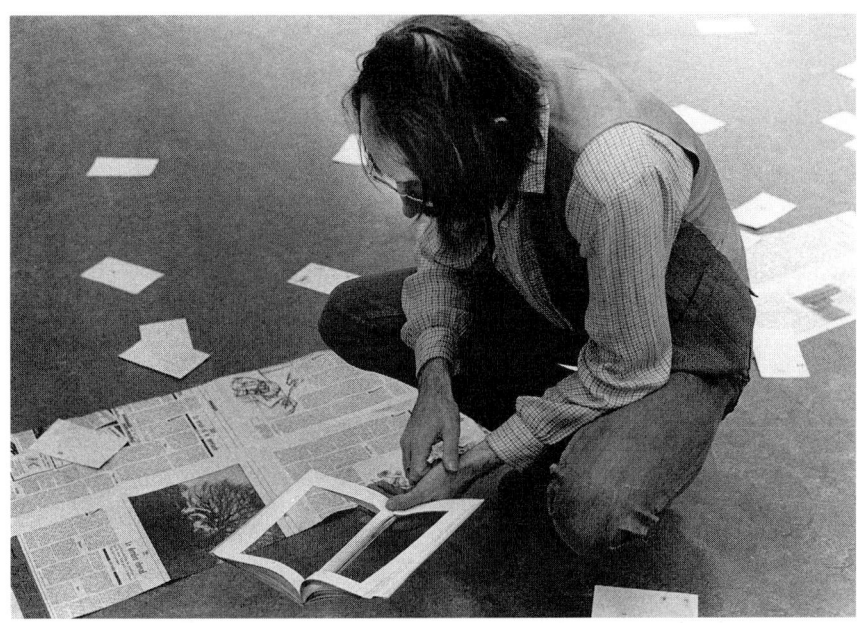

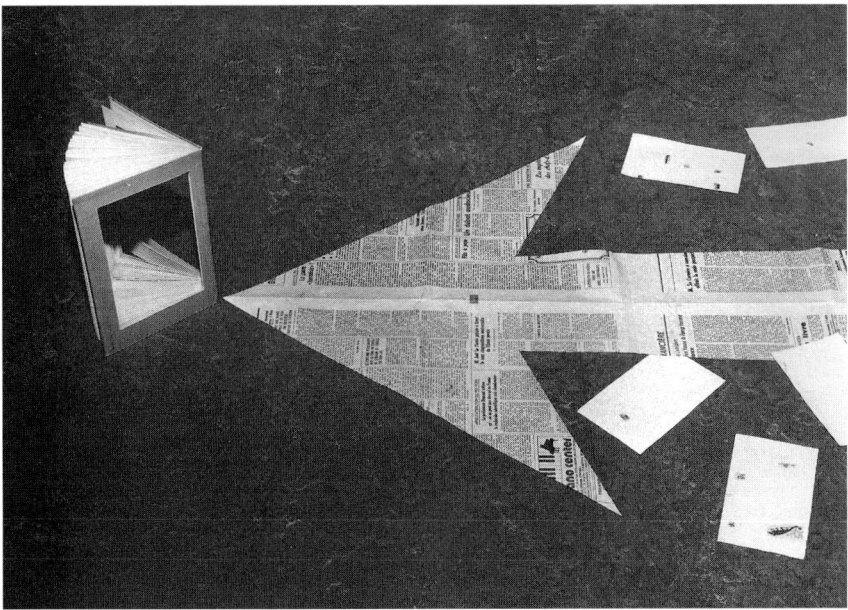

"a book is an object within a class of similar objects / a book is an event (accumulation) of discrete particles, an operation—opus, / through spheres of knowledge / turning turning turning / mind-moving / page by page"

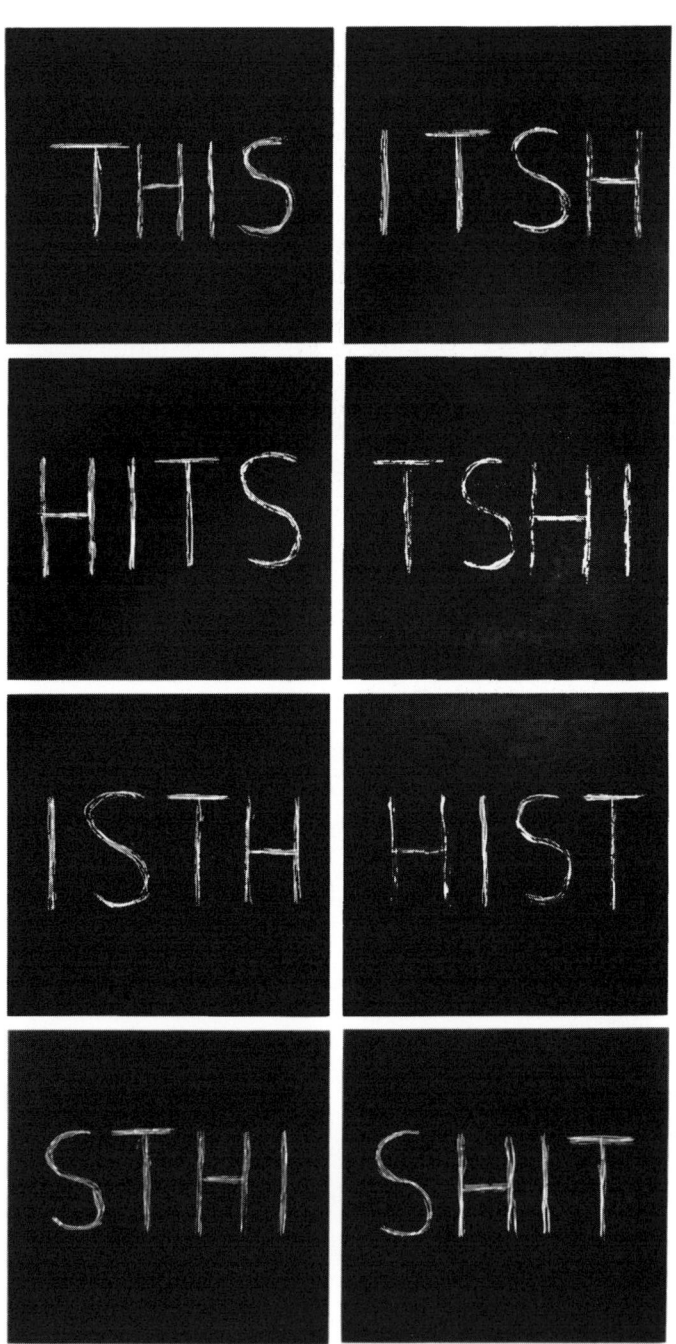

Untitled
Oil on laminated panels, 1981.

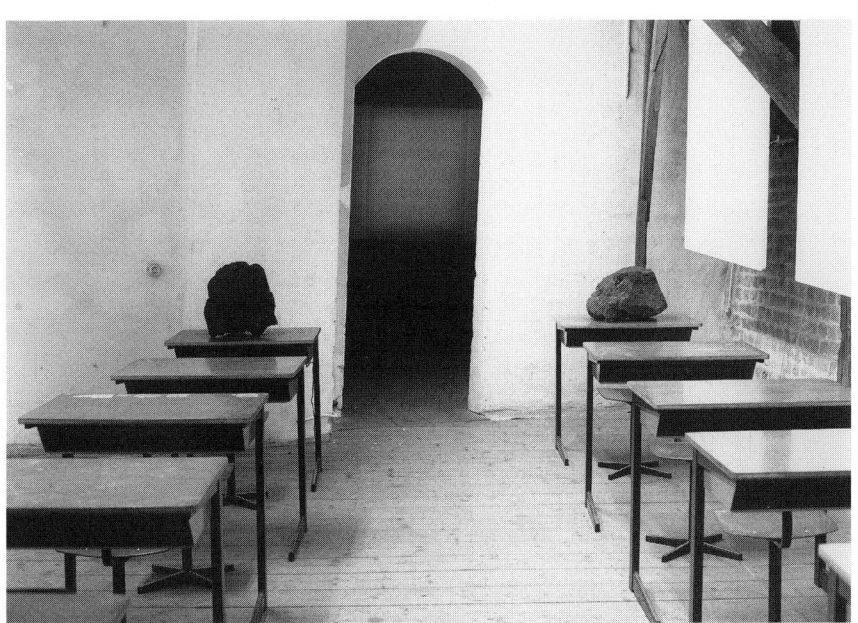

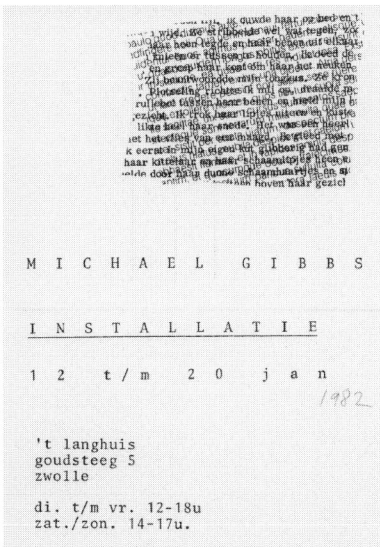

"'It consisted of about a dozen old school desks with chairs, on two of which sat a large rock. Two speakers hidden inside the desks relayed a twin-track tape, one track being a piece of 'body text' written in Latin and spoken by a student I'd hired from the Classics department of the University of Amsterdam, the other track a pornographic story read from the Dutch by by Harry Hoogstraten. Both recordings had been made in my darkroom. A sequence of slides depicting writing exercises from an old school book I'd found was projected onto a free-standing screen." Installation, 't Langhuis, Zwolle, 1982.

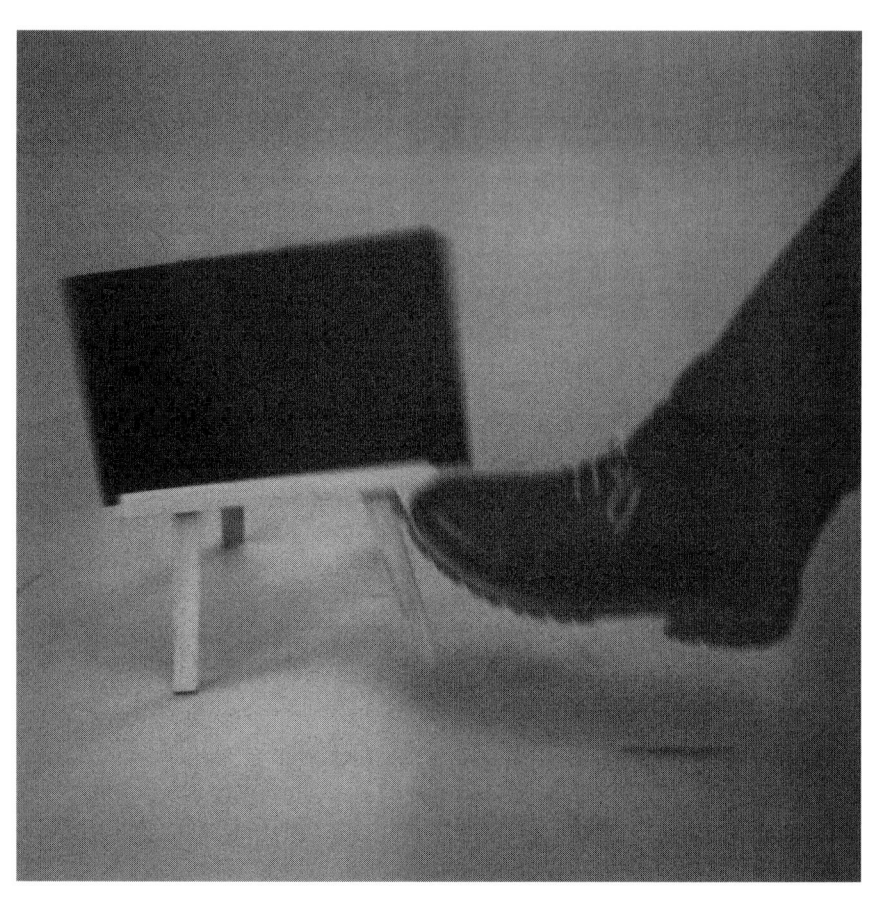

Untitled
Photograph on canvas, 1983.

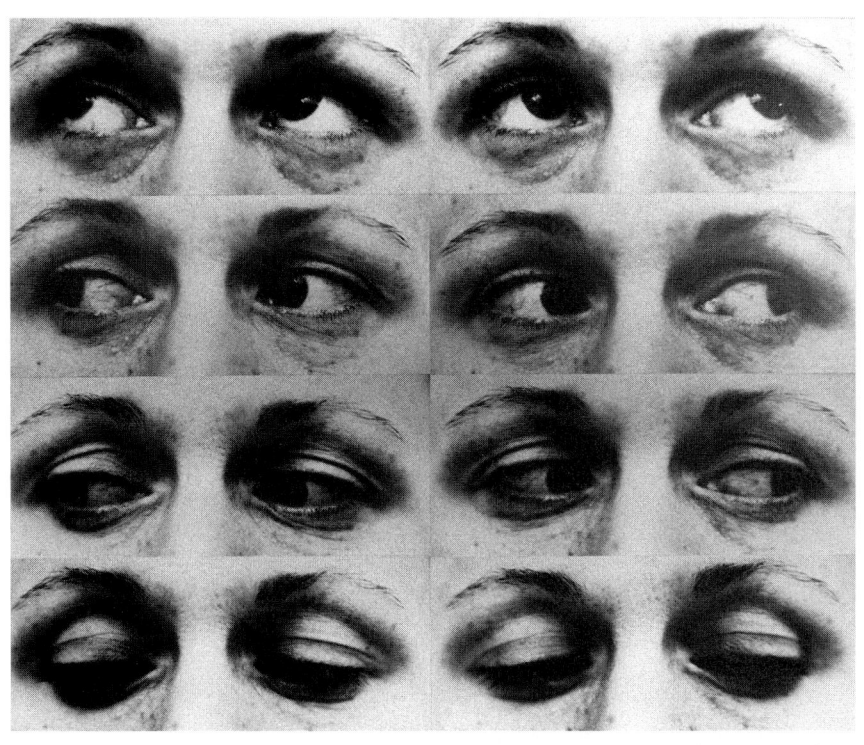

Reading You
Composite photographs, 1983.

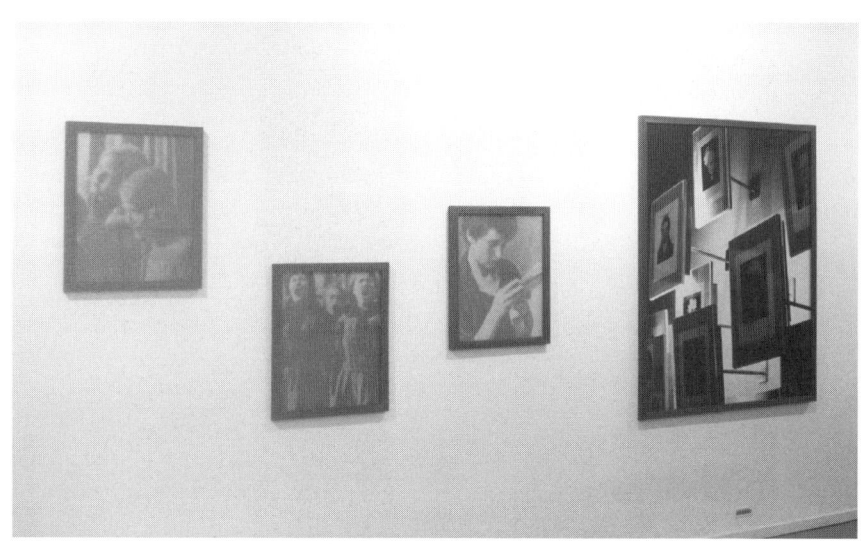

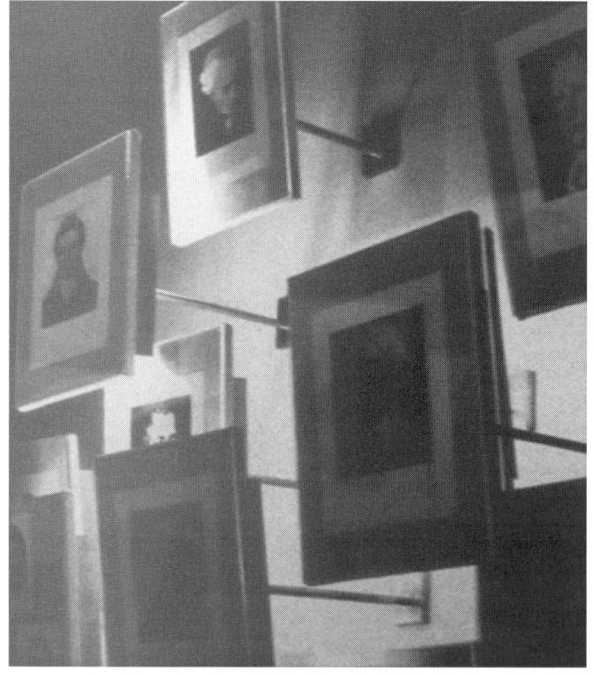

Installation
Framed photographs, 1983.

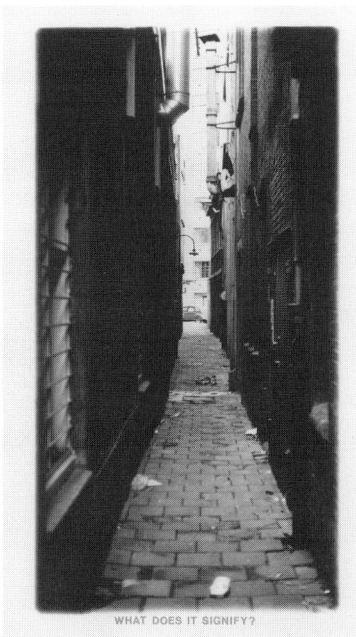
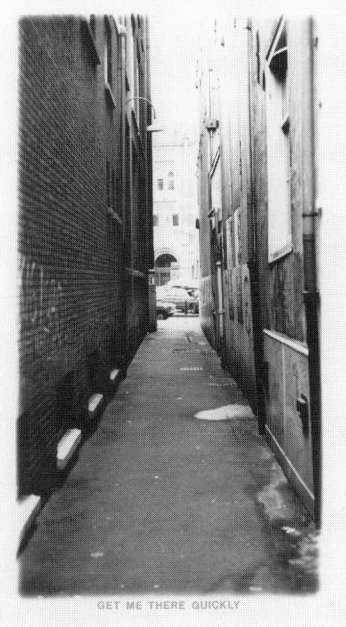
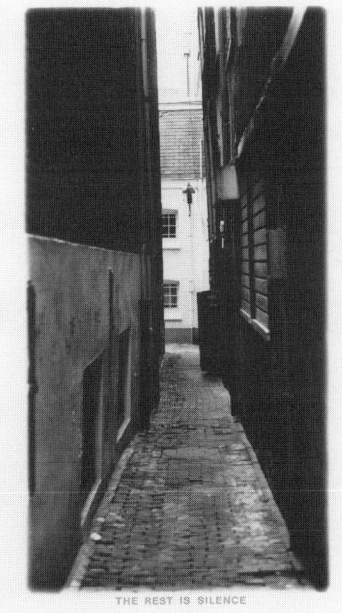
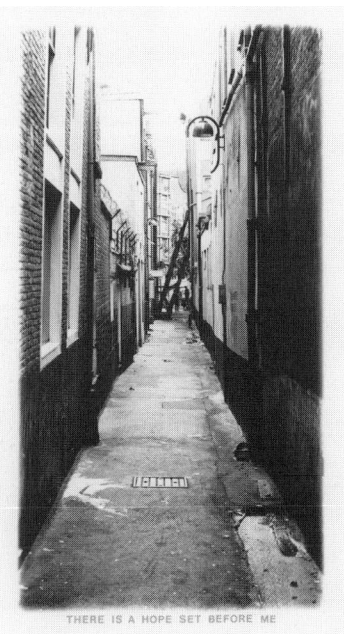

Passages
From a series of ten large-format black and white photographs on linen of alleyways in Amsterdam, each with gold text of famous, but anonymous, 'last words', 1982/84.

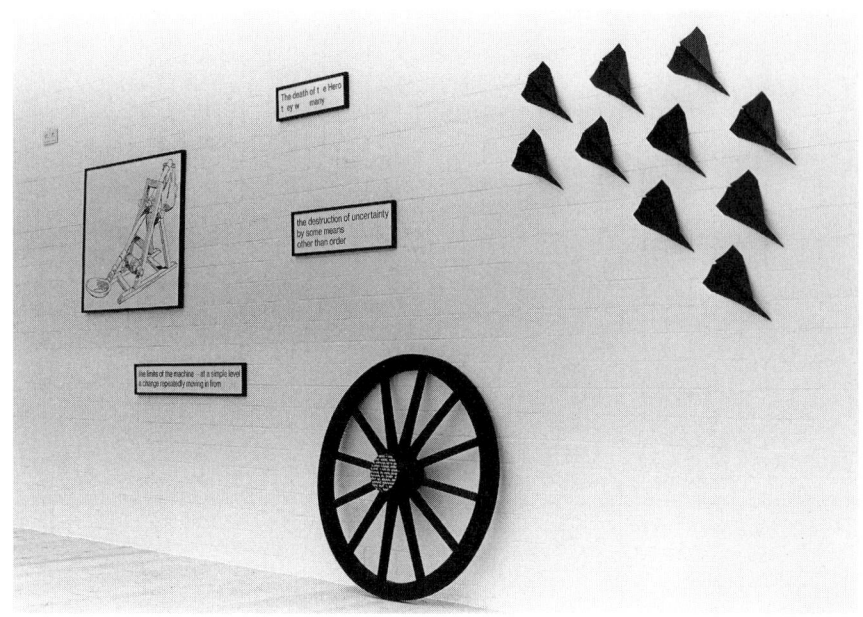

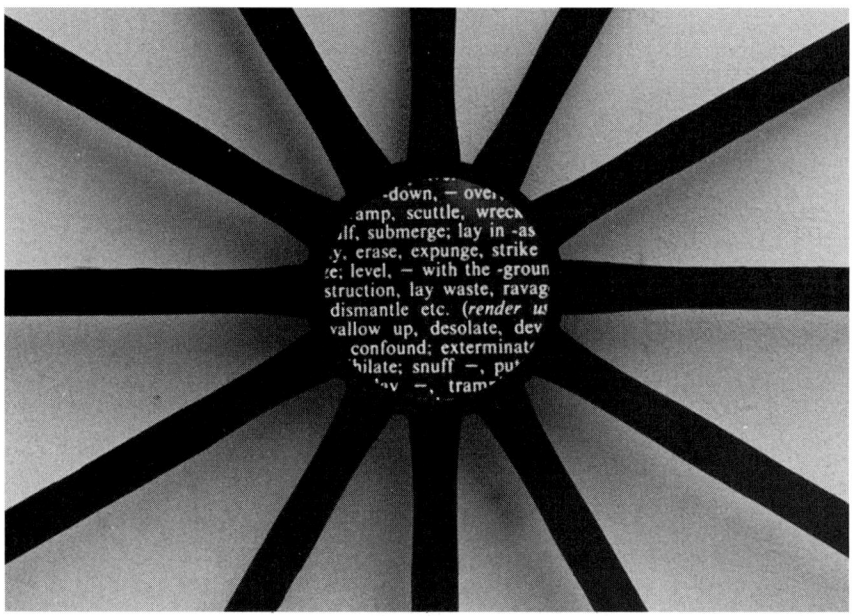

Installation
Galerie Waalkens, Finsterwolde, 1984.

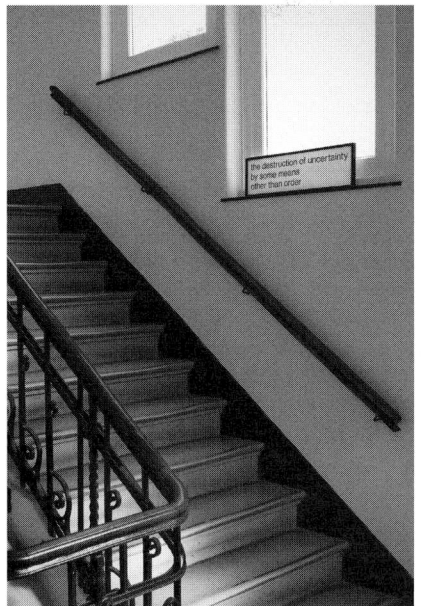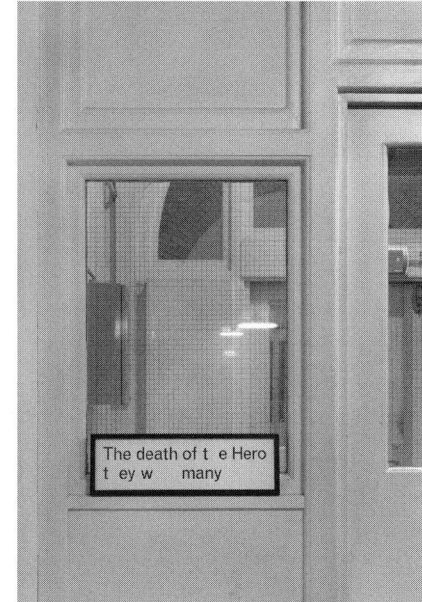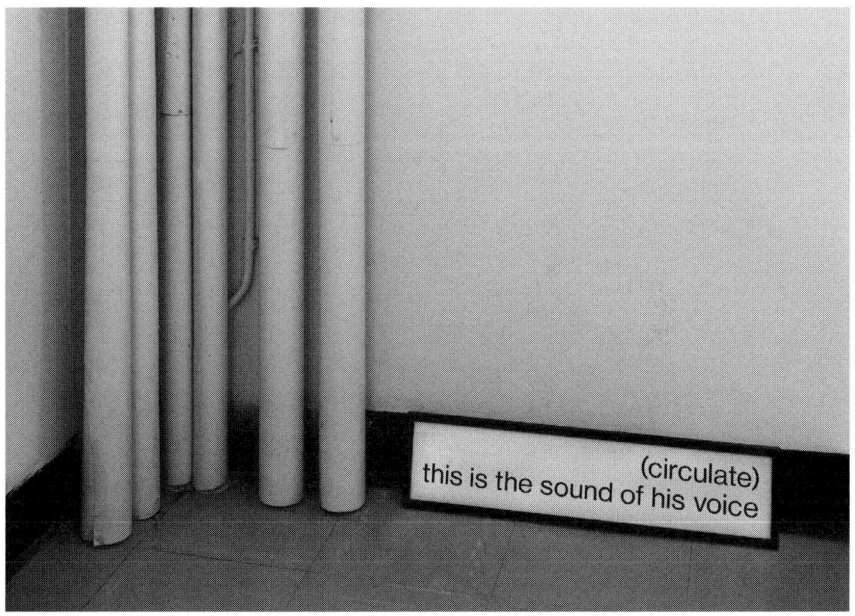

In and around the studio, 2016.

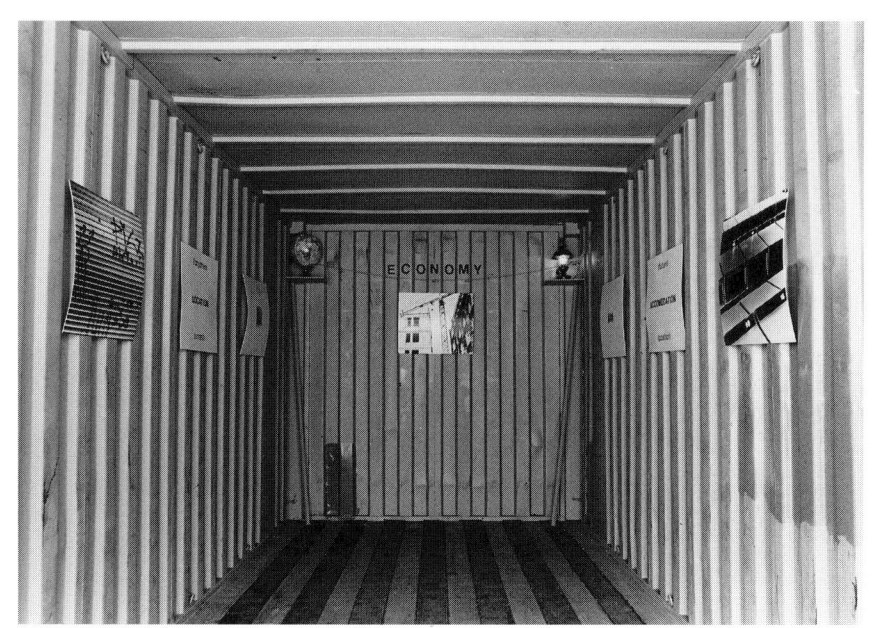

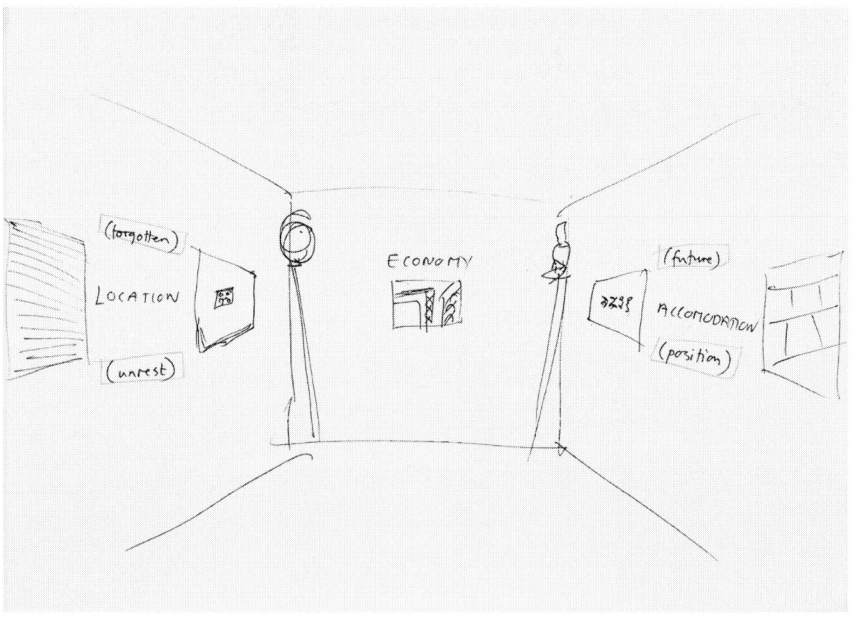

Economy
Shipping container, photographs, texts, lamps; Edelweiss, Amsterdam, 1985.

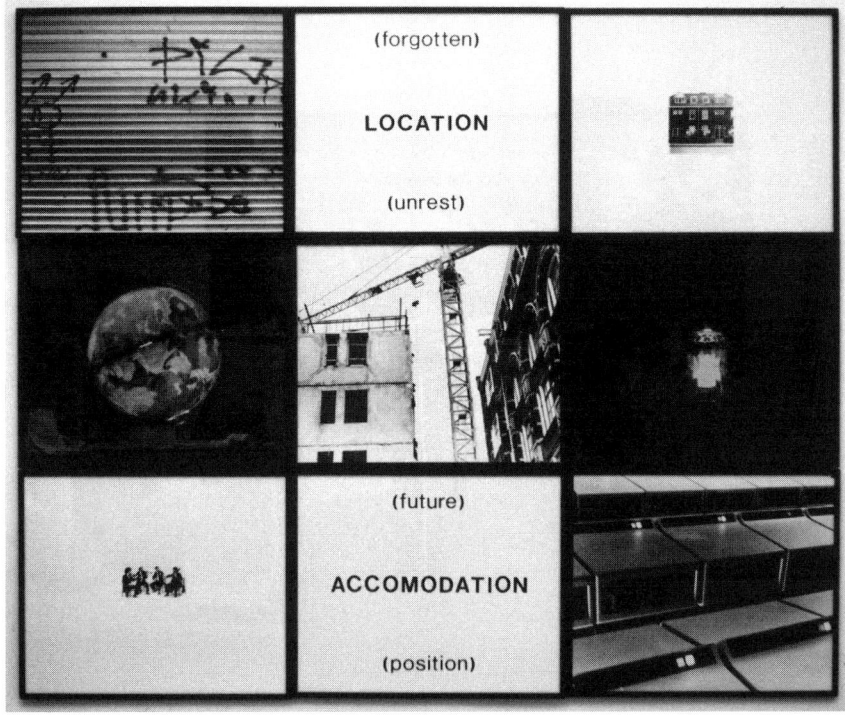

Economy
Framed photographs and text, 1985.
"Word and image can also exist in art on an equal basis. Much of the work that interests me personally at the moment uses a combination of photography and texts (either static on the wall, or off the wall—and off the page as well—as installations and performances). There are many ways in which texts can be used to contradict, reinforce, subvert or complement the meanings offered by images, while the images themselves can be ambiguous and open to multiple readings."

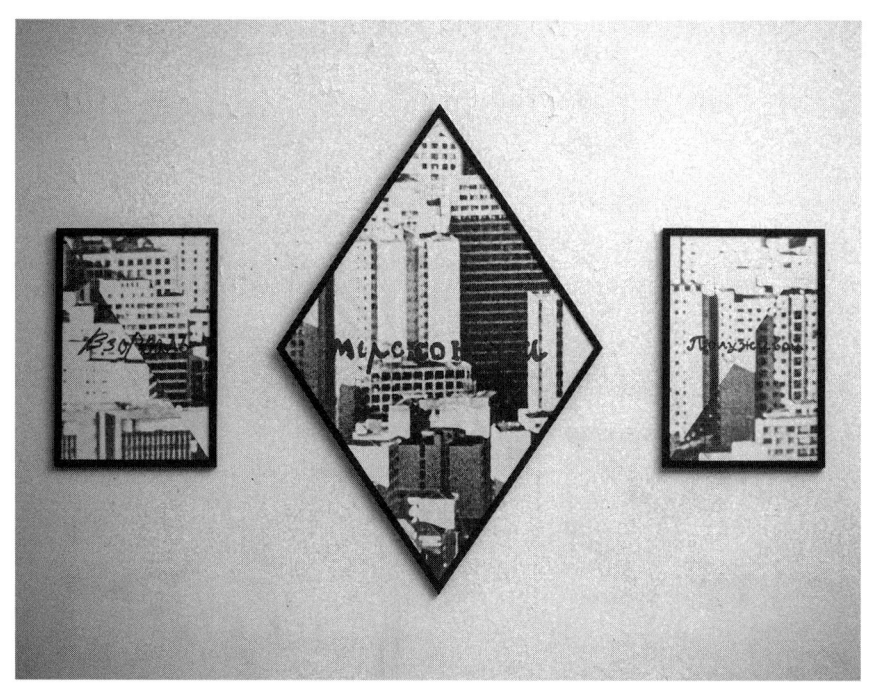

World Backwards
Left: "Explodity"; Centre: "World backwards"; Right: "Half-alive".
Framed photographs and text, 1985/6.

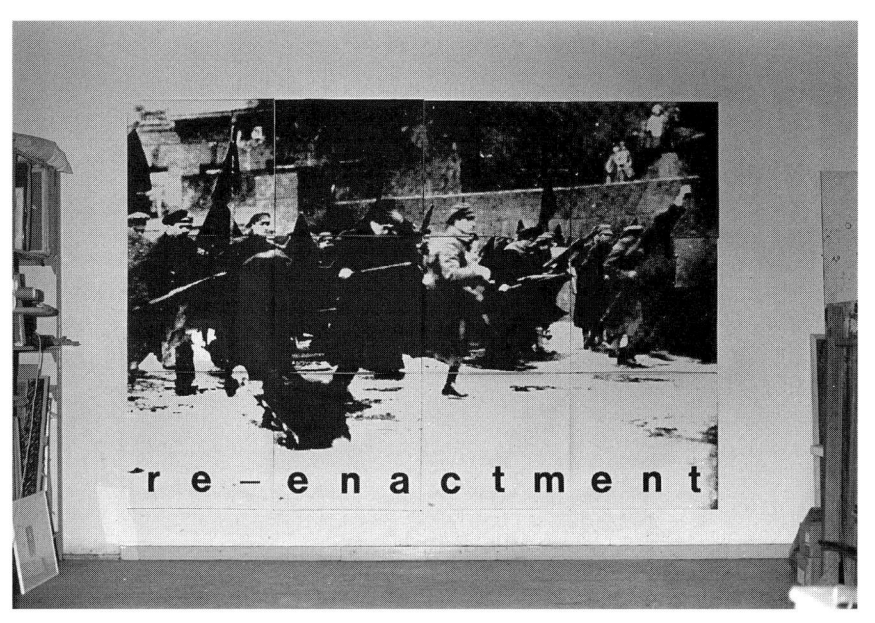

Re-enactment
Composite photograph and text, studio view, 1986.

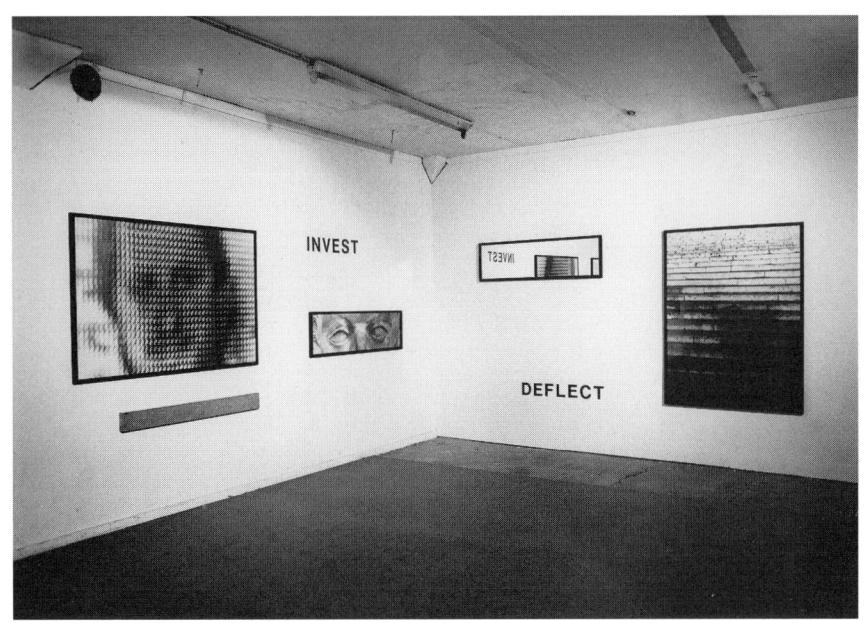

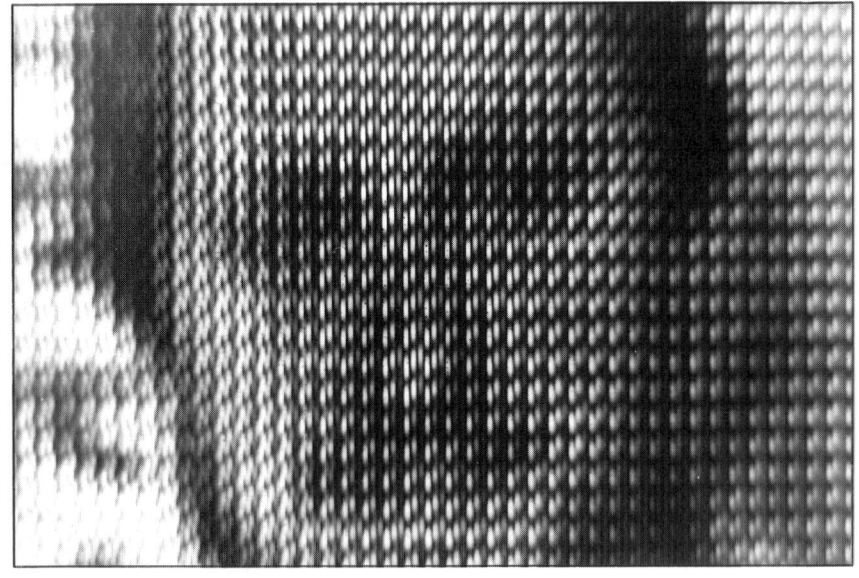

Installation
Framed photographs, mirror, zinc, text, De Fabriek, Eindhoven, 1987.

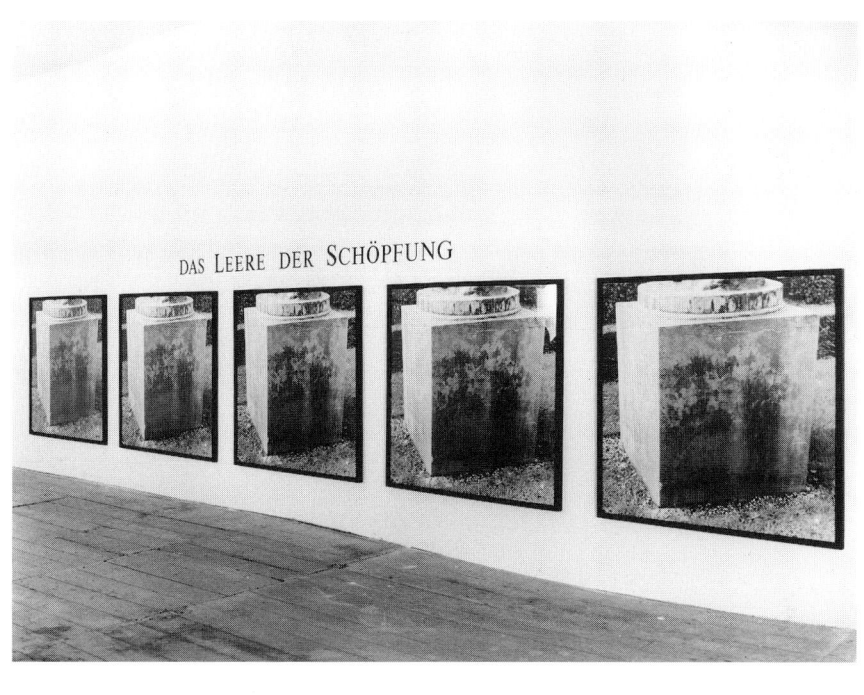

Das Leere der Schöpfung
Framed photographs and text, 1988.

EFFACE   *FORGET*

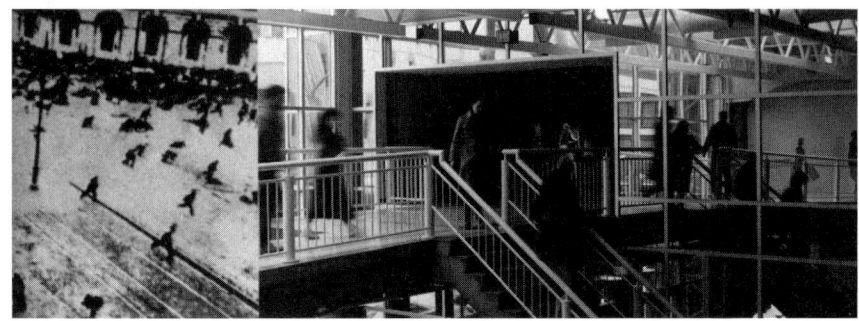

REFLECT   *ATTEND*

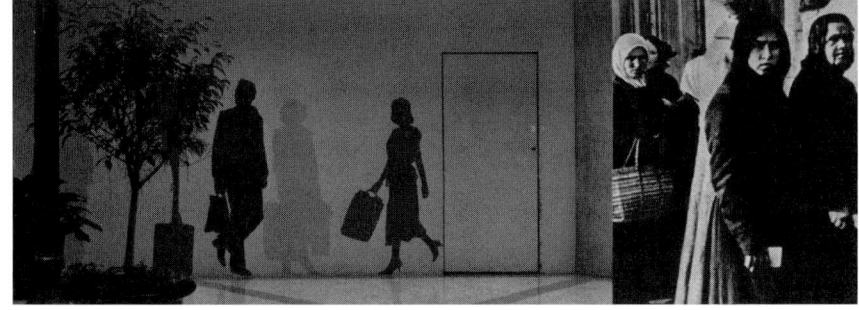

Efface / Forget; Reflect / Attend
Colour, black & white photographs and text, 1989.

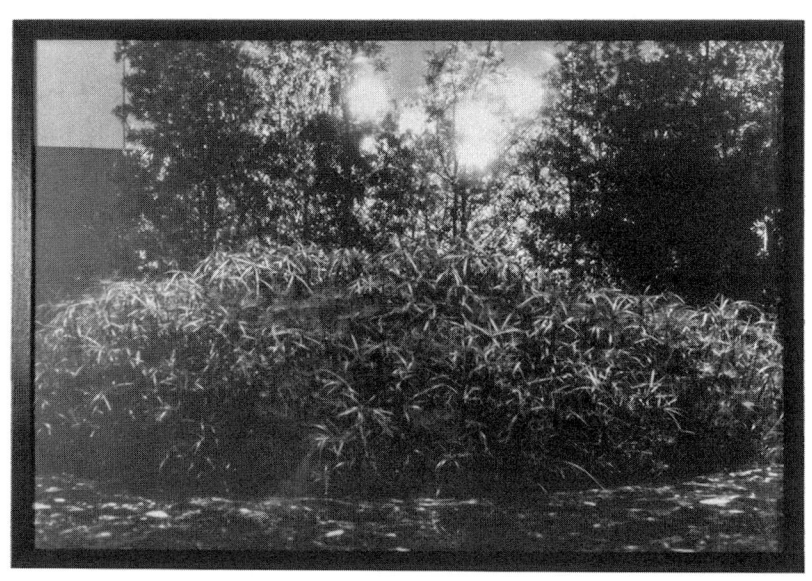

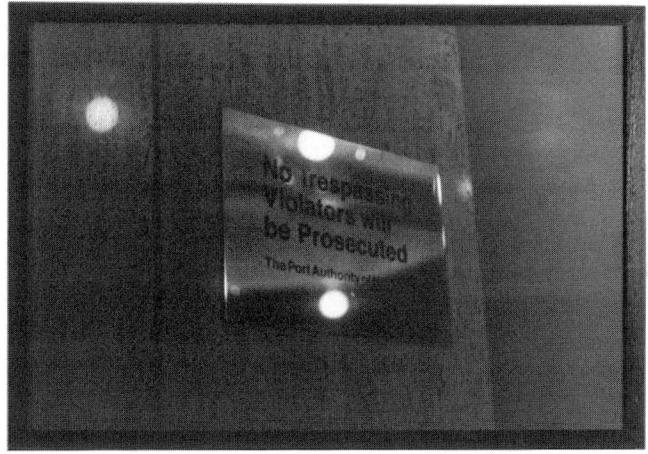

Terminal
Framed photographs, 1990.

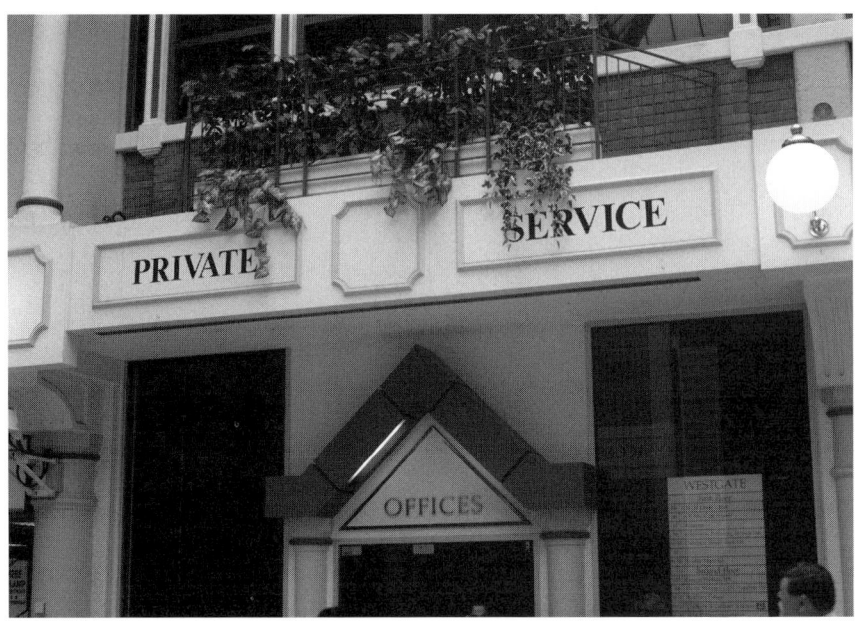

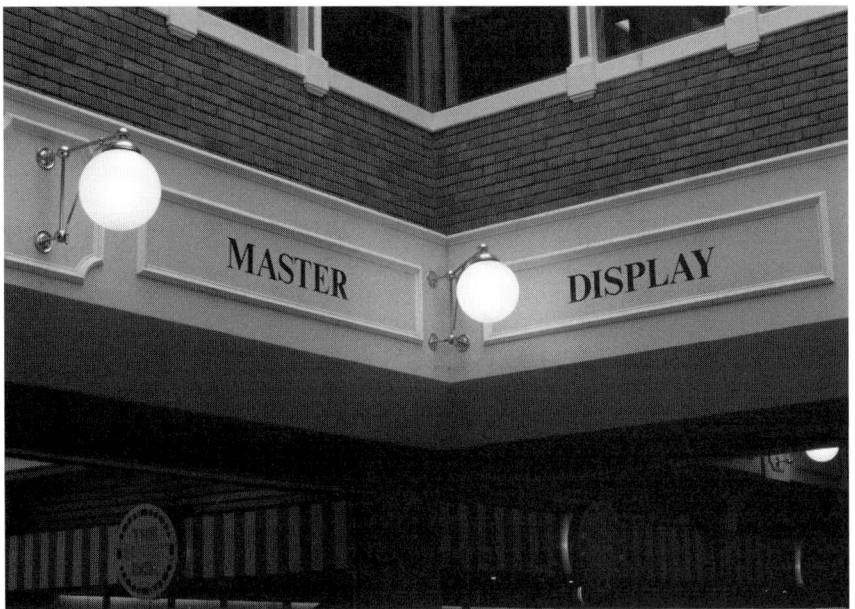

Words for Westgate
ASSENT / DISPOSE / DESIRE / CONCEAL / PRIVATE / SERVICE / PUBLIC / VISA / ACCESS
MASTER / PROMISE / DISPLAY / RESIST / POSSESS
Installation of fourteen words in the Westgate Shopping Centre, Oxford for the symposium
'Art Creating Society: Art as Social Process' at the Museum of Modern Art, 1990.

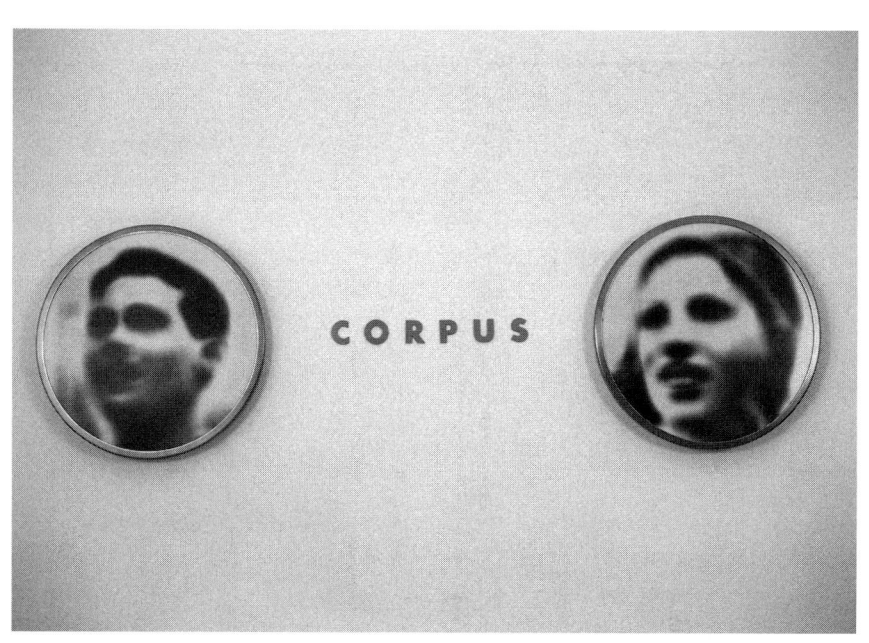

Corpus
Framed photographs and text, 1991.

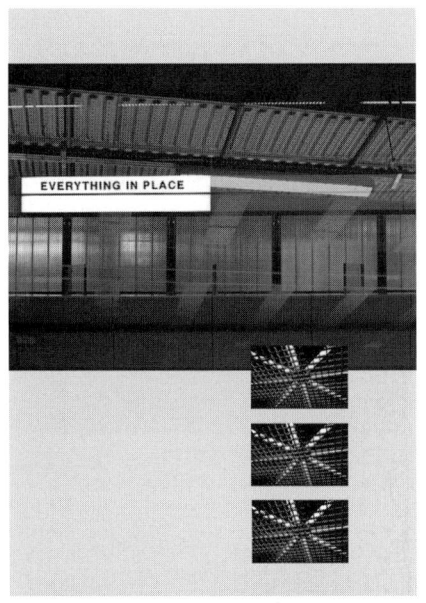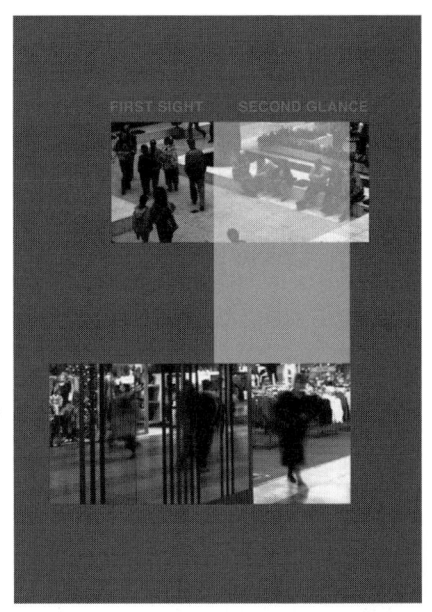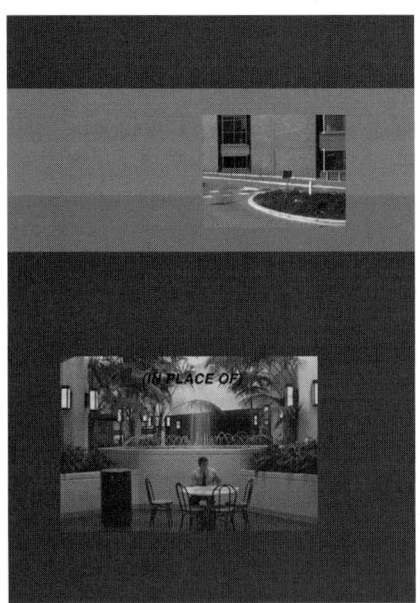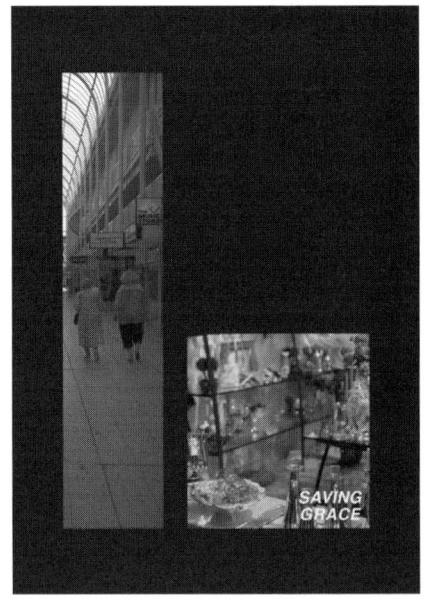

Poster series
Inkjet prints, 1994.
Online: nondes.home.xs4all.nl/posters.html

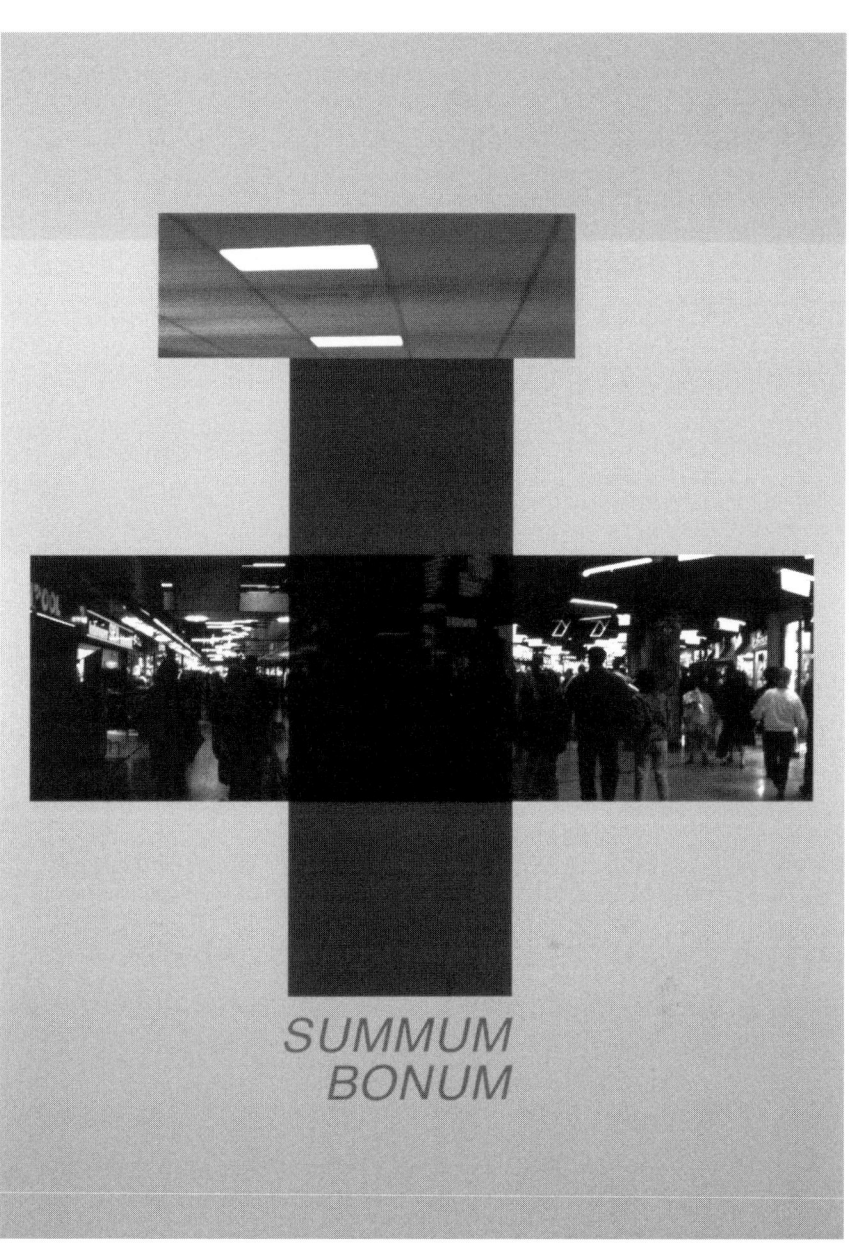

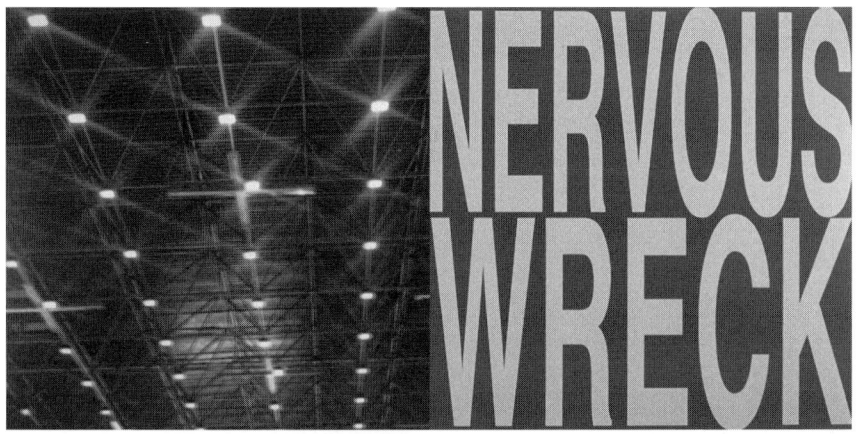
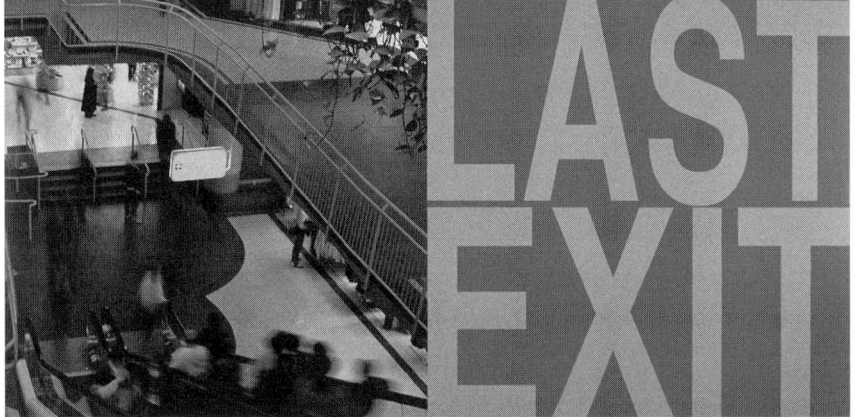
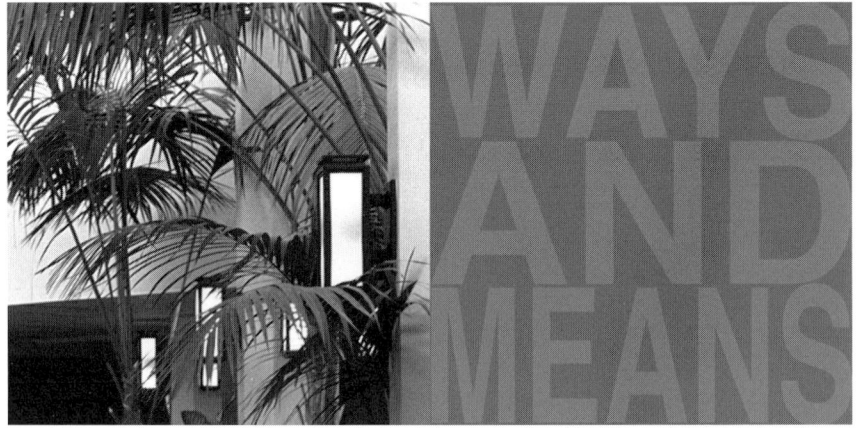

Common Boundary
Magnaprint on aluminium, 1995.

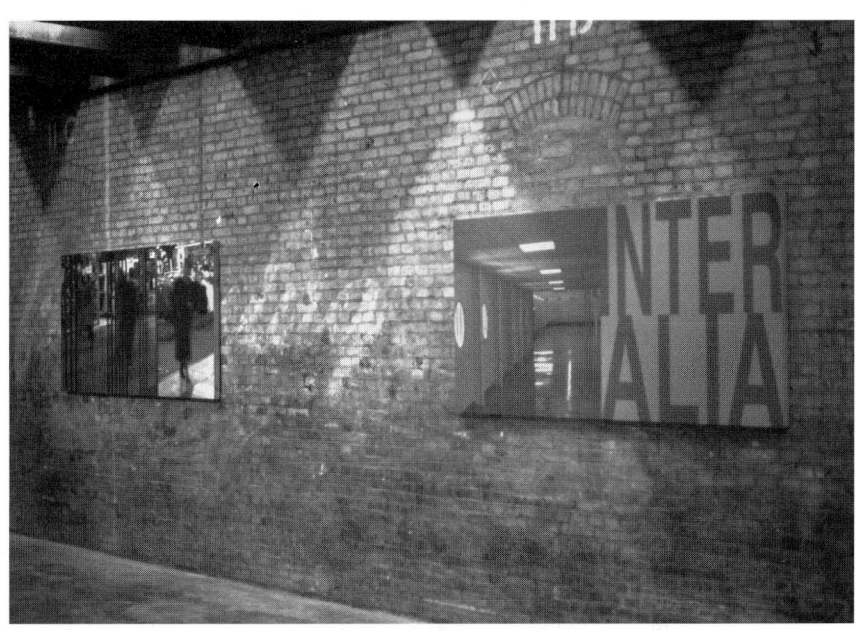

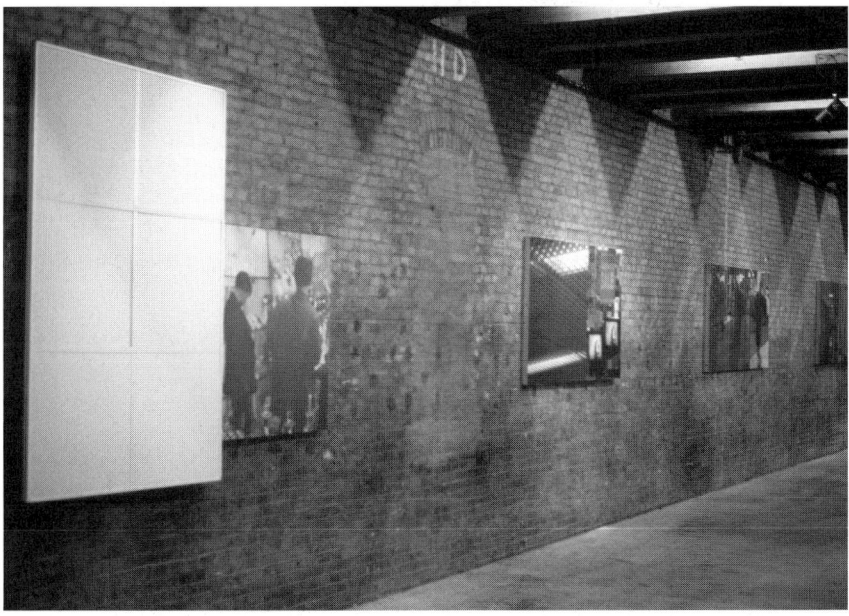

Installation
De Veemvloer, Amsterdam, 1998.

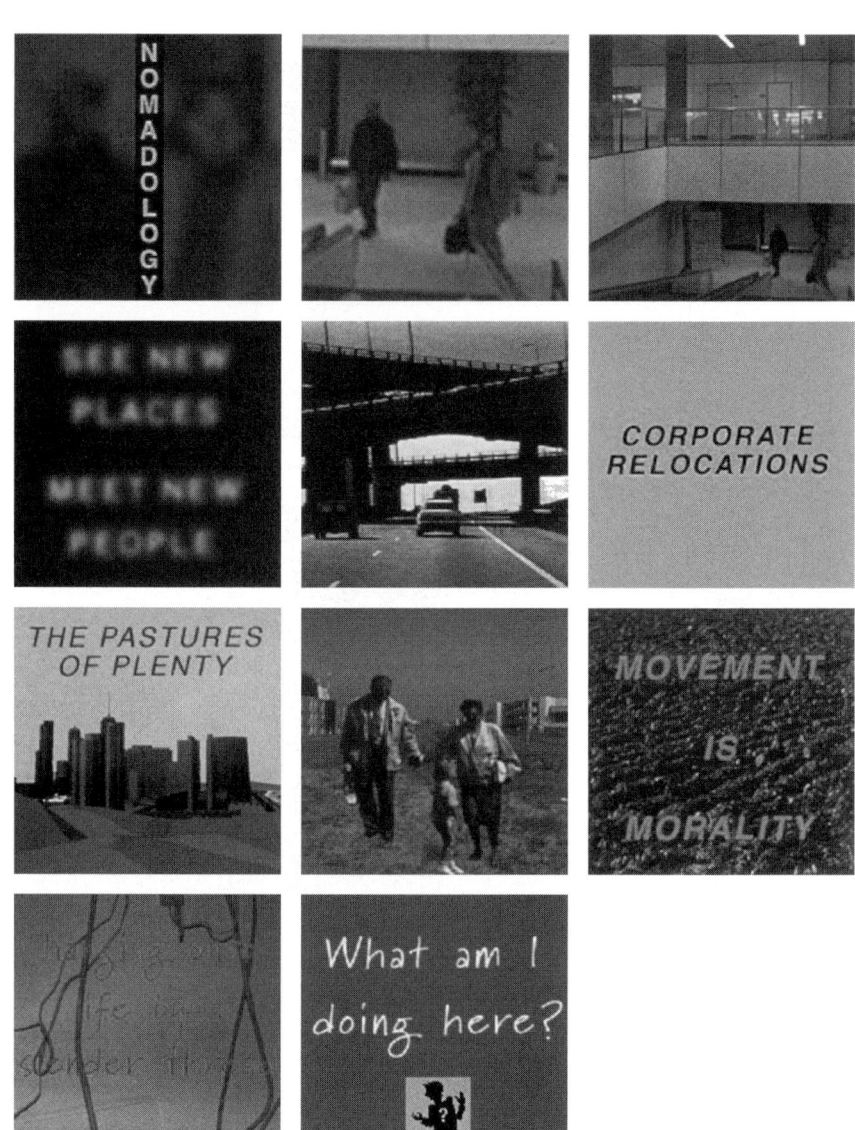

Nomadology
A sequence of images on the web, 1996.
Online: nondes.home.xs4all.nl/sneeze/nomadology/nomadology.html

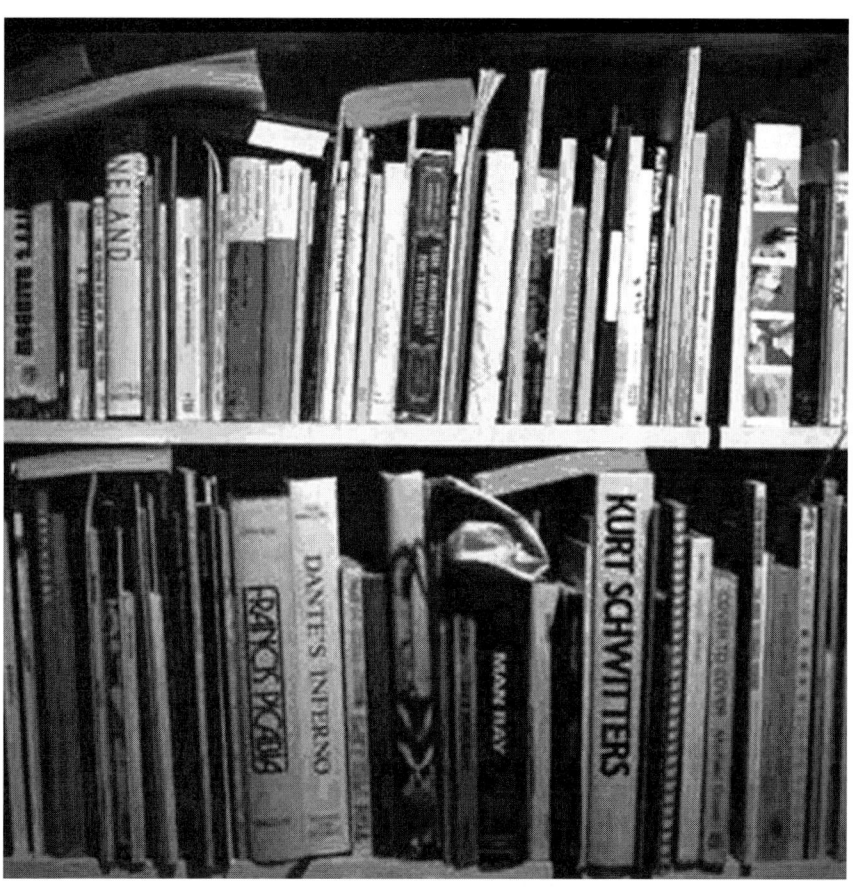

Ex Libris
By clicking on an individual book a new page opens to provide a description of each title in this cross-section of 125 volumes from Michael Gibbs' private library, 1998.
Online: nondes.home.xs4all.nl/exlibris/shelves.html

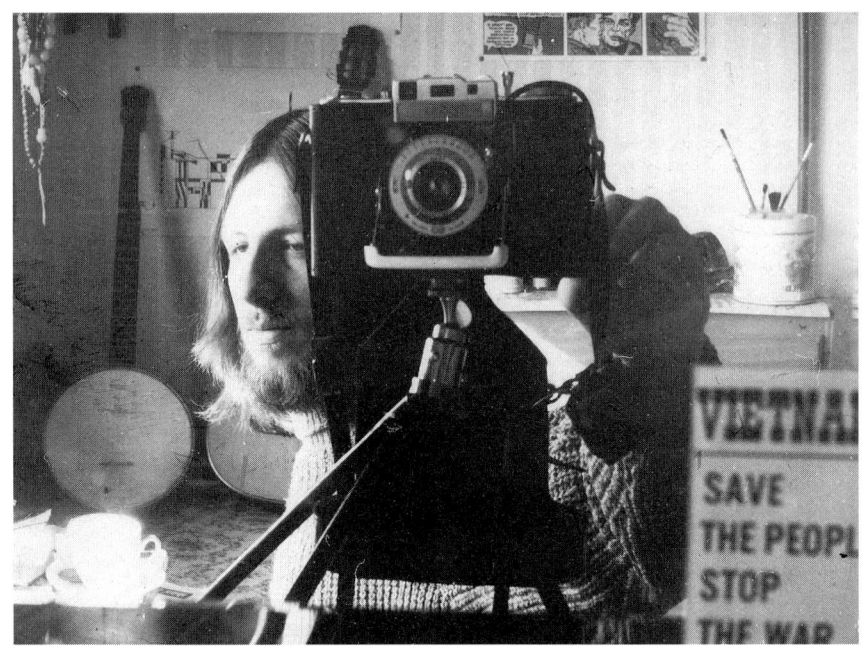

Self-portrait in mirror
Photograph, c.1970.

DONALD GARDNER

Subverter of Categories

I first met Michael Gibbs in 1968 when he was nineteen years old and a student at Warwick University, where he was organising an alternative arts and poetry festival. My group of street poets was among the groups and individuals whom he had invited to perform or present work. Right from the start Michael seems to have known what he wanted and this festival was an ambitious and subversive presentation of the avant-garde. In my case, we had a shared interest in the poetry that was coming out of the USA which we saw as a breath of fresh air in the rather cautious British scene. It was 1968 and the universities were in turmoil. I have a vivid memory of Michael in that year of student revolt, pale-faced, very young but already urbane, a Situationist in the English midlands. I also recall that he was interested in everything as long as it was *different*. During the last years of the sixties and early seventies we left footprints in many of the same places—Better Books, the ICA, Compendium Bookshop and the London Arts Lab—but didn't actually cross paths until some years later.

I caught up with him again in the 1980s when I moved to Amsterdam and we became friends. I saw a number of his performance pieces which seemed to me subversive of the notion of action, a sort of anti-performance. A staging of introversion and irony. His non-judgemental approach to anything that came his way, a notion that art happened where and when you allowed it to happen, was, I felt, typical of the 1960s which he saw as representing the last avant-garde. Despite the variety of media with which he worked, his activities—literary, extra-literary and artistic—formed a continuum that originated in his student days at Warwick. Non-rhetorical, value-free—I know nobody who was as non-judgemental as Michael.

Of course the sixties meant different things for different people and Michael's enigmatic reserve was almost the polar opposite of the overtly ideological character of much of the work of that time. However his cultivated hesitancy was more than a style statement; it was a way of creating space for the work of other people. Unlike for example, André Breton, Michael did not found a school but there was something of the Surrealists in his desire to appear in the company of others, to define himself in terms of a movement. Thinking of Michael means thinking of the many other artists whom he promoted and who were travelling in roughly the same direction as he was.

From 1984 onwards, I saw a lot of Michael. While we occupied very different positions on the spectrum of literature, we had interests in common. Browsing through his bookshelves, I found the works of Artaud and Bataille, as well as Burroughs, Ed Dorn's *Gunslinger* and Tom Philips' marvellous, illustrated translation of the *Inferno*. I admired his mischievous playing with language, which always reminded me of Marcel Duchamp, with its Sphinx-like punning and deadpan humour. The subtitle of his website, *Nondescript* is "things that are neither one thing nor the other" and I think his greatest pleasure came from everything that eluded definition. His work in poetry was always a visual thing, just as his artworks were always literary. Perhaps the best description of someone who so eluded being defined is indeed to use the term he coined for himself and speak of him as a 'Langwe Jartist', a discreet subverter of categories, someone who never minded the gap between disciplines, forms or media.

GERRIT JAN DE ROOK

Concrete poetry and language art 1965–1985

Michael Gibbs published his first-ever concrete poem 'Walk' (1965) in his final collection of poetry, *Legend* (2004). The poem is composed of letters that have been cut out and pasted together. [see p.97] This playful fascination with letters, words and language was to become typical of his entire body of artistic work.

Gibbs had been visiting the ICA in London from 1965, and this is where he first came into contact with contemporary trends in the arts. In 1966 he attended the *Destruction In Art Symposium*, where he got to know the work of Fluxus artists such as Yoko Ono and Wolf Vostell, and Viennese Actionists such as Günther Brus and Otto Muehl. Through art programmes broadcast on television he learnt about the happenings of Jean-Jacques Lebel, and the avant-garde music of John Cage; the *International Times* kept him informed of the underground films of Andy Warhol and Stan Brakhage. In the legendary London bookshop Better Books, managed since 1966 by the leading propagator of the new poetry, Bob Cobbing, he read publications by authors such as Ernst Jandl, Augusto and Haroldo de Campos and Jiří Valoch. In this mecca of literary developments he also came across the figurative poems of Apollinaire and the language concoctions of the Dadaists. Cobbing suggested that Gibbs make contact with John Sharkey, who in turn, advised him to submit a number of his poems to an international exhibition of avant-garde poetry in Buenos Aires in 1969. His name is there, on an impressive list of 114 poets from fourteen countries.

In the summer of 1967 Gibbs went on a two-month journey hitch-hiking through a dozen European countries. Turkey was his final destination, where he was caught smoking a joint and landed himself in jail. However, this did not hinder him from purchasing a fashionable sheepskin jacket and returning to England as a long-haired bearded hippie.

Out of the amalgam of these sources of inspiration and possibilities, it was Gibbs' fascination with language that determined his artistic direction. The relative simplicity of the requirements of this medium—a crayon or a typewriter—undoubtedly played a role. Between 1967 and 1970 he studied English and American Literature at Warwick University. His future direction was evident in the first issue of the magazine *Kontexts*, which he published in spring 1969 with Paul Merchant and which contains their concrete poems, supplemented by those of four of their fellow students. [see p.103] In his final year at Warwick he wrote an essay on the work of William Burroughs and John Cage.

In summer 1970 the second issue of *Kontexts* appeared. Gibbs had widened his connections and the journal included work by figures such as Alan Riddell,

Paul de Vree, Bob Cobbing, Nicholas Zurbrugg, Peter Mayer and Dom Sylvester Houédard. [see p.104] In October of the same year he had his first one-man show, in the library of Warwick University. The exhibition was accompanied by a text in which he explained his ideas about concrete poetry:

> "concrete poetry is possibly the first truly international poetry movement—a universal form of poetry that cuts across nations and languages—the poetry of the global village—its beginnings lie deep in history in the origins of language itself / in hieroglyphics in the word as sign as picture / ancient chinese picture texts / english emblem books / and the master calligraphers of the middle ages / by the 20th C artists and poets began to rebel against the staleness and restrictions of print technology—mallarme wrote 'un coup de des' juggling with typography / apollinaire explored the possibilities of shaped poems / futurists such as marinetti (and later wyndham lewis and the vorticist blast / and dadaists man ray hugo ball raoul hausmann and sound poets theo van doesburg and schwitters all experimented with word and typography (…) concrete poetry is between poetry and painting (apollinaire said 'i too am a painter') its methods and subject matter are diverse: abstract typograms (houedard) patterns of print (kriwet mayer furnival) pastoral word plays (finlay) permutations (gysin achleitner) etc etc communication on a variety of levels / the arrangement of the poem's visual elements (words and/or typography) together with its semantic and phonetic associations constitute simultaneously the meaning and dynamism of the poem / 'tension of thingwords in spacetime' / form is content / the concrete poets have revolutionised poetry / they have discovered new forms of expression for 20th C man and have abolished the linear structure of conventional poetry that is also the linear framework of authority"

In October 1970 Gibbs pursued his studies further, doing postgraduate research at the American Arts Documentation Centre of Exeter University and embarking on a thesis on 'New Structural Methods in the Contemporary Modern Arts'—a title he later changed to 'Chance Operations in Modern Arts'. Director of the institute was Dr. M. L. H. L. (Mike) Weaver, who was also the organiser of the *First International Exhibition of Concrete and Kinetic Poetry* held in Cambridge 1964. He invited David Mayor to Exeter to carry out research into the Fluxus movement. Mayor and Gibbs became friends, and Gibbs participated on the project 'Fluxus West in England' which resulted in a travelling Fluxus exhibition, *Fluxshoe*, held at seven venues in the UK until August 1972. It included work by the artists of the Beau Geste Press—such as Felipe Ehrenberg and Martha Hellion—whom they first met in June 1971. The Beau Geste Press also published Gibbs' first collection of poetry—*Lifeline* (1972)—as well as two books that he compiled with others: *DRECK, bits & pieces from the frontier* (early 1972, with David Mayor and intended as the house journal of the American Arts Documentation Centre) and *Ginger Snaps: a collection of cutups, machine prose, word and image trips* (March 1972, with Hammond Guthrie), which included work by figures such as William Burroughs, Allen Ginsberg and Tuli Kupferberg. Beau Geste also printed the fourth and fifth issues of *Kontexts*.

Gibbs published issues 3, 4 and 5 of *Kontexts* while still at Exeter. They had a print run of a maximum of 250 and the poems included show that his network had widened considerably. *Kontexts* 3 (1971) contained work from Yugoslavia and Latin America, *Kontexts* 4 (1972/1973) was devoted to the United States, while Czechoslovakian poets and artists were dominant in *Kontexts* 5 (1973), which also had work by Robert Lax from the USA and Ulises Carrión from Mexico—whom he met through Beau Geste. [see pp.105–107]

A shift also occurred in his ideas about poetry, partly due to the discussion provoked by the travelling exhibition *Sound Texts? Concrete Poetry Visual Texts* (1970–1972). Concrete poetry—as an aesthetic play with the alphabet—was pronounced dead, and visual poetry, a more socially engaged combination of language and image or object, took its place. In *Kontexts* 3 Gibbs wrote: "What is needed is a terminology (not a definition) sufficiently flexible as to allow variety and maximum opennes [sic]… so let us adopt (as the Italians seem to have done) the term 'visual poetry' which not only encompasses concrete and 'spatialist' [this tendency was propagated by Pierre Garnier and others] poetry but also extends into the area of graphic images". And in the anthology compiled by Peter Finch, *Typewriter Poems*, (1972), he said: "dissatisfied with tendency towards typographical decorativeness and simple typewriter games (have virtually ceased using typewriter medium) more interested now in some sort of global/social relevance concrete poetry needs to develop but somehow remain poetic".

On 26 October 1971 he wrote:

STATEMENT ON POETICS
"visual poetry (postconcrete) and the poetics of vision: the feeling-seeing. i try to say much with few words (sometimes even no words), to achieve a kind of profound simplicity in which there is no superfluity. the poem is the result of momentary awareness, and i feel it is important to preserve this instantaneity by making the poem itself an event on the page.

for the sake of convenience you can call me a 'concrete poet', but for me the term 'concrete' means gomringer et al, and i'm not that. they were working within a specific discipline which i find too limited for my purposes. my work is predominantly visual and nonlinear but i still write syntactical poetry because i write what i see, & i use whatever means is best to express my vision. i'm stretching the limits of language (and experience), playing with words, inventing new languages, combine word/image, etc. i share the view of korzybsky that there is no need to go beyond words, beyond the arbitrary limitations on experience imposed by the tyranny of syntax, and hence i admire the work and ideas of wm. burroughs, brion gysin, & co.

it all comes down to this: how to express the ineffable? the void? perhaps to renounce art altogether as a serious intellectual activity and just live *playfully* ???? (to be continued)."

In 1973 Peter Finch's publishing house Second Aeon, published Gibbs' collection of concrete/visual poetry *Connotations*. Despite his regrets about the poor quality of the printing, it still gives an impressive picture of the varied methods he used to deal with language. On the back flap he states that: "I'm concerned with the reduction of language in its structural elements—taking it apart to see how it works. Words don't always mean what they say—their patterns and forms reveal inner processes and events, ambiguous connotations of meaning".

Gibbs makes generous reference to his sources of inspiration: Dom Sylvester Houédard, Andy Warhol, Robert Rauschenberg, Brancusi, Mallarmé and Yves Klein. Another leitmotif is the presence of Buddhist concepts such as mindfulness, Tao, haiku, tantra and mantra.

In the meantime Gibbs abandoned his studies in Exeter. In March 1974 he departed for Amsterdam for an exhibition of his work at the In Out Center gallery, which was possibly due to the initiative of Ulises Carrión, who had now moved to Amsterdam. To accompany his exhibition he produced the booklet *Extinction* that consisted of a series of photographs where the letters of the alphabet were set on fire. [see pp.112–113]

On his return to England a month later, a great deal had changed: his employer, for whom he had worked for the past eighteen months had gone bankrupt and the Beau Geste group had split up. He got a job as a teacher, but showed little enthusiasm for this work and at the end of 1974, when he received an invitation to show his work in the Agora Studio in Maastricht and was able to combine this with a lecture and workshop at the Jan van Eyck Academie, he decided to stay on in the Netherlands. The workshop resulted in his book *Scriptimages*, printed on the Academie's presses. The combined sixth and seventh issue of *Kontexts* were also produced there.

Kontexts 6 & 7 (spring 1975) had as its subtitle "a review of visual / experimental poetry and language art". [see p.118] Concrete/visual poetry is still a pronounced presence, but it is supplemented with language reductions, semiotics, essays about artist's books and Dada, calligraphy, narrative photography and graphics, video, conceptual art and language experiments. Richard Kostelanetz, Lawrence Weiner and Maurizio Nannucci are mentioned as collaborators and Carrión's essay 'The new art of making books' will become the most quoted source from the magazine.

In the journal *Fun-dangos* 5 (1975), published by Agora Studio, with a.o. Raúl Marroquin as editor and Michael as contributing editor, Gibbs restates his views of twentieth-century literature: "19th C. concepts of linear order, of time and space, have been superceded [sic] in 20th C. literature by strategies of *silence* and *synthesis* (including a return to source). External reality proving too chaotic and indefinite has resulted in withdrawal into the self. into the solipsism of Beckett where the self is the last remaining sign of life / or into the private realism of art". One of his conclusions in the article is that "The experimental poet is a 'languagedesigner' he escribes rather than describes. LANGUAGE AS A GAME in which the given structure and rules of the game (grammar/message/situation) predetermine the moves in the game (words/signs/gestures/actions) and progressively limit the possible alternatives, the earlier move conditioning thoose [sic] that follow".

In June 1975 Gibbs moved to Amsterdam where he assisted Carrión in making contact with publishers of concrete and visual poetry for the artist's bookshop, Other Books & So. He kept in touch with Maastricht and printed *Kontexts* 8 (spring 1976) again on the hospitable presses of the Academie. The sub-title was altered slightly to "an occasional review of visual poetries and language arts". Ulises Carrión was now 'contributing editor' and Other Books & So was the editorial address. Just as all the issues of *Kontexts* are different in form, this one too looks different. *Kontexts* 8 resembles a newspaper and is concerned especially with performances, sound poetry (Jackson Mac Low, Henri Chopin, Arrigo Lora Totino), cut-ups (Burroughs, Brion Gysin) and computer poetry (Greta Monach). [see p.119]

In Amsterdam Michael earned some money giving English lessons and—with John Liggins—he produced the *6 Plays* (1976) by Carrión in letterpress at the Drukhuis, a printing press next door to Other Books & So. He also embarked on the time-consuming compilation of his book *Pages* (1976), which was inspired by Jorge Luis Borges and consisted of the successive numbered pages from other books, so that out of the chaotic variety of content, typography and language another book emerges that is about everything and nothing.

Further developments

From this account so far one can see how Gibbs' ideas about the poetic use of language changed over the years. The first five issues (1969–1973) of *Kontexts* were concerned with concrete poetry, in 1975 he turned instead to "visual / experimental poetry and language art", while in 1976 his theme was "visual poetries and language arts" and *Kontexts* 9 & 10 (February 1977) contained 'Langwe Jart'—a term invented by Gibbs. He describes the contents as "the development of a more conceptual, rather than purely visual (or 'retinal') approach to language experimentation, together with related processes in the fields of photography, video, performance and music". [see p.126]

In an undated note (1974?) he describes Langwe Jart as: "visual art in any form/media/inter-media, in which the principle idea is related to linguistic (and para-/meta-linguistic) expression and invention in terms of writing, speech, words, letters, syntax etc. (i.e. language systems.) my own particular contribution in this new genre was initially 'concrete' and visual poetry, but more recently I have been concerned with exploring the basic elements of language in terms of minimal verbo-visual structures—this led me to a number of works which use the visual possibilities of one of the most basic linguistic structures: the alphabet".

In July 1975, at the opening of the exhibition *Internationale Visuele Poezie* in Utrecht, he presented his more physical relation with language with a performance in which he wrote the letters of the alphabet with his own blood.

In *Dremples* (spring 1976) he described Language Art as follows:

> "It's true that all artists make use of language in one way or another (the language of form, colour, imagery, etc.), but what distinguishes language art is its concern with language as a system possessing an infrastructure, and a wide range of external forms. While the visual poets have emphasised the plastic (surface) elements, the conceptualists have concentrated on the semantic (sub-surface) ones. Ways of seeing and ways of thinking."

Another possibility he explored, that involved working with language in the presence of an audience, was sound poetry. He attended the '8th International Festival of Sound Poetry' at the Poetry Society in London (May 1975). On the occasion of the sound poetry event 'Text in Sound' at the Stedelijk Museum in Amsterdam (April 1977), of which he was one of the organisers, he presented *Kontextsound*: "a compilation of sound poetry, textsound compositions, poésie sonore, auditive texts, optophonics, verbosonics, lingual music". It included the sound poetry of Sten Hanson, Ilmar Laaban, Bernard Heidsieck, François Dufrêne, Gerhard Rühm, Arrigo Lora-Totino, Jeremy Adler, Katalin Ladik, Theo van Doesburg and others. Gibbs also attended the international sound poetry festivals in Stockholm (1977), Toronto (1978) and New York (1980) and in 1978 he worked on the audio cassette *Sound Proof* no.0, published by Carrión, which also included work by Carrión, Greta Monach and G. J. de Rook.

In his performances he harked back to a subject that was already present in his 'Connotations' collection, namely Zen Buddhism.

> "Tonight, he will adopt the lotus position on stage, flanked by two guttering candles behind him, a projector will flash illuminations of mandalas from ancient Tibetan prayer books, and as it does so, he will chant a translation of the prayers related to the mandalas but chopped and rearranged like a blast from a spiritual scatter gun. 'I'm interested in magic, but in twentieth century terms. And to me, the spinning of a prayer wheel or the casting of sticks in the *I Ching* is no different from the random number tables in a computer. That's our kind of magic, and I'm not afraid of it'." (*The Globe and Mail*, Toronto, 21 June 1977)

In a manuscript he throws further light on his approach:

> "Random Selection Sutras are based on an ancient Tantric text, the Kamakalavilasa. The original verses are treated word by word by progressive elimination determined by dice-throws, peeling off layers of words until only the 'seed-words' remain. The evolutionary process in reverse, from the complex to the particular. Tantric thought holds that the world and all that is in it was created by the divine utterance of the alphabet—names *and* things sprang from the alphabet, which is both seed and sprout. With the RSS [Random Selection Sutras] the listener is able to make his own verbal creations grow from the seeds he hears the sounds of the cymbols [cymbals] which punctuate the recitation, or the random-treated mandalas which are projected, are intended to be aids. The first 10 Sutras are scheduled for publication later in 1977, together with a cassette tape version which uses tape-recorder techniques to achieve the word elimination procedure."

Like a number of his other plans for books, this idea was never realised.

In summer 1977, Gibbs travelled for three months in Canada, the USA and Mexico. He visited George Maciunas and had conversations with a large number of artists such as Jackson Mac Low, Richard Kostelanetz and Lawrence Weiner in New York, Anna Banana and Bill Gaglione in San Francisco and John Baldessari and Chris Burden in Los Angeles. He then stayed in Mexico for a month where he met Felipe Ehrenberg. He returned to New York by way of Austin, Texas, where he stayed with Loris Essary. Back in New York he had meetings with Allen Ginsberg, Charles Bernstein and Ray di Palma of the L=A=N=G=U=A=G=E-group, Jill Kroesen, Carolee Schneeman and other artists and writers. He was stimulated by their kindred ideas about language and in 1983 he looked back on these contacts:

> "When I first encountered this concerted, serious effort at renewing poetic language I was immediately attracted. I could appreciate their use of words, or fractions of words, as things in themselves, freed from their role as referents to an outside world. They dealt with language as opaque material, not as formally as the concrete poets, who often did little more than make patterns, but with an awareness of the philosophical implications of their work." (*Menu 1*)

One result of this journey was his book *Deciphering America*, with work by twenty-six artists from the USA, five from Canada and two from Latin America.

Gibbs presented a summary of ways of working with text in his book *Selected Pages* (1978). He starts by listing sixteen approaches to dealing with texts, which vary from "kindly" to "with contempt". After that printed texts are juxtaposed with handwritten ones, 'translated' into graphic symbols, crossed out, converted into numbers, subjected to word reduction or to being read on the basis of another language. They are cut into ribbons and composed all over again, rendered illegible, subjected to memory tests or else—partially—erased.

At the end of 1978 he presented his project in a show with Ania Bien, John Liggins and Pnina Reichman at Gallery A+ in Amsterdam, which the owner Harry Ruhé put at their disposal for four months. In 1982 and 1985 he also had one-man shows in Ruhé's Galerie A.

He dealt with books in his performances and exhibitions in a similar way to how he dealt with language in his publications. He deployed all his emotions: he threw them around, pronounced them dead but he also got them to sing. "The sounds of the making, and the inherent sound of the finished object (the page / the book / the reading) are what interest me. How the sound of typing a sonnet differs from that of free verse. How the pages of a book can be flipped, thumbed or slammed shut, to produce a symphony of 'tome tones'." (catalogue: *Sound Poetry Festival*, Toronto, 1978) In his exhibitions he made objects of them (1977); in his artworks he deconstructed, reconstructed and reduced them.

Later he remarked: "I have an emotional relation with books, a sort of love-hate relation. The book is a metaphor for me, an erotic symbol". (catalogue: *The Absent Words*, 1980) A striking example of his physical approach is his *Wounded Book* (1979) in which he staunches the bleeding wound of the book with a real sticking plaster. [see p.135]

In the period from 1977 to 1983, performances, installations and video played an important role in Gibbs' work. Stéphane Mallarmé's unfinished work 'Le Livre' in particular formed an important source of inspiration: "Each reading of the Livre would be a performance or séance in which it would adapt itself to its circumstance".

Gibbs was active on a number of different fronts during this period. From November 1978 to November 1982 he published twenty-eight issues of the magazine *Artzien*, which he edited (after early 1982, with Harry Ruhé as co-editor). [see pp.112–113]

In 1980 he published an *Artzien Audio Cassette* (with work by Hezy Leskly, Dirk Larsen, Ulises Carrión, Robert Joseph & Pier van Dijk, Remko Scha and others). In 1980–81 he also contributed to a number of audio cassettes published by Rod Summers under the latter's VEC label. Halfway through 1983 however, he declared: "But sound poetry itself seems to have run out of steam, or to have become less relevant nowadays when more interesting work is being done by visual artists such as Lawrence Weiner and Laurie Anderson". (manuscript)

From 1975 to 1981 he also produced work in the field of stamp art, partly thanks to the Stempelplaats gallery run by Aart van Barneveld, the partner of Ulises Carrión, and made a number of books with stamps. From 1976 to 1984 Gibbs contributed to some thirty international exhibitions of Mail Art and twenty of artist's books. In the period from 1968 to 2015 his concrete/visual poetry and language art was included in more than eighty issues of around sixty different journals and to fifty books. He also presented this work in a dozen solo shows and around thirty group exhibitions.

This article could not have come about without the generous support of Eva Gibbs-Gonggrijp who gave me permission to study Michael's posthumous writings. It has been translated by Donald Gardner.

GUY SCHRAENEN

The Bloody Alphabet, or how to crack it

It may seem overdramatic, but if one could imagine somebody offering his life to 'the word', it would be Michael Gibbs. He was, as Andrew Wilson writes, "a gentle and tolerant believer in the worth of art—its social, cultural, political and aesthetic worth. Art excited him and was the core of his life". He entered the world of art when he was very young, in particular the world of language, as some might enter religion. For him, dealing with language was a kind of mystical attitude, which culminated in his public performance, *The bloody alphabet*, where he writes letters and sentences such as "These letters are my flesh and my blood" with blood on a large sheet of paper. [see p.120]

Michael Gibbs was discrete in appearance. His humble and unsophisticated demeanour was accompanied by that of a careful observer, with an alert eye, never putting himself into the foreground. He was very aware of the role he had chosen in his particular but essential segment of the art world—the investigation of language in all its experimental aspects and its diffusion by publishing. His body of work should be considered as a work in progress. It comprises both his own art, which includes experimental poetry, essays, performances, photo works, graphic works, artists' books, sound works, internet projects and his teaching and publishing activities. The latter included his magazine *Kontexts* (1969–1977), a key journal for experimental poetry and language art. As well as comments and critical texts on recent publications, *Kontexts* included contributions by William Burroughs, Ulises Carrión, Henri Chopin, Bob Cobbing, Mirtha Dermisache, John Giorno, Brion Gysin, Clemente Padin, Jiří Valoch, Edgardo-Antonio Vigo, Paul de Vree and many others. (The reason for the inclusion of so many names here is not to undermine the importance of Michael Gibbs and his work, on the contrary, it is also a tribute to his involvement with this group of artists who he promoted incessantly.) [see pp.103–107, 118–119, 126–127]

As a publisher, he founded Kontexts Publications (1968–1983) to publish his own books as well as his colleague's, including Ulises Carrión, Robert Lax, Jackson Mac Low and Jan Voss. In collaboration with Harry Ruhé, founder of Galerie A in Amsterdam, he published the art journal *Artzien* (1978–1982), a magazine which is described as a "fearless, idiosyncratic review of art in The Netherlands, focussing particularly on the marginal and the new, written mostly by artists, and featuring interviews". [see pp.138–139]

Through his engagement with the global network he also contributed art works to many artists' magazines such as *Schmuck* (GB), *Ovum* (Uruguay), *De Tafelronde* (B), and *Blocknoot* (NL). But his work shouldn't be placed in some kind of nostalgic universe, his intellectual agility meant he began using new technologies in the 1990s, exploring the possibilities and limitations of the internet. While searching to find interesting information on Gibbs, I fell on Nondescript

Productions, the name of the web-project he maintained. What I discovered there gave me the feeling "Yes! One can do something creative and imaginative within the internet biotope!" Rather than producing eternally repeated loops for the digital world, he used the internet in its most positive way, as a critical and imaginative tool. He described the internet project *Why not sneeze?* as "a combination of a magazine and a laboratory for experiments... for critical art on and about the internet". In *Ex Libris*, a digital version of his eponymous, hand-written work from 1978, (nondes.home.xs4all.nl/exlibris/shelves.html) he placed a detail of a bookshelf in the centre of a completely black window. By clicking on the spine of one of the books, the screen opens to a lapidary description. One can move from book to book and undertake a voyage into his private library, as well as gaining an insight into his pragmatic way of explaining. [see p.171]

Born in 1949, Michael Gibbs began his artistic and editorial career while still a university student. In 1974, he moved to Maastricht and then to Amsterdam, meeting artists and finding a favourable atmosphere to develop his activities. In Maastricht he had the opportunity to collaborate with Agora Studio (1972–1985) which promoted innovative ways of working with printed matter, early video art, and later, media art. In Amsterdam, he held his first exhibition at the In Out Center (1972–1974), this venue was an early artists' initiative founded by an international artists collective from a variety of cultural backgrounds, including Michel Cardena and the artists Raul Marroquin, Ulises Carrión, Hreinn Fridfinnsson, Kristjan and Sigurdur Gudmundsson, Hetty Huisman, Pieter Laurens Mol and Gerrit Jan de Rook. In 1974, he performed *Extinction* where he doused a polysterene alphabet in petrol, set it on fire, and extinguished it. [see pp.112–113] On the occasion of this performance, he published the artist's book *Extinction* under the name of In Out Productions. In 1975, following the closing of the In Out Center, one of its members Ulises Carrión, founded Other Books and So, in Amsterdam, the first bookshop-gallery of its kind. Here Michael Gibbs traced an inspiring atmosphere for further collaborations, presentations of his publications and a daily meeting-place. He organised an exhibition of his artists' newspaper collection in 1976 under the title *Newspaper Art / Art Newspapers*. [see pp.123] Some years later, after Other Books and So had closed, he developed, as did many others, including myself, a close relationship with the artists' collective Boekie Woekie, who still have a bookshop/gallery in Amsterdam today. Here they promote their own publications, as well as stocking books by other artists and publishers that are unobtainable elsewhere—"regardless of their author's fame", as Jan Voss, one of its founders, points out. Michael Gibbs developed their website and presented his works here in 2004, and in 2009, which was to be his last exhibition.

The intellectual spirit of the international avant-garde art scene, which Michael Gibbs belonged to, was a far cry from today's celebrity art market. It is for this reason that such a critical and independent artists' network is so often overlooked, despite it being indispensable in defining the intense and creative atmosphere of the open and cosmopolitan Amsterdam at that time. Its historical significance can't be reduced to the established galleries and art institutions, as expressed in the exhibition and catalogue *In & Out of Amsterdam* (MoMA 2009). This title in fact refers to the name of the In Out Center—used without citing its source—and proves thereby the negation within the discourses in the predominant art scene.

Aware of the activities of Michael Gibbs and having already collected his publications, my first personal encounter with him was at the then recently opened bookshop gallery Other Books and So, which became my favourite venue in Amsterdam, and lead to a close relationship with both Michael Gibbs and Ulises Carrión. Here I discovered numerous publications, and I also had the chance to show the work of my own publishing house and organise exhibitions on Eduard Bal, Mirtha Dermisache and the thematic exhibition *Typewriter Art*.

My contact with Michael Gibbs grew into both a professional relationship and a friendship, and I had the privilege to collaborate with him on several occasions over the years. I published the book *5 coloured alphabets in black and white* and I included his project *This is a limited edition of one million copies, of which this is no...* several times in my publications. [see p.137] I presented his publications, such as the series *Publishers as no others* in the Weserburg Museum Bremen, alongside Hansjörg Mayer Publications (GER), Something Else Press (USA), Beau Geste Press (GB), Eschenau Summer Press (CH), Giorno Poetry Systems (USA) and others. I also showed his books in several exhibitions in the Serralves Museum Porto and recently in the exhibition *It is not new it is a book* in the Museo Reina Sofia Madrid. He also contributed to the special stamp issue of *Libellus* 8 and to the mail art project *Aeropus I*.

In 1976 I invited him to perform the piece *Public Publishing Project* at the Small Press Festival, held in the Galerie Kontakt, Antwerp, where there were also performances and films by Ulises Carrión, Raul Marroquin, John Liggins, François Dufrêne, Eduard Bal, and others. For the Small Press Festival catalogue, Michael Gibbs wrote a clear statement, which proves his engagement as an artist, publisher and champion of the small press scene:

> "The small presses are small only in the size of their editions and their fund; in vision and courage they are far greater than the established (commercial) publishers and booksellers who market books like brands of coffee? A small press edition is a sacred object, evoking reverence (or at least respect) for its author, editor, and printer (who may all happen to be the same person."

In 1985 a conversation between Michael Gibbs and myself was published in the series *A Survey of Alternative Spaces called Sound—printed—visual* in the Belgium magazine *Artefactum*. This series commented on various artists' initiatives such as the Exchange Gallery (PL), Revue OU (F), Studio voor experimentele muziek (B), Club Moral/Force Mental (B), Artpool (H) and also *Kontexts*. In this interview his uncompromising point of view is clear:

Michael Gibbs: The first issue of *Kontexts* appeared when I was still at university. The idea then was to publish some concrete and visual poetry. Sending my small scale publication abroad I got feedback, people sent me material and so the magazine became international. It more or less stayed in the area of concrete and visual poetry but expanded into other areas. So it included works by different types of artists. In some way they were people as myself who fitted between visual art and literature.

Guy Schraenen: Did you work independently from financial aid?

MG: Yes. The first books were published quite cheaply by stencil, with a low budget. Each time I wanted to print something, I had to do it the cheapest way possible.

GS: After *Kontexts* you published another magazine, *Artzien*, in Amsterdam this time. Contrary to *Kontexts*, which published artists' works, *Artzien* spoke about art.

MG: Yes, but there were sometimes essays and interviews in *Kontexts*; however it's function was very different. My aim with *Artzien* was to provide a platform for artists to be critical on the art scene around them and to write about art.
In most of the art publications or newspapers, the writings are done by critics; those are little more than journalists who are only giving informations. I hoped that artists would be able to write about art in an intelligent, critical and polemical way. It maybe didn't work out as I hoped because the Dutch culture is more a visual than a written orientated culture.

GS: Don't you believe it is better to have a publication where artists show their work than where they explain their work?

MG: In some ways, yes, but I don't restrict an artist just in making artworks. At least that is not how I would define my own activity. I think that one of the functions of an artist should be to put himself in relationship with the world.

GS: Is that the reason of your activity as publisher?

MG: Certainly, but at the same time it was also a means to enter a field as an artist. Above all, when I was living in England, in Exeter, there were very few artists around I could communicate with. Publication seemed to me another possibility of communication. So I could situate my own work within a movement and thus escape from a local situation.

GS: Actually you seem to have restricted your publisher's activity. Why?

MG: There are two reasons. The first is financial. The second is that there are not enough artists around whom I feel interested to publish. In the beginning, my activities were in the defined field of Language Art. Actually, I don't feel attached to any kind of movement except for a general critical approach.

GS: There is also a big problem to diffuse publications as yours...

MG: Yes. Booksellers do not want to sell publications of small publishers which stay on their shelves and they can't make enough money out of it.

GS: However a contradictory situation exists: on one hand it is difficult to diffuse this kind of publications, on the other hand, after a few years they are out of print and get very expensive!

MG: But who buys such publications? The collectors!

GS: They are buying because they are interested in them when valuable, but they have no curiosity of discovery.

M.G. The whole argument of producing for collectors is not valid.

GS: Why don't people buy when it is easy to buy, which would permit the publisher to pursue his activities. Those publications are important tracks of todays artistic production.

MG: I believe there is very little public interest. In any case there are archives for such a kind of material, like the one of Ulises Carrión in Holland and yours in

Antwerp, which interested people can have access to. Such places will be necessary to write history. But do we need a larger public? I don't think so. It is aimed towards a circle of artists and friends, not to a public. To reach that sort of high public should not be the focus of our activities. If they are interested, they will come to us.

Michael Gibbs' attitude, was always an intellectual support to my activities as a publisher and collector of artists' publications. The magazine *Kontexts* and his book works have a prominent place in my collection (now in the Center for Artists' Publications, Museum Weserburg, Bremen) and are significant examples of freedom, engagement and imaginative working processes. Even if he never had the intention to surprise the viewer with glamorous aspects of his publications, but by simplicity and discreteness, the changing format of the issues of *Kontexts* show the permanent adaptation possibilities without ever departing from his concern with language art and experimental poetry. In particular the last issue of *Kontexts* (9 & 10) is the result of a perfect combination of content, material and the coloured mimeographed printing technique: a tactile and visual delight. [see p.126] For this final issue, he wrote an editorial, reflecting on his role as editor/publisher:

> "Since the first Issue, produced at Warwick University in 1969 in the form of an envelope containing 8 poem-cards, *Kontexts* has steadily grown to the present bulk of 90 pages; it seemed that, were the magazine to continue, it would have to keep expanding, eventually to control the poor publisher's life completely.
>
> There has also been a spreading out of the type of work that *Kontexts* published: initially devoted to 'concrete' poetry (hence the title, from the german 'konkrete'), it very soon became involved with visual poetry, and more recently, as particularly exemplified in this issue, the development of a more conceptual, rather than purely visual (or 'retinal') approach to language experimentation, together with related processes in the fields of photography, video, performance and musics.
>
> There are unfortunately too few journals which are willing to present original work by unknown artists and writers. The policy is generally to wait until a 'movement' appears, and then to use it as a peg, or a prop, to support the new trend, with the subsequent exclusion of any other new developments. *Kontexts* has never harboured a coterie; true, there have been some contributors (among the hundred or so included to date) who appear in more than one issue of *Kontexts*, but even these 'regulars' work in widely different fields.
>
> The format of the magazine has also been flexible, *Kontexts* is as far as I know the only small press magazine (not to speak of the larger presses) which changed its format every issue. Economics had something to do with this, but it evolved as a principle that the material received for each issue should determine its format, not the other way round, as is usually the case."

Language and its link to the image is the basis of his work, whether in his own book works, his visual works or his performances. One can consider his œuvre as a visual and intellectual deconstruction of all of its elements in order to reveal and transform its role and its aesthetic and, by doing so, its effect and function within the broader cultural context. Many of his artists' books deal not only with language but also with the book itself. In various ways he examines the concept: what a book is, what it can be, what it means.

One of his first artists' books, *Extinction*, is a photographic documentation of the performance, described above. On the cover, the title "Extinction" is printed five times, but fading out line by line.

In *Selected pages*, he bundles pages of several of his own books. On one of the pages one can read many words chosen from pages of a conventional book and a hand-written sentence at its centre: "from a book, chose the most beautiful word on each page. destroy the rest of the book".

The front cover of the *Wounded book* has a real plaster fixed in the centre. The imagined blood of the wound beneath seeps through all the inside pages, which have a red coloured cut at their centre. [see p.135]

The book *Pages* can be seen as a reconstruction. It assembles one hundred pages from different books, following the sequential numeration of the diverse pages. The simple, but intriguing idea behind the postcard sized book *5 coloured alphabets in black and white* and part of the series *ColleXtion* can be explained in the artist's own words, namely by his "note on procedure" on the first page of the book:

> "5 random sequences of 26 different colour crayons writing the alphabet A–Z. The coloured alphabets are transferred to a photo-electric stencil via a photostatic process with reduces all the colours to different shades of black and white."

Legend, published by Boekie Woekie in 2004 is a "selection of previously unpublished texts produced between 1966 and 1984, including the author's first ever concrete poem, language poems, text drawings and other in between genres".

In 2005, he revised and expanded previously published texts and republished them in three volumes in a slipcase. All three books deal with his extended relationship to the book and to language, considering all possible kinds of writing and reading and their meaning. Two of these volumes, both titled *All or nothing* are an anthology of blank books. [see p.76] Both include an essay on white works and books, followed by a selection of white pages in books. One of the two volumes is printed white on white, an actual literal illustration at the limits of signification. This is, as far as I know, one of the rare books signed by Michael Gibbs; and signed with white ink! The third book, *SomeVolumesFromTheLibraryOfBabel*, consists of a theoretical reflection on several other authors who have analysed language: the title reference to Jorge Luis Borges' idea of a total library. [see p.26] Michael Gibbs writes here without spaces between the words, making the text *almost* unreadable. This 'artessay', both artwork and theoretical essay, is followed by pages by artists who have expanded the limits of writing.

Michael Gibbs wasn't only the "unsung hero of concrete poetry", as B. E. Mitchel calls him, but also evidence that an artist who could be considered as a destructor of language is in fact—as so many artists of his time—an essential component which makes the machine function. The quotation in his essay *All or nothing* of the often dispraised French poet Jean Cocteau: "All texts are only alphabets in disorder" points towards the purpose of his subversive attitude.

By creating unexpected images and meanings, Michael Gibbs questions the alphabet as a tool of the power system. His cracks appear to create disorder, but in fact he puts everything in a new place, and forces us to look beyond the limits of our conventional language.

Still today, the work and engagement of Michael Gibbs offers discoveries. It proposes a way beyond the ossified and conformist art world which attempts to dictate our behaviour and functionality. If he and his fellow campaigners are considered marginal, their actions are the seed in the darkness of the soil which emerge to bear fruit.

With thanks to Maike Aden for research.

MARGA VAN MECHELEN

Performances[1]

What do you remember of a performance after forty years? Of course one person will have more memories than another person. Most likely one remembers the artist when they are the performer. An image of how he or she moves, relates to the objects, if present in the room, or to the audience. Probably also what we might call the essence of the content of the performance, sometimes not more than a feeling or a rather vague idea, and of course we might remember shocking or unexpected things. If we summarise *The Name of the Game* (1980), a performance Michael Gibbs did at de Appel in Amsterdam, in this way, we see a slender man, with straight long hair and a beard, looking older then he was at that time, who moved through space without paying much attention to the public. He carefully arranged sheets of paper onto a large sheet of glass resting on three trestles. [see pp.140–141] People will remember the bricks and the breaking of the glass and presumably also the little girl that together with Gibbs piled the bricks onto the sheet of glass. Talking about the essence of the content of the performance, we don't think about those bricks, the glass or the girl in the first place but about language. Is it because we already knew more about the artist, and recognise other motifs that often return such as slide projections of words or spoken language on a tape recorder? Here the performance is concentrated on sheets of A4 blank paper, details known by descriptions in the literature.[2] There were slides projected, forty in total, with just one word on each slide and a tape recording that played spoken texts. These were constructed from the same words as the ones in the slides. The texts one could hear through the loudspeakers were later published in *Artzien* (vol.2, no.2/3).

The performance was very well orchestrated. Numbers played an important part: the sheets of paper in five rows of seven, the exact number of sixty bricks and forty slides etc. At the same time 'chance' was involved. The sheet of glass had to break, but when and how? Not immediately though. The first ten bricks were thrown towards the glass but were not supposed to hit the glass. It becomes more clear from his notebook that to a certain extent he also wanted to prevent the performance from being killed by defining. "Rather, let it be related to, the connotations are what make the work live in the imagination."[3] Nonetheless in another note he reveals his own thoughts, put between brackets: […]; herein he talks about "virgin pages awaiting the 'imprint'". "Fragile inviolability." And when the bricks fell before the glass, he sees "the pages tremble in fearful anticipation of violation". At the end of this notes, he formulates a kind of conclusion, the quintessence of the performance: "the violation effected—the weight of language proves too great for its supporting surface".[4]

Gibbs moves not only in this performance but in other performances as well between a structural approach with which the notion of connotation is connected and a use of psychological terms.[5] The word imagination from the quote above is an indication of it, or elsewhere: words like 'suggestion' and more in particular 'association'. It was Roland Barthes who replaced the word 'association', still used by the structural linguist and founder of modern semiotics, Ferdinand de Saussure (1857–1913), by the more structuralist linguistic term 'connotation'. Gibbs deliberately wants to keep both concepts at work. As Kees van Gelder stated, "he followed (the later) Barthes in his critique on empirical thinking and the doxa. Instead he pleaded for the 'para-doxa', as the non-acceptable".[6] Within his orchestration the connections between words and objects, as for instance the bricks, though maybe not so clear at first sight, are all the same made. In his notebook of September 1978–March 1979 these interrelations are explicitly mentioned.[7] Not the one we might have recognised already: a sheet of paper versus a sheet of glass, but here the equation of words and bricks: "bricks=words". Also the throwing of the bricks is connoted to a throwing of words by the voice (or the writing impulse). Another document underlines the idea of structural relations. Here he speaks about the parallel of composing a text and building a wall of bricks. An arrow, which is an indexical sign, leads us in his notebook to a word that has a pivotal significance in his work: ventriloquism, the disconnection of sound and source. In the invitation for the de Appel performance most of these elements are also mentioned: "Let the work live in the imagination not giving the whole story right away", "use processes of extrapolation, bricks=words, throwing (the voice) ventriloquism".[8] We come back to that crucial word 'ventriloquism'.

An unexpected element in *The Name of the Game* is the appearance of a child. The presence of the child in what is called so far an orchestration, now makes us think of a better word, namely 'game' or 'play'. We associate the second word in particular with playfulness, a free, undetermined and creative life, with things in another space and time than that of normal life. However, the English word 'play' leads us also to plays that know certain rules which one is obliged to obey. Thanks to the regulated system of a play the viewer is able to recognise the state of being with all the necessary information about the history of the game and at the same time as a moment in a diachronic process that leads to the question: what might be the next step (within a restricted number of possibilities)? This first meaning of the word 'play' is often more interesting to philosophers and anthropologists than the second meaning; Johan Huizinga and Roger Caillois both recognised in 'play' the foundation of culture. However, in the performances of Gibbs we oscillate between the two readings of the word 'play', like other artists related to Fluxus did before him or parallel to him.

Becoming a performance artist

Gibbs started doing performances in 1975 when he was invited by the owners of the Agora Studio, Ger van Dijck and Theo van der Aa, and the Jan van Eyck Academy to come to Maastricht.[9] In fact, his move to performance was a gradual process, after many years of concrete poetry readings and his association with Fluxus artists. The performance *Extinction* in the garden of the Jan van Eyck, recorded by Raul Marroquin, [see pp.112–113] was closely related to the exhibition of his concrete and visual poetry a year earlier at In Out Center in

Amsterdam. In conjunction with the performance, he published a booklet under the same name, *Extinction*, featuring a disintegrating alphabet. In Maastricht he set fire to an alphabet of large letters cut out of polystyrene with a hard-board template, which was doused in petrol, ignited, and put out with a fire extinguisher.[10] In 1974 and 1975 Gibbs stayed in The Netherlands most of the time, enjoying friendship with the founder of Other Books & So, Ulises Carrión, and the other artists involved with In Out Center and Agora Studio, most of them foreigners like Gibbs. Two performances followed in the summer of 1975, one in 't Hoogt in Utrecht, *Bloody Alphabet*, [see p.120] the other one called *Een gedicht voor Vincent* (A poem for Vincent), during which he cut the word 'oor' (ear) out of the word 'voor' (for). [see pp.115] He became interested in random structures, which led to his performance *Random Selection Sutras* at Kosmos, a famous meditation center in Amsterdam. It developed into a bigger project with the exhibition and performance organised by Harry Ruhé at Gallery A, Amsterdam, in cooperation with Albert Waalkens of Gallery Waalkens in Finsterwolde. Curator and Fluxus collector Harry Ruhé describes the original idea of the performance called *Propagation Piece*, [see p.130] and what people could expect from the project. Gibbs, he said, intended to sow "book" seeds and promised to travel to the remote village of Finsterwolde to see how it, the literature, grew. But he changed his mind and decided to sow "ideas" instead of "books". Waalkens, who was a farmer as well, helped him with this next step by ploughing a piece of land; otherwise the 'ideas' would not grow. The idea of "seed-words" was not new to Gibbs, he had mentioned them in *Random Selection Sutras*. *Random Selection Sutras* were based on an ancient Tantric text, the Kamakalavilasa. Gibbs described how: "The original verses are treated word by word by progressive elimination determined by dice-throws, peeling off layers of words until only the 'seed-words' remain… With the RSS the listener is able to make his own verbal creations grow from the seeds he hears".[11] Though this project in Finsterwolde is quite conceptual it is at the same time also Fluxus-like in spirit. It is serious and playful at the same time, even funny, like the tone of Ruhé's description.

More than a year later he made the first performance in which the word 'Ventriloquism' was introduced.

Ventriloquism

The Art of Ventriloquism took place at Gallery A+ in Amsterdam on September 2, 1978. [see pp.132–133] The gallery was a temporary initiative of Gibbs, Pnina Reichman, his wife at that time, Ania Bien who had also just settled in The Netherlands, and his good friend John Liggins who had arrived in Amsterdam at the same time as Gibbs. During the performance Gibbs projected thirty-six slides, a full slide roll. These slides were based on phrases and illustrations from a booklet called *Secrets of Ventriloquism*, written by a Professor Foxtone. The booklet has a subtitle: "How to acquire this amusing art and other illusions", and on the cover, a ventriloquist with a doll on his knee. His booklet became famous, but Professor Foxtone himself disappeared into history. Both the title of the booklet and the professorial status of the author suggests that this is real art or real science. Ventriloquism is usually associated with the theatre, vaudeville in particular, while the performance itself depends on skilled acting, and humour. Earlier in the century it had appealed to the Dadaists, and had been included on the bill in their cabarets. In the performance, Gibbs assumed the role of ventriloquist, sitting next to the projection screen holding a female puppet. A tape played a recording of him reading the entire booklet, his voice restricted as if it were a live ventriloquist's performance.

There is much more to say about ventriloquism besides that it is based on a disconnection of sound and source. You might also characterise it as a phenomenon existing between two voices that have only one source and that this source is the creator of these voices and lets them communicate. Ventriloquism belongs to show business, to low art; but due to modern communication technology it may have gradually changed. Only extraordinary and convincing qualities of the two antithetical voices, such as adult and child, animate and inanimate, calm and agitated, and humour, can save this 'art'. Though there have been many variations throughout its history, the relation of the two voices is broadly the same, more so in the twentieth century. The puppet in general is cheeky while the man (it was mostly men who were ventriloquists) is calm, as an adult should be, keeping contact with the audience in an attempt to let them identify with his thoughtful approach to the childish behaviour of the dummy. It is concerned with a way of acting that is based on two specific things: 1. the projection of oneself outside of oneself and 2. this projection is a 'vocalised' projection.[12] In many of his performances, Gibbs, the actor and performer, literally projects the basic elements of communication, namely words. This performance gives voice to Professor Foxtone, who is the screenwriter and at the same time the dramatist of the ventriloquism. In other performances by Gibbs it seems as if the audience is the puppet, that is promised a certain freedom to act and to speak, though within certain boundaries. David Goldblatt, in his article about Nietzsche and ventriloquism opens up another possibility: the ventriloquist is not the conductor but the receiver of all the sounds around him which he gives back to the world in the form of concepts, and therefore in words. So the artist-ventriloquist becomes a medium, like the puppet is a medium.[13]

Reading—listening

Six months later, on the 28 April 1979, Gibbs performed at Bedaux b.v., a gallery run by Jacoba Bedaux, in a room quite similar to the performance room of de Appel, both having a balcony. The performance is called *Piece in a Minor Key*. In *Artzien*, May 1979, a couple of weeks after the performance, Jan van Raay writes a description of it. He mentions four tape recorders, two of them placed on the balcony and several different coloured lights. When the performance starts, the room is lit by only blue light. Gibbs begins to run between the tape recorders and switches them off and on, in the meantime turning the blue light off and the reddish-orange one on. It becomes apparent that the texts on the tapes refer to his own personal history. Van Raay describes the scene as "A barrage of words, feelings, thoughts, information. You strain to hear, to select from the bombardment and chaos. [...] One tape whispers... secrets? Shadows of words, dark and musty".[14] In the next part of the thirty-minute performance, Gibbs stands on the balcony with a large book in his hand. When he turns the pages things fall out of the book. Dead leaves and sand drop from the balcony to the floor below. Van Raay draws attention again to the whispering sounds that were heard during the first part, a sign of secret things. In his own short description of the performance later that year, Gibbs said that "It expressed my interest in the physical nature of the book, and in the spatio-temporal dimensions of reading and listening".[15] Through being interested in the physical nature of the book, he says, it can also function as a sound producing instrument. He stresses this aspect in a text that accompanies two performances with the same title *Tome Tones*. [see p.134]

The first was on May 13, 1979 at 't Turfschip in Breda, during an event called *Breda schaam je* [Breda, shame on you]; the second one a year later in New York on the occasion of the '12th International Sound Poetry Festival'. In New York he conducted a kind of orchestra that made sounds with books: by turning, flipping, rustling the pages and slamming the books shut, using an amplifier to increase the volume of these actions. The book can be seen here as like the dummy of the ventriloquist, who is able to give voice, or at least noise to it. He invites his reader to "listen to fragments of narratives, pick up threads, weave in and out of phrases from various languages. piece together the words, pile them on top of each other until they tumble down and flutter to the floor, pick them up again and improvise or improve on them. speak with tongue in cheek, practice *ventriloquism* [italics mine], let the typewriter have its say. only the voice that erases can say the true thing".[16]

Clearly, this quote, in relation to the works just described, expresses what he summarised in his report of the year 1978/80 as his interest in "the spatio-temporal dimensions of reading and listening".[17] In this same report, in the same sentence he mentions his "other" interest, namely "the physical nature of the book".[18]

The book

The book is undoubtedly central to Gibbs' oeuvre. In his early years when he presented himself as a poet it was indeed the most 'natural' medium, first for his concrete poetry, then later for visual poetry, but the book became an important element of his performances between 1975 and 1980 as well. In his report of the year 1978/80 he accentuates his interest in "the physical nature" of the book, obviously to differentiate it from the function it usually has for a writer. Being a writer, a poet, and a visual artist, this distinction between the disciplines should be made, however, the dividing line was certainly not so sharply drawn in the beginning. His move from poetry to performance was a gradual process, and the position of the book in this process is fundamental to it. More and more it became an object that he could torture, or more constructively, give a voice, like the ventriloquist does to his puppet. *Tome Tones* is a good example of this category. In the catalogue of his later performance in Schiedam he talks about his love-hate relation towards the book, an emotional relationship and at the same time a metaphor and erotic symbol.[19] The booklet *Extinction* that he published on the occasion of his exhibition of concrete and visual poetry at the In Out Center, showed the disintegration of an alphabet and this returned in a different way to his first performance in Maastricht in which he set fire to an alphabet of cut-out letters. What became so characteristic of his later performances we can see in this example: the opposition of two movements, both going in different directions. Firstly, the physical creation of letters and an alphabet, which can be considered as the primordial status of the book and language, and secondly the demolition of it in order to make it invisible.

In his CEAC performance *Open Page / Closed Mind* and *Closed Page / Open Mind* presented in Toronto in 1977, Gibbs again plays with opposites. [see pp.128–129] In *Open Page / Closed Mind* he specifically discusses the avant-garde and what is the significance of a precursor. The performance is centered around the book by Renato Poggioli, *The Theory of the Avant-Garde*, published in 1968 and not read by Gibbs before the time of the performance. The performance is recorded and from what Gibbs says about the avant-garde one might conclude that he wanted to stress the necessity of prior historical knowledge in order to understand language and specifically, in this instance, the avant-garde. He further elaborates by offering his thoughts and comments on the notion of the avant-garde and what he considers as its history. In the second part of the performance, *Closed Mind / Open Page*, Gibbs talks about the book based on what he actually sees from the outside without reading the text that is inside. On the one hand, his words deal with the book as an object in its own right, on the other, the title is there to function as a source for interpretation and elaboration. Like the title of an artwork, the title of a book can be considered as the most condensed form of the book's content. In this way Gibbs is giving a voice to the book; it is no longer only a physical object but something that contains a spirit within and behind its cover, or as the title of this performance suggests: a mind. In this way the attention is taken away from the performer and given to the author of the book. Herein Gibbs demonstrates continual engagement with language and pathways to comprehension. The book, the body, the voice, channels, move the words and structure around, experiment with meaning, push boundaries to understanding.

Three years after the Toronto performance, Gibbs had an exhibition at the Stedelijk Museum in Schiedam, entitled *The Absent Words*. [see pp.146–147] In addition to showing a project consisting of nine photographs, he decided to do a performance as well, under the same title, dated November 1, 1980.[20] The title is important as it refers to the famous book of Edmond Jabès, *Le livre des questions*, published in 1963 by Gallimard and of which a few parts were published in English a few years before (*The Book of Questions* in 1976 and *The Book of Yukel/Return to the Book* in 1977). In the seventies, Jabès was considered to be the most important French poet since Mallarmé, in particular within the circle of *Tel Quel*.[21] Both Jacques Derrida and Maurice Blanchot wrote about him and contributed to the dissemination of his poetry. Gibbs selected a few fragments from the English translation and typed them on two sheets of paper. In one of these fragments he made a few changes, not with a typewriter but with a pen. In the text he twice crossed out the word God and replaced it with "the word". "~~God~~ the word had to be absent so that man could push back his limits in reading ~~God~~ the word." (Reb Abassis). The performance started with a sound tape that he had used before for a series of performances that carried the same title as the tape: *Ghostwritten under Pressure*. On the floor is an arrow one metre in length, made out of six unfolded sheets of newsprint taken from *Le Monde*. Gibbs walks around the arrow while repeating in French the sentence: "tout/tout/tout au monde..." based on a sentence of Mallarmé: "Tout, au monde, existe pour aboutir á un livre". Then he threw pages out of a book on the ground; these are from a Laroussse encyclopedia. The text on the pages is painted white; but here and there are tiny illustrations in the form of old-fashioned stickers. On top of the arrow he laid a book, the text cut-out. After putting this book at the top of the arrow, he returned to the other side of the arrow, sat down in a cross-legged position and started doing something with another book, the *Anthologie du Français Classique* by Henri Sensine. He looked at the pages, licked them while the audience listened to the soundtrack of the video *2ième Poème Symboliste* [The second symbolist poem]. Then he took the cut-out book and used it as a window through which he looked in the direction of the audience and walked along the line of photographs. De Rook sees the 'cutout book' as a crystallisation of Gibbs thoughts about chance and writing. All texts and images fit in it, so it has a potential freedom in use.[22] On another tape, the so-called Zebra Code Words can be heard. These are a combination of five letters that are used in telegraph post to replace the names of different types of wood and measurement. They come from *The Timber Trades Journal Zebra Code Third Edition (code word ZEBRAIC)* compiled by And Carstensen for the use of timber merchants, shippers, traders, shipbrokers and others and published by William Rider & Son Ltd in London in 1919. In *Artzien* (September 1980) he published a page from this book under the title *Some Sounds*. [see p.145] Finally he lays the book on the floor with the front downwards and the back visible. In a formal pose he reads: "Ce peuple alors contrainct de se ranger... casi en panos menores... Ik zal er eens over nadenken... Kom, ik geloof dat het tijd is... aan wij hij geschiedkundige... [??] La foule est là... I l y a aurait tout un livre à écrire". This is not the first time that he mixes up languages.

The Book of Books

In this performance Gibbs quotes Mallarmé and with good purpose. Van Gelder considers Gibbs as the one who carries on what Stéphane Mallarmé intended with his unrealised project 'Le Livre' [The Book]. Mallarmé envisaged a total art work that contained theatre, music, poetry etc. Only notes are left of this project in which chance played an important part. Gibbs, living in a different time, was able, so Van Gelder states, to adopt "a broader angle of attack, from within the visual arts, with slides, video, sound tapes and, maybe in the future, computers".[23] For this reason he calls the project *Book of Books*. So the role of chance in the work of Gibbs has not only to do with John Cage, Marcel Duchamp or Fluxus, but with Mallarmé too. However, there is always a counterpoint to what Gibbs is doing; he always has paradoxes to hand, or at least something that regulates his a-methodical approach. The way he uses language is against a linear reading supportive to the narrative of a text, and it is mainly visual media that gives the audience the most free space to infer, to associate, or to imagine. This does not imply that he is researching the features of the media or that he considers the media as pawns in a total art work, that one should experience simultaneously. Van Gelder says that such an idea is unknown to the age of historical relativism, that Gibbs represents. "Gibbs is idealist and anarchist at the same time."[24]

During a performance at The Bank, in the Haarlemmerstraat in Amsterdam, he presented himself as a twentieth century oracle. When a person in the audience asked him: "Why am I here?", he answered: "So that you can ask such a question and so that you can be prepared to receive an unclear answer".[25] One could say that the relativist speaks to the idealist and that the post-structuralist, following the footsteps of Roland Barthes and Jacques Derrida, speaks to the anarchist.

In general, in his installations we see the same motifs and media return, for example in the installation he made for the Loa Gallery in Haarlem (25 November–17 December 1977) where he hung books from the ceiling, like a rain of books, and covered the floor with books, while offering to the spectators book-hats, book-shoes and book-umbrellas. [see p.131] Almost a year later in the art space Sudurgata 7 in Reykjavik (16 September–1 October) he made an installation divided into four parts which he called "narrative versions". Although it seemed to be about narrative structures, for example the series of twenty-five photographs called *The Time of Day*, he introduced here the same procedure as in his later performances. In one of the rooms the spectators were invited to walk through leaves, reading pages of their choice and so creating their own stories. In comparison to his performances, the participation of the audience played a larger role in his installations. In one of his last works, *The Demon of Analogy, Taal/Ruimte/Taal [Language, Space/Language]* at Lokaal 01, in Breda, he invited the audience to repeatedly write the letter V with gold-painted pens. He was not present but he sent slides to the art centre as well as the pens. The audience could hear on a sound tape how he translated letters from Mallarmé's poem, 'La Démon de l'Analogie' into piano keys and sounds. In the meantime slides were projected forwards, backwards, forwards etc.

Connotation–Association; the verbal and the visual

As stated earlier, Gibbs does not make an epistemological choice between structuralist notions such as connotation and its psychological 'equivalent', association. In his publication *Connotations* he states, "I'm concerned with the reduction of language to its structural elements—taking it apart to see how it works. Words don't always mean what they say—their patterns and forms reveal inner processes and events, ambiguous and connotations of meaning".[26] Like the many diverse interpretations and meanings that Gibbs ascribes to the book, so the construction of a book can be a vehicle and instrument for instigating performance. In Gibbs' *Public Publishing Project*, conducted at the 'Text, Sound, Image, Small Press Page Festival', at Galerie Kontakt, Antwerp in 1976, he produced a series of books in an edition of fourteen copies with one being produced each hour. [see p.122] The project had a structured format: 1. Writing, 2. Cutting, 3. Cutting, 4. Collating, 5. Binding, 6. Titling, 7. Signing. In this project, the making of the publication placed the emphasis on revealing the process, versus creating a unique object with the printed edition of fourteen. The public and collaborative act of production and assembly relates to performance, where the structure and fabrication of the publication is made primary. Much like Gibbs' earlier Fluxus performances, the combination of different media emphasises the tactile, aural, visual, and interactive within publishing and a residue is left from the performance in the printed edition. It is the extreme perimeters of language and the structure of a book, that continually unfold in the performances. The sound poetry festivals that Gibbs participated in and co-organised were an opportunity for him to work in a more fluid manner, where a publication could combine performance, sound and visual poetry, in essence a gesture rather than a resolute form.

Word play, in performances such as *Tome Tones* shows an interest in the structural relationship between words as bricks and their connection to objects, but also the disconnection in sound and source. Similarly, in his installation *The Demon of Analogy, Taal/Ruimte/Taal [Language, Space/Language]* where the focus is less on narrative structure but rather on an interactive performance with the audience, and a playful experimentation between the objects and sounds. Playing with words and substituting one object for another, such as in ventriloquism is also a concern. Gibbs takes notice of Mallarmé's fascination with the word 'penultimate' and adjusts this to "ultimate pen" in the performance. The 'penultimate' precedes what is considered last and necessary for the end of something, where the 'ultimate pen' literally has the last word. With reference to an "endless circle there can neither be an ultimate or penultimate" from Gibbs' thoughts on the performance, there is no clear ending or linear direction of what is spoken or written. The viewers, forced to reconcile the sounds of the piano keys within the enclosure of the room and the gold painted pens hanging in the circle on the wall are faced with a question of where is language coming from and who is directing this language? It is open ended with no clear answer but an internal act performed on behalf of the audience. The sound of the piano notes, "derived" from Mallarmé's poem create a rhythmic word/letter/sound play much like in *This/Shit* as in "THIS/SHIT; THIS, HITS, STIH, ISTH, SHIT en TISH; Tixe/Exit". [see p.148] Here again he pays tribute to French literary theorists of the late sixties and early seventies, predominantly the authors of *Tel Quel*, with their interest in palindromes and anagrams going back to Ferdinand de Saussure's study of the anagrams that he started in 1906 but left unfinished. While he was primarily searching for codes to decipher the intentionally hidden text, *Tel Quel* authors and Michael Gibbs were more focused on what we already called the para-doxa and all disruption of the clarity of meaning.[27]

I am grateful to Eva Gibbs-Gonggrijp, Emily Henderson and Gerrit Jan de Rook for all their help in realising this article.

1 This contribution is written in close cooperation with Emily Henderson, who also contributed to the picture editing.

2 Being the translator of the book *De Appel. Performances, installations, video, projects 1975–1983* (Amsterdam: de Appel 2006) he approved the description of this performance in the book (p.228). There is also a handwritten concept of the performance.

3 Black notebook September 1978–March 1979, archive Michael Gibbs.

4 Ibid.

5 In 1973 he published his first collection of concrete and visual poetry under the title *Connotations* (Second Aeon Publications).

6 Kees van Gelder, 'The Idealism of Michael Gibbs, and his criticism thereof', *Artzien*, no.25, Summer 1982, n.p.

7 Notebook September 1978–March 1979, archive Michael Gibbs.

8 Uitnodiging De Appel [Invitation De Appel], January 1980.

9 Much work on behalf of the ordering of Gibb's performances has been done previously by Gerrit Jan de Rook. We rely on this work in which we also found a number of important quotes and references to the sources and other publications of and about Michael Gibbs. The document is called 'Performances 1977–1985' (unpublished), but contains also descriptions of a couple of installations.

10 This description is partly based on William Allen's article about Michael Gibbs' experimental poetry (Bill Allen, 'Michael Gibbs: Unsung Hero of Experimental Poetry', *if p then q*, no.2, Autumn 2008 (Manchester: if p then q)).

11 Handwritten note, with the intention to be published later in 1977, archive Michael Gibbs.

12 These features one can find in David Goldblatt, 'Nietzsche and Ventriloquism'. *Historical Reflections*, vol.21, no.3. Fall 1995, pp.419–435.

13 Goldblatt relates this to Nietzsches philosophy of the will that he rightfully disconnects from a traditional idea of intention. Like many semioticians Nietzsche claims that "intention is only a sign and symptom that needs interpretation". Nietzsche (BGE…) quoted by Goldblatt, p.423.

14 Jan van Raay, 'Piece in a Minor Key Review', *Artzien*, May 1979., n.p.

15 Michael Gibbs, 'Tome Tones' ('t Turfschip, Breda, the Netherlands, May 13, 1979).

16 Typewritten short biography with a paragraph called 'speaking metaphorically' (February 1980; archive Michael Gibbs. The texts opens with the sentence: "books are normally so silent they don't converse with each other. writers, though can make quite a bit of noise".

17 Notebook 1978/80, archive Michael Gibbs.

18 Ibid.

19 Pieter Heynen in his review of this Schiedam exhibition and performance, in *de Volkskrant*, 18 November 1980, refers to what he says in the catalogue. He also mentions the invisibility of words on the pictures of bookcases, shown in the exhibition, which he sees as central to the whole exhibition. Language is present but without words.

20 The exhibition contained not only photographs, but also collages and drawings; in a little room he showed documentation about his performances, both photos and texts.

21 De Rook is not sure about what were Gibbs main sources for his knowledge about the *Tel Quel* group; in particular Jabès, Barthes, Blanchot, Derrida and George Bataille were important to Gibbs. He mentions two possibilities: the journal *Curtains* of Paul Buck, founded in 1971 and an article in *New Wilderness Letter* 5/6 (1978). In those years there was a great interest in Tel Quel in the surroundings of the Dutch journal *Raster* as well.

22 Unpublished overview by Gerrit Jan de Rook of the performances and installation of Michael Gibbs. See note 9.

23 Van Gelder 1982, n.p.

24 Van Gelder 1982, n.p.

25 Michael Gibbs, *Report on my activities* 1980/81, archive Michael Gibbs.

26 Michael Gibbs, *Connotations*, see note 5.

27 One other author of the *Tel Quel* group, Julia Kristeva, introduced a new concept, 'paragram', in reference to Saussure and she in particular points to unconscious contents in the articulated texts. This determined her approach of Stéphane Mallarmé in her dissertation *La revolution du langage poétique. L'avant-garde a la fin de XIXe siècle: Lautréamont et Mallarmé*, Paris: Éditions du Seuil, Collection Tel Quel, 1974. See also my 'Julia Kristeva and the Legacy of Émile Benveniste', in Inna Semetsky (ed.). *Edusemiotics: A Handbook*, Springer 2017.

JOHN HELD JR.

Michael Gibbs & the Development of a Network Across Cultural and Language Borders

The late 1960s/early 1970s were a time of social, political and poetical alternatives. The Beat poetics of a decade previous were growing tired and in need of renewal. Fluxus artists had begun to weave graphics and text into conceptual and intermedial configurations that drew upon the earlier experiments of Apollinaire, Marinetti, Schwitters and a succession of other visual, concrete, found and sound poets. The post-war baby-boom generation of English artists, inspired by the 1966 *Destruction In Art Symposium* (which Gibbs witnessed at age seventeen) and the 1972 *Fluxshoe* exhibition, which travelled England, played with concepts of poetical communication across cultural and geographical boundaries.

Michael Gibbs was one such artist in this growing global network of correspondents engaged in intense international discussion about the future of visual/found/concrete poetry. Fluxus artist Dick Higgins did much to promote this activity in small edition books via his Something Else Press, but it was in the smaller zine publications that could be distributed affordably in the postal system, that stimulated the growth of a network across cultural and language borders. Built upon the backs of Fluxus, Ray Johnson, Gutai and other far-flung groups and individuals using the postal system to distribute art and information in the previous decades, publications of an avant-garde nature proliferated in a new environment of open international discussion, which became known as Mail Art.

By the time of *Fluxshoe*, a wide net of correspondents had been woven between Latin and North America, Eastern and Western Europe, Japan, Australia, and points between. An important means of communications across these borders were limited editioned, self-published magazines, referred to as zines. Several of these gathered and distributed news of general interest to the developing Mail Art network including announcements of exhibitions and projects of interest, and the reproduction of contributed textual and visual works. *File* magazine, produced by General Idea of Toronto, Canada, comes to mind, as does the less polished International Artistic Cooperation (IAC), edited by Klaus Groh, who did much to spread Mail Art, as the network was beginning to become known, in Eastern Europe.

Gibbs participated in and witnessed first-hand the organization by David Mayor and Beaux Geste Press of the *Fluxshoe* exhibition, while he was a student at the University of Exeter. He moved to The Netherlands in 1974, having two exhibitions that year—one in Amsterdam, another in Maastricht. The following year he contributed to the *Internationale Visuaele Poezie* exhibition, which travelled to Rotterdam, Amsterdam and Utrecht.

He had, by this time, been the editor of *Kontexts*, a magazine of concrete/visual poetry, since 1967. [see pp.103–107, 118–119, 126–127] He would continue editorship of the publication until 1977. By the fourth issue, published in 1972, he had established relationships with and presented works by Ken Friedman (USA), Gabor Tóth (Hungary), Richard Kostelanetz (USA) and David Mayor (England). The following issue was even more international in scope, introducing works by Jiří Valoch (Czechoslovakia), J. H. Kocman (Czechoslovakia), Ulises Carrión (Mexico/The Netherlands). Following issues contained works by Lawrence Weiner (USA), Henri Chopin (France), Jackson MacLow (USA) and Dick Higgins (USA). All of these artists were active participants in the expanding Mail Art network.

Gibbs' contacts expanded when he travelled to America, Mexico and Canada in the summer of 1977, meeting correspondents and making new connections with such artists as John Baldessari, Anna Banana, Lowell Darling, Felipe Ehrenberg, Albert M. Fine, Peter Frank, Dick Higgins, Alison Knowles, Jerome Rothenberg, Carolee Schneemann and Lawrence Weiner. This resulted in the book, *Deciphering America* (Kontexts Publications, Amsterdam, The Netherlands, 1978).

In 1979, Gibbs joined forces with Harry Ruhé, director of Amsterdam's Gallery A, and a champion of Fluxus related art activities, in the publication of twenty-eight issues of *Artizien*. [see pp.138–139] The magazine has been described as a "fearless, idiosyncratic review of art in The Netherlands, focusing particularly on the marginal and the new, written mostly by artists, and featuring interviews with such luminaries as General Idea, [Marina Abramovic], Vito Acconci, [Davi Det Hompson], Reindeer Werk, Al Hansen, Milan Knižák and Lawrence Weiner".

The Mail Art network was beginning to proliferate in an explosion of magazines, serving as an umbrella for various marginal artistic mediums and movements such as rubber stamp art, artist postage stamp, photocopy art, collage, poetry, Neo-Fluxus, Neo-Dada and Neoism. By 2002, I had personally collected some 3,700 periodicals, consisting of 655 titles published in thirty-four countries. These were eventually placed with the Museum of Modern Art in New York.

Editors of these various Mail Art zines overlapped with correspondents in related fields. Gibbs was focused on visual language and various forms of experimental poetry, but this did not deter an interest in allied fields, including rubber stamp art. His contribution to rubber stamp art consisted of textual stamps, such as "ART IS LANGUAGE", "LANGUAGE IS NOT ART", "PRINTING MATTERS", and "REMEMBER FLUXUS?", which he contributed to Gerrit Jan de Rook's, Stempelkunst (exp/press, Utrecht, The Netherlands, second edition, 1976).

In the process of this widespread interaction over several decades, Gibbs also amassed a substantial archive of visual poetry and mail art. It was one of eight archives examined by Hungarian art critic, Géza Perneczky, in the compilation of his important reference guide, *The Magazine Network: The Trends of Alternative*

Art in the Light of Their Periodicals 1968–1988 (Soft Geometry, Köln, Germany, 1993).

Gibbs' publishing activities continued after the advent of the Internet, conducting website workshops at the Split Academy of Art and Zagreb Academy of Art in Croatia during 1999, and publishing the online art magazine, *Why Not Sneeze?*, from 1996–1999. Since his passing in 2009, Gibbs has been recognised as an important contributor to the global cultural and social fabric that paved the way toward today's interwoven digital participatory society.

HENRIETTE DINGEMANS

Why not sneeze?

I met Michael in 1996 in Amsterdam during the premiere of a movie about Joseph Beuys. I walked up to him and said, "I saw a photo of you in Brion Gysin's studio in Paris". Indeed, he had met Gysin and Burroughs a couple of times for interviews.

Michael told me about his plans on the World Wide Web. From an artist's point of view, the internet is an extremely attractive proposition. It offers an inexpensive means of distribution to a potential audience of millions, bypassing museums, galleries and the art press. Yet it is not as simple as that. Making pages of ones artwork for the World Wide Web is very much like do-it-yourself desktop publishing—but, how to get them to the people who might be interested. In those days it was only available to people who where fortunate enough to have a sophisticated computer and an internet connection—and who were interested in art? In this respect the idea of an online art magazine sprouted to mind. Michael decided to create such a platform.

At the time I was experimenting with an Amiga and welcomed the idea, so within a week I started helping him in his studio in Amsterdam. As an artist in his laboratory, Michael orchestrated his experiment in a very meticulous way. Every ingredient was interesting, from a historical and artistic point of view. For example the server he used, xs4all, was started by Rob Gonggrijp with a group, called CCC (Chaos Computer Club)—a combination of political activists and techno freaks who later became Europe's largest association of hackers.

Of course there was the Apple—Quadra 605—computer and Netscape 2.0. with a SCSI port. We constructed the site in pure HTML, there were no WYSIWYGs, typing out the HTML codes gave us great pleasure, and we were able to see it appear in the web browser at the end of the day. Uploading the webpages through a 56k modem—the pinnacle of modem technology in the nineties—had to be done in the early evenings when America was going to sleep.

Why not Sneeze? [www.nettime.org/Lists-Archives/nettime-nl9805/msg00014.html] was launched in May 1996: "a site for critical art on and about the internet", "a combination of a magazine and laboratory for experiments" and "a platform for everyone professionally involved with art and media". The site wanted to explore "the possibilities and limitations of the medium" and was looking for "art projects and theories that make innovative use of the unique possibilities offered by the net". It wanted to be a site that is "constantly under construction", dropping old projects and initiating new ones.

Anyone who has tried viewing art on the internet will know that, more often than not, it's an extremely frustrating experience. *Why not Sneeze?* was unique in this way, because it was created for Netscape 2.0, and typed out in HTML with the use of a small gif images, the site downloaded quickly and was accessible to all net uses. This was another important aspect of the site. As there was nothing more tedious than staring at an almost blank screen, this—even with a fast modem and telephone networks—means that images trickle down the screen at a painfully slow speed, leaving you twiddling your thumbs and getting nervous about the size of your telephone bill. In this way surfers stayed longer on *Why not Sneeze?*. Michael's hot list preventing surfers from drowning in the sea of data on their search to find a hot spot.

Michael was also fascinated by the 'Palace' environments that have sprung up all over the world during the last year. Essentially, they are an extension of the text-based MUD (Multi-User Dungeon) and MOO (Multi-Object Oriented) environments, which offered visitors the possibility of navigating around 'virtual worlds' that consisted purely of verbal descriptions like "You are standing outside the Library; press X to enter". Once inside the various rooms, you could chat to fellow guests and describe the actions you wished to take. Although everything was mediated through whatever you typed on your keyboard, and this involved knowing a fairly long list of keyboard commands, the MOOs and MUDs managed to instil an uncanny feeling of presence. He once 'attended' a ball at the MediaMOO hosted by the Massachusetts Institute of Technology, and "really felt that I was in a ballroom surrounded by other guests whom I could talk to if I wished. I could even order drinks, but, of course, managed to stay sober the whole time!"

Michael had made an appointment to meet up with his good friend Lawrence Weiner—who was on his boat in Amsterdam—to do an interview about his collaboration with Adaweb and his exhibition at Leo Castelli's gallery *then, now & then*, (15 February–15 March 1997), where Weiner launched *Homeport*.

"THE PARTICIPANTS IN HOMEPORT TO FUNCTION AS THE NAVIGATOR OF A SHIP IN NOT_KNOWN SEAS AS OPPOSED TO THE ROLE OF A PILOT BOAT LEADING (WHAT) THAT ALONG A PRE_KNOWN ROUTE"

Lawrence Weiner's *Homeport* [www.adaweb.com/project/homeport/] uses the Palace environment as a novel means of presenting his textual and graphical works. Appropriately, the work was included in the exhibition *Port: Navigating Digital Culture*, held recently at the MIT List Visual Arts Center. Weiner's thinking behind his concept: "Once within Homeport there is no means of proceeding without mixing what is perceived as (a) reality & what we must consider dream space or reality based on assumptions not necessarily correct". Weiner compares navigating through *Homeport* as a voyage through uncharted seas, where all assumptions have to be left behind. Prospective voyagers should not be put off by the censorious voice that announces "Sorry, Members Only" as you enter, nor by the built-in avatars that tell you to fasten your seatbelt and ask if you want coffee, tea or milk. Once you start to find your way around and discover the nine hidden passageways (or 'portholes') that are embedded in the various pages, you pass through a series of well-known Weiner formulations in various typographic styles and embellished with the artist's typical lines, arrows and boxes. "STARS DON'T STAND STILL" leads to "IN THE SKY" and then "FOR ANYBODY". Or "WHEN IN DOUBT PLAY TIC TAC TOE & HOPE FOR THE BEST".

Why not Sneeze? has been invited to many digital platforms in Holland, as well as abroad to give a talk. One of these invitations was in 1997 by Milan Knížák who at the time was Chancellor of the Academy of Art in Prague. Shortly after arrival we were invited up to the Chancellor's chambers where Milan Knížák gave Michael a warm embrace and sat down to talk about old times. We sat around Milan Knížák's mirrored coffee table with gold and platinum diaspores running around, one of his latest pieces he had created. As we left he gave Michael another bear hug and said that he was looking forward to Michael's Fluxus evening at the Academy. There was a handsome turn out. We had set up three long tables and each table had seven piles of blank pages. The piles were numbered and the participants were invited to collect the pages. These were later stapled together, and folded to form a book. As the participants left Michael presented a red bookmark with the logo of *Why not Sneeze?*, to poke it in the blank book, inviting them to join him on the net.

Michael loved giving lessons in HTML and challenging the students to think about hyperlinking and multidimensionality. True to his earlier works with Fluxus and concrete poetry he was very conscious of the content/context relation and less interested in meaningless image culture. He was invited to start an internet department at Grafisch Atelier in Haarlem. Here he was able to present his concern with 'the public domain' by giving talks about people who were transforming their world though the digital age, like the Mexican photographer Pedro Meyer who in 1993 created the first CD-ROM about Photoshop and photography. The Canadian interactive media artist George Legrady would drop in and give a talk about his work with digital media. Michael provided a platform for people to talk about the pro's and con's of the digital age and get inspired. His department became very popular. But at a certain stage a conflict with the managers arose and Michael called for a staff meeting; the majority of the staff were in agreement with him and there was a staff walk out.

After leaving Haarlem Michael turned his attention to his hometown Amsterdam and became involved in collaboration with people from the video world at 'Vrij Media Café' (September 1999–October 2000). It was a place for meetings, exchanges, discussions, showing films, video, performing music, dance and spoken word, in short all forms of 'time based arts'.

ROB PERRÉE

The dialectical view of Michael Gibbs

A remarkable new work. Two portraits of young people, each mounted in a circular, polished steel frame that lifts them away from the wall and makes them into objects. Between the two, like a hyphen, stands the word "Corpus". [see p.165]

The peculiarity of this recent work by Michael Gibbs does not reside in the vagueness of the black and white photographs. His pictures are almost always vague in themselves or made vague by enlargement. The origin of his images should not be surprising either, for he regularly draws from visual material that in one way or another is connected with the Russian Revolution. Nor is the combination of image and text strange. On the contrary, this forms one of the essential characteristics of his work.

The surprise lies in the formal presentation of the piece. This is the first time he has deliberately broken away from two-dimensionality. It seems as though, through the choice and presentation of the material that carries his message, or rather: his formulation of a question, he wants to make a claim to the test of aesthetic criteria. Florentine *tondi* have acquired a twentieth century variant. Sandro Botticelli's circular frames, manifesting themselves as wall sculpture, recur in contemporary form through an artist from whom I would not immediately expect it, since his work until now has been largely conceptual.

Michael Gibbs comes originally from England and has lived and worked in The Netherlands since 1974. In the early seventies he was primarily active as a composer/performer of visual and concrete poetry. In addition he published the magazines *Kontexts* (1969–1977) [see pp.103–107, 118–119, 126–127] and *Artzien* (1978–1982) [see pp.138–139] which was "the mouthpiece of many artists on the fringe".[1]

That might appear to be an improper activity for an artist, in the same way that his writing criticism could be seen as an aberrant sideline. But words have run like a thread through everything that he does. They also have a prominent place in his 'visual' work. In his case it has to be said for making no distinctions between the two forms of activity. All these activities are to be considered as expressions of his calling as an artist.

I have put the word 'visual' between marks because Gibbs' decision to use the medium of photography and the way he employs it, do not result from its supposed visual qualities. For him it is primarily a scriptural medium. "Just as words retain traces of the development of history, so too does the photographic image."[2] It is a barrier to oblivion, a means of storing memories.

It is indeed a direct rendering of reality, but it also says something about reality. "Photographs are not to be 'read' merely on the basis of a recognition of the visual facts that are presented in them, in correlation with an identifying caption, for any photograph is already a representation of several layers of meaning, many of which are contingent or hidden. A photograph may be said to contain a polysemous 'floating chain' of signifiers, a hidden agenda of cultural and semiotic texts and linguistic propositions. In this sense, a photograph does indeed reveal something about reality, and this is always more than what is purportedly revealed at first glance."[3]

For Michael Gibbs the photographer is therefore not a magician who conjures up the moment, and photography is not a reservoir of technical possibilities. He is scarcely interested in technique, otherwise he would take no pleasure in rephotographing existing images, and his own photographs would have to go well beyond the level of snapshots. The way that he uses photography turns it into a linear medium, like a language. He sees the photograph not as a summary but as an element in a discourse within a greater whole in which 'real' words also play a role.

In *A Place…* (1991) two square photographs of equal size hang next to each other. They are of considerable size, printed in black and white and are placed in matte black frames. Between them is displayed the text: "A place for this future to be found". The image on the left suggests a living room, vague and dark, where the lamps provide a 'warm' atmosphere and a scarcely visible figure to the left awakens curiosity. The right-hand image is sharp. We see a fragment of the interior of an austere building, shot from below. Two convex, umbrella-like shapes stick out above a wall in the middle of the photograph. No people are present. Whatever the photographs mean, or whatever they refer to, they stand squarely against each other and by their juxtaposition are evidently part of a dialectical process. The text which has been added is no explanation, but a catalyst for the process.

The photographs are atmospheric; through association they elicit words that lead to a meaning. That meaning is a question, certainly, because Gibbs has no desire to give answers. That is difficult because, as is clear from the above quotation, he realises that an image has different layers of meaning. In principle, the viewers are free to formulate their own question. In practice, however, this freedom is relative. Gibbs steers perception by introducing ingredients that determine a direction because of their subjective nature. The viewer is creatively engaged, but only within these limits. Michael Gibbs' themes can be read in these ingredients. He is interested in cultures and how these change over the course of time (in this respect the current upheavals in Eastern Europe are a source of rich inspiration). The marxist cultural philosopher Michael Bakhtine has influenced his thinking in this area. Bakhtine's study of Rabelais, written in 1971, places the sixteenth century French writer against the background of the popular culture of his time (not only would he find this concept appealing, but, as a man of the word, Gibbs would surely be fascinated by the verbal artistry of Rabelais himself).

For the artist from Croydon, buildings are cultural signs, symptoms of particular cultural issues. In this, he comes close to the ideas that Walter Benjamin formulated in his unfinished *Passagenwerk*. The arcades of the nineteenth century have a twentieth century equivalent in the indoor shopping centres and mails that appear in his work, either as images or as the physical context for his work. These buildings are the skin under which a fin-de-siècle feeling lies hidden. I don't know whether Gibbs "yearns for doom in order to die in beauty", as I once heard a learned but particularly animated professor say, but in a number of works the sense of an end is unmistakably present. In *Terminal* (1990) he places a photograph of a sign on the wall of a bus station reading "No Trespassing. Violators will be Prosecuted. The Port Authority of N.Y. and N.J." next to a photograph of an artificial garden in the foyer of another large building in New York. [see p.163] Both images imply terminations that are a spur to reflection.

In *Living Debt/Dead Credit* (1989) a classical staircase is confronted with a modern one situated in the heart of a shopping centre. Above the old staircase stands the text "Living Debt", and above the new one "Dead Credit". In *Turn of the Century* (1991), the text, identical to the title, says it all. As history and utopia encounter one another in the photographs that are used, the meaning of the work cannot escape a turn of the century feeling. In various works he combines photographs of the Russian Revolution with other images, as in *Efface/Forget* and *Reflect/Attend* (both 1989). [see p.162]

How the historical material fits within this thematic whole is not so easy to determine. The origin of the dialectical structure of his works is implicitly indicated. But this is not the most important explanation, it seems to me. The revolution photographs that he integrates are like archetypes, icons consecrated to a defunct 'religion', to an intellectual inheritance the echoes of which still resound even while its foundation is progressively undermined, Perhaps they symbolise the bankruptcy of Lenin's utopia. They remind us of a reality that has been tripped up by its own ideals.

Michael Gibbs' working method has a lot to do with the way he ultimately presents his 'texts'. He collects photographic images from everywhere, without knowing at the time what he is going to do with them. He takes his own photographs in the same way. Yet the images all have something in common: they possess a sort of universality. It doesn't matter who the people in the photographs are exactly, or where the places shown are located.

His texts come into being in the same way. For the most part, he takes them from existing books or essays by the thinkers who inspire him. They do not need to be identified any more than the photographs do. Gibbs files all this material away, and at the right moment certain elements coalesce. These then become fragments of a greater whole. They become components of a constellation.

In his essay 'The Graph of Photography', [see p.46] Michael Gibbs quotes the strict demands that Victor Burgin puts to his viewers: "The work is not to be consumed at all, it is to be produced in the active process of looking, reading, composing, interpreting". As Gibbs comments: "The viewer/reader is required to work… to 'unpack' the condensations." Burgins work, he continues, is "the result of, and the occasion for, a great deal of reading". He could just as easily say the same about his own work. Not that Gibbs and Burgin are dealing with the same themes, but the ways in which they use photography and especially the way they address the viewer are comparable. "A single picture always requires a context for it to become understandable, including not only the context pertaining to the circumstances in which it was taken, but also the conditions under which it is viewed. Thus, despite the fact that the photograph can have nothing added to it, it nevertheless suffers from an irremedial lack; lacking presence, it requires a supplement, another form of writing, another 'graph' inscribed onto the graph of its traces."

1 Frank Gribling, 'Kunst, Kunstenaars en de Kunstwereld in Amsterdam, 1960–1980: Feiten en Samenhang'. In *Amsterdam 60/80. Twintig jaar beeldende kunst/Twenty years of fine arts*. (Amsterdam: Museum Fodor, 1982), p.21.

2 Michael Gibbs, 'The Graph of Photography', published in Dutch translation in *Een Woord voor het beeld*, ed. Van Alphen/Visser, Uitgeverij SUA, Amsterdam, 1989. Original English version published in this collection: see p.46.

This article was published in *Perspektief* no.43, February 1992.

BAS VROEGE

Being one and the other

The magazine, *Perspektief*, that I published together with a group of young artists, photographers and art historians, became bilingual with issue no.11 in 1982. We needed translators, and we found Michael Gibbs, I do not remember how. It may have been via Ulises Carrión whom one of us knew or it may have been through Michael's own magazine, *Artzien*. [see pp.138–139]

In March 1985 he wrote his first piece for the magazine, 'Appropriate Strategies'[1], dealing with plagiarism in postmodern photography. Was it because he was inspired by the issues raised by the other editors, or irritated by the lack of depth in the articles he was supposed to translate and which, one way or the other always sounded more intelligent in (his) English than in (our) Dutch...

I failed to ask what triggered him to start writing about photography and he was much too nice a person to tell us the truth. That worked: as of issue no.23, published early 1986, he became a member of the editorial board. His first article was immediately spot on: it challenged the notion of traditional documentary practice in photography. That was unheard of in the Dutch scene where the humanist documentary approach was synonymous to documentary at large. Its meaning was hardly questioned. In his historically well-founded article entitled, 'Documentary and its discontents'[2] [see p.38], Michael introduced the notion of a new critical documentary as practiced by American artists Allan Sekula and Martha Rosler. Their work could be seen as a critique of traditional documentary practice: photographs cannot speak for themselves, was their message, they need context to become meaningful. Until then, many believed, a photograph could tell more than the proverbial thousand words...

That piece fuelled both an internal as well as public debate on the 'new' postmodern documentary that led to numerous articles of *Perspektief* in the years to follow. They would prove to be a binding force for some older generation photographers like Oscar van Alphen who had long battled for a critical, theoretical approach to photography as well as a younger generation of photographers or academics with the aspiration to become image makers, such as philosopher Ton Hendriks. As a 2006 master thesis by Stefan Lalleman has revealed[3], in no other country and in no other photography related magazine, were so many articles, essays, polemics on the new documentary published. It destroyed ignorance, supplanting it with representational doubt. If Michael did not manufacture that bomb, he was for sure among the people who ignited it, in the Netherlands and beyond as Lalleman's study has proven.

Raising questions was more his nature than providing answers, though. But, it differed from the role he took on as an artist or a theoretician. He tended to be more explicit in his critical writing than in his own photo-text works. In his article 'The dialectical view of Michael Gibbs' [see p.206], critic Rob Perrée writes about the latter: "The text which has been added is no explanation, but a catalyst for the process. The photographs are atmospheric; through association they elicit words that lead to a meaning. That meaning is a question, certainly, because Gibbs has no desire to give answers".[4]

The response to his writing and occasional curating—for the 1990 'Fotografie Biennale Rotterdam' dealing with documentary for cultural environments he made 'Critical Realism'[5]—can hardly be described as a response to 'just' raising questions. In a polemic article entitled 'A quagmire, not a goldmine—a plea for the conservation of realism in documentary photography' published in the Dutch quality newspaper *NRC Handelsblad*, documentary photographer Marrie Bot responds fiercely to the practices and theory of the new documentary. She emotionally claims the spokesmen of the new documentary to be stealing at will from postmodern philosophy while "making use of preachy and bombastic language that… physically make it impossible to read their texts".[6]

To many in the art world, Gibbs' important role in the documentary photography debates of the 1980s, may sound like his secret life. Not just because we undoubtedly share memories of a caring, committed yet modest man, both in his capacity as a son, a father, a partner, as well as a friend, a teacher, or a colleague. Until his very last moment, in everything the contrary of a noisy, let alone opportunistic or irresponsible radical.

Secret, before all, because his 'real' work as I feel it—hidden in turn to most involved in photography—was being a conceptual artist, a concrete/visual poet. Moulding minimalist wordings into textual sculptures that, ideally, were to live on paper pages. Stencilled pages held together by staples driven in manually, as in the days of *Kontexts*, the magazine he ran from 1969 to 1977.

Sure, he made works that would function on the wall, elegant ones too; sure, some museums printed his concrete poetry in beautifully produced catalogues; sure, he experimented with text/image/sound works to function on the World Wide Web. Save from his early performances: how much more immaterial can one formulate a piece of art? Prevent the commodification of the object, make sure the meaning of the work does not get contaminated by any other than intrinsic, artistic values than in the form of a web-based piece?

The functioning of the art market has been one of the recurring themes in Gibbs' writing, for *Perspektief* as well as for *Art Monthly*, a magazine he contributed to until the end of his life. But his aversion to the market was expressed in its most explicit form in an article he wrote in 1992 for *Kunst & Museum Journal*, 'The Art of Forgetting—The Lost Idealism of the Sixties' [see p.13]:

> "Artists are more concerned today about whether their work will sell or whether they'll be given another subsidy, than about how their work may engage with society. Even much of the so-called 'socially-committed' art that has been emerging in the US recently seems more committed to publicity and art market mechanisms than to any broad-based social idealism. The experimental art of the sixties and seventies was born in (and borne upon) a wave of revolutionary fervour that now seems to have totally subsided. When we hear the word 'revolution' today it is more likely to be in the context of an advertisement for a new car or some other product of consumer technology.

What has happened is that most of the new, challenging art forms and ideas of the sixties—visual and sound poetry, performances, artists' books, 'alternative' spaces, 'Free Universities', etcetera—have either been consigned to oblivion or valorised by the art market and museum economy… Fluxus, for example, was virtually ignored by dealers and curators until its driving force, George Maciunas, died in 1978, whereupon they appropriated the movement, sanitised it of Maciunas's revolutionary anarchism and remoulded it in their own image in the form of revivals and retrospective survey exhibitions, all of which coincidentally served to vastly increase the market value of Fluxus multiples that were once ridiculously cheap or even free. Fluxus today means nothing more than a section of the 'collectables' market; like the other historical avant-gardes, it has been reduced to items in dealers' catalogues."[7]

Gibbs' critical stance towards the art world and the art market and the fact that he lived to that, certainly did not make his life easier, economically speaking. He had to continue doing translation work and he picked up teaching on a more permanent basis as of 1998 at the Design Academy Eindhoven, and as a guest lecturer at the Master's in Photographic Studies at the University Leiden. Some of the Leiden students were thrilled that they were now being trained by the author, they had gotten to know in their academy/BA period by his articles from the eighties and early nineties.

Both in Leiden and Eindhoven, his uncompromised thinking has without any doubt ignited the critical capacity of a new generation of artists, curators, critics, and designers. We will have to make sure that his writing and his art will remain available—in his spirit: cheaply!—to new audiences in times to come, on the web and hopefully also on paper as, however hard he tried in cyberspace, immateriality for Michael and his generation is best represented by words on (cheap) paper. May this book be the first publication, linking the many identities—or should we say: sides or talents—Michael Gibbs represented. For him these qualities were inseparable.

"Things that are neither one thing nor the other" reads the sub line to the Nondescript Productions website.[8] The 1990s site hosted by xs4all—then an idealist organisation that had grown out of the Amsterdam hacker scene—brought many aspects of his life together. 'Nondes', as it was referred to, may sound ironic today but beware: it is the (word)play of a man being one and the other, who took (words and) play seriously, who approached play as a revolutionary act.

Michael lay in state in a cardboard coffin, carrying his picture. Visitors wrote their farewell messages around it, on its surface. The combination of the words and the picture could not have been more appropriate: "[The photograph] suffers from an irremediable lack; lacking presence, it requires a supplement, another form of writing, another 'graph' inscribed onto the graph of its traces".[9]

"Never finish your article with a quote" is how a former Leiden student remembers some of Michael's advice, given during the critical writing course he taught.[10] May I be forgiven this one time, using his own words…

1 Michael Gibbs, 'Appropriate Strategies—Michael Gibbs on the nature of plagiarism in post-modern photography', *Perspektief* no.20, Rotterdam, 1985.

2 Michael Gibbs, 'Documentary and its discontents', *Perspektief* no.23, Rotterdam, 1986.

3 Stefan Lalleman, 'Naar een nieuwe fotografie—De rol van het tijdschrift *Perspektief* binnen de internationale ontwikkelingen op het gebied van de documentaire fotografie', Master thesis, University Leiden, 2006.

4 Rob Perrée, Michael Gibbs and the dialectical view, *Perspektief* no.43, Rotterdam, 1992.

5 *Oppositions*, the main exhibition for the 1990 Fotografie Biennale Rotterdam (curated by Bas Vroege, organised by *Perspektief*) investigated documentary practice manifesting itself in cultural spaces. *Critical Realism*, focusing on current practice in the US, took place at the gallery of *Perspektief* (centre for photography) and was curated by Michael Gibbs. Included was the work of Andres Serrano, Alfredo Jaar, Nancy Burson, Donald Moffett and others. See also *Perspektief* no.39, 1990.

6 Marrie Bot, 'Een modderpoel, geen goudmijn. Pleidooi voor behoud van realisme in de documentaire fotografie', *NRC Handelsblad*, Rotterdam, 2 November 1990 quoted from Stefan Lalleman, 'Naar een nieuwe fotografie', see 3.

7 Michael Gibbs, 'The Art of Forgetting—The lost idealism of the sixties', *Kunst & Museum Journal*, Stichting Internationaal Kunst- en Museumtijdschrift, Amsterdam, 1992.

8 Nondes, nondes.home.xs4all.nl (the site may eventually be moved to nondes.nl).

9 Michael Gibbs, 'Het schrift (graph) van de fotografie', in *Een woord voor het beeld*, Uitgeverij SUA, Amsterdam, 1989 (English version published in this collection, see. p.46).

10 Anecdote by Aleksandra Kononiuk, expressed in an email to the author, July 2016.

Based on the text, 'So Long, Michael', read at the memorial service for Michael Gibbs in Amsterdam, 29 December 2009.

MICHAEL GIBBS

Biography

1949
Born Croydon, England.

"Michael Gibbs and I grew up in New Addington, a modern development on the outskirts of the London Borough of Croydon. Isolated by its location it had a strong sense of community and independence. Surrounded by open spaces, farms, woodland and golf courses it had been farmland until the 1930s. Intended to be a garden village, the post-war housing shortage nudged Croydon Council to take over the development of what became one of the largest local authority estates in the country. Michael lived at the southern end of the estate and attended Fairchildes Primary School which was only a few minutes from his house. A new school, distinguished by the enthusiasm of a mostly young teaching staff imbued with post-war optimism and bordering on verdant countryside.

Post-war desire for a change for the better had seen major changes in the education system. Between the ages of ten and eleven every child sat what was known as the eleven-plus exam during their final year at primary school (aged ten to eleven). In theory the top 25% would go to grammar schools where they would receive an education suitable for university entrance, the next 10% to technical schools, and the remaining 65% to secondary modern schools which would offer a broad general curriculum discharging pupils at the age of fifteen. The reality was different and few pupils from Fairchildes Primary School passed the exam. Michael was one of the exceptions and achieved a place at John Ruskin Grammar School which he attended from 1960 to 1967 (I was there from 1959 to 1966).

Michael and I shared a common interest in much of the alternatives to the mainstream. Michael's interest in Dada and Surrealist art started early and unlike most of his contemporaries he appreciated that these were more than just art movements, but movements that also encompassed writing and poetry. It was Michael who discovered Better Books, one of the centres of the blossoming London underground scene and the Indica Bookshop. Les Cousins and Bunjies, two of the original folk cafés of the 1960s were also popular destinations. Michael was the first boy to wear a Dada badge to school. As an alternative to being sent home with long hair, it was suitably intellectual.

Intellectual yet full of good humour: on New Year's Eve 1966 several of us braved the cold and joined in the traditional Trafalgar Square celebrations. Not content with just being there, he and I jumped into the fountains (sadly the last year the fountains weren't boarded up) and arrived at Les Cousins club somewhat wet. We gained admittance and were rewarded with hearing Paul Simon sing at 3am. Michael always seemed to know someone who could get you into rather different parties in Croydon, where ska was the only music played on very loud sound systems and substances were available of which our headmaster would not have approved.

Hitchhiking in Europe in the summer of 1967 I missed the rendezvous with Michael at Rostock, perhaps fortunately for me as Michael was arrested in Istanbul and spent the night in an infamous Turkish prison. Ever the archivist, he managed to acquire a copy of the newspaper containing details of his arrest (this may or may not have included a photo of him behind cell doors!). An early association with publishing alternative material was made with friends of Tony Elliott, founder of *Time Out*. Michael and I gave out free copies of *Time Out* in Hyde Park prior to the Rolling Stones free concert in the summer of 1968.

Michael read English and American Literature at the University of Warwick, one of the new plate glass universities established during the 1960s. He found it stimulating, not only for the heated differences of opinion with his English tutor, one Germaine Greer, but also for the contact he had with other visionary poets. During his time at Warwick Michael started *Kontexts*, the magazine of visual and concrete poetry. First published in 1969, a total of ten issues were published until 1977, by which time Michael had moved to the Netherlands and was publishing other poets.

Realistic as to the potential difficulties of being able to live solely on income from writing and publishing Michael quickly learnt Dutch, initially teaching English as a foreign language and becoming an accomplished translator. He went on to become a leading European sound poet, an eloquent writer on digital art, an accomplished translator from Dutch into English and an important figure in European small-press publishing. I'd like to think that Michael was inspired by the optimism of the 1950s and 1960s, attendance at relatively new places of education and growing up in a new community. What I am sure about is that he was as much of a pleasure to have known in those early days as he was in later life."

—John Byford

Education

1967–70
University of Warwick, England. BA (Hons) English and American Literature.

1970–71
University of Exeter, England. Post-graduate research at the American Arts Documentation Centre.

1971–72
University of Exeter, Department of Education. Certificate in Education.

"To start with, a simple name like Mick, my first sight of him—lean, sad eyes and very long hair—it was after an event at Sigi Krauss Gallery, London 1970/71. A group of people came to our flat at Duncan Terrace in Islington, together with Felipe Ehrenberg, there was David Mayor, John Plant and Mick.

We already had the idea of moving to Devon as a group of artists. There was a common idea, to share a large space for both working and living, in a sort of collaborative association around art and production.

Spring came and we made a short visit to Mexico. During this time a more definite idea started to form, aided by Felipe's experience of being involved in an art collaboration with the bilingual magazine *El corno emplumado / The Plumed Horn*, edited by the poets Margaret Randall and Serjio Mondragón. It was a very successful international magazine that came to an end because of its political content, publishing international writers whose work reflected the politics and difficult times of the sixties.

The move was planned; first the decision was to go to Devon because Chris Welsh and Madeleine had contacts, David was at Exeter University and Mick Gibbs was living in Exeter as well. As a very nice gesture he offered us temporary accommodation and we stayed at his flat for a short period. We started looking for a place that had specific characteristics to fulfil all our needs, sufficient space and facilities for each others work.

All day long we were combing the countryside, until unexpectedly we came across Langford Court South in Clyst Hydon, near Cullompton, an hour from Exeter. It was a manor house, half occupied by the owners and half empty. It took time to negotiate as it hadn't been rented before and we decided to move nearby into a small B&B till the negotiations were done.

We went to London and picked up all our belongings. Our friend Jay Landesman sold Felipe a Fiat 500 for a pound, and we fitted everything we had into it. During the second trip we had to abandon the machine.

Amongst all the bits and pieces was a Gestetner mimeo machine, an important tool that gave the name to the Beau Geste Press. We moved into Langford and bit by bit everything and everybody started to fit in. Activities were organised and we had frequent artist visitors, not only from England, but from the United States, Europe and Latin America. This accelerated the plans to establish the BGP community as printers, editors and collaborators.

Langford Court South became the focus for the activities around BGP and the atmosphere of the house gave space for encounters and collaborations. The location of the place, not only because it was surrounded by beautiful and peaceful landscape but also for the creative energy and effort of each persons work, was an important part of the enchanted magical world of continuous creativity.

Reunions of writers, poets, visual artists, theatre actors, film makers, composers and musicians, were common, and several projects were developed under the thatched roof of the house. Small editions, printed matter, visual art and of course the technical part had to be improved with more equipment.

Mick Gibbs was among the artists and friends present at those important moments, as well as another close friend, Michael Leggett, a film maker always collaborating with his video-works; Allen Fisher was also always participating, Pierre Joris, Opal L. Nations, Anthony McCall, Carolee Schneemann, Kristjan Gudmundsson and Solveig, Michael Nyman, Michael Carr Jones, Serjio Puente and Ada Dewes, Serjio Pitol, Ulises Carrión, Raúl Marroquín, Servie

Jansen, Jan Hendrix, Alison Knowles, Eric Andersen, Takeisa Kozugi, Ryu Koike, Takako Saito, John Steinbeck Jr., and Klaus Groh remain as part of the BGP family, and many more that I would like to mention. All are very dear and appreciated.

I think those times which we all experienced together, the strong will and feelings, built deep relations that are still alive and shining, even nowadays when we see each other again.

Among all the connections, it is the one with Ulises Carrión, first of In Out Center and then Other Books and So. in Amsterdam, that is most important; as well as Marroquin and the Jan Van Eyck Akademie in Maastricht who created several collaborations. We all travelled to Amsterdam often, it was a centre of action, and our relations and friendship became more dependent on the net of connections which were made by the way we distributed our work.

Years later the circumstances of each one of us had radically changed, but we shared the experience of being part of the Dutch community. Mick Gibbs in Amsterdam, and me in Maastricht attending the Jan Van Eyck Akademie and with a new family. All are now stories from the past, not sad, but nice to remember."

—Martha Hellion

Solo exhibitions

1974
In Out Centre, Amsterdam.
Studio Agora, Maastricht.

1975
Warwick Gallery, Warwick, England.
Fignal Gallery, Amsterdam.

1977
Galerie Waalkens, Finsterwolde (NL).
Galerie Loa, Haarlem (NL).

1978
Verlag/Galerie Leaman, Dusseldorf.
La Mamelle Art Center, San Francisco.
Gallery A+, Amsterdam.
Gallery Sudurgata 7, Reykjavik, Iceland.

1979
Galerie Da Costa, Amsterdam.

1980
Stedelijk Museum, Schiedam.

1982
Galerie A, Amsterdam.
't Langhuis, Zwolle (NL).
Art & Behaviour, Amsterdam.

1983
Ruimte Morguen, Borgerhout, Belgium.

1984
Galerie Waalkens, Finsterwolde.

1985
Galerie A, Amsterdam.

1987
De Fabriek, Eindhoven.

1989
Galerie Witzenhuizen-Meijerink, Amsterdam.

1990
CEPA, Buffalo.

1992
Galerie Van Kranendonk, The Hague.
AIR, Amsterdam (installation 'Innocence and Experience', also at: Fotograficentrum galleri iNDEX, Stockholm and Zone Gallery, Newcastle-upon-Tyne).

1994
Camerawork, London (installation 'Heaven and Earth', also at Street Level, Glasgow).
Flatland Galerie, Utrecht.

1996
Boekie Woekie, Amsterdam.

1998
De Veemvloer, Amsterdam.

2001
Galerie de Boer-Waalkens, Finsterwolde.

2004
Boekie Woekie, Amsterdam.

Group exhibitions

1972–3
'Fluxshoe' tour of England.

1973
'A Conceptographic Reading of Our World Thermometer', Calgary, Canada.

1975
'Internationale Visuele Poezie', Rotterdam, Amsterdam, Utrecht.

1976
'British Artists in The Netherlands', British Council, Amsterdam.

1978
'Photopoetry', Polytechnic of Central London.
'Artwords & Bookworks', LAICA, Los Angeles.

1979
'Sprachen Jenseits von Dichtung', Westfalisches Kunstverein, Munster.
'The Open and Closed Book', Victoria & Albert Museum, London.

1983
'Fotografie', Galerie Suspekt, Amsterdam.
'Wort fur Wort', Kasseler Kunstverein, Kassel.

1984
'3 Fotografen', Galerie De Annex, Amsterdam.

1985
'Taal in het Beeld', Makkom, Amsterdam.

1986
'Perfo photo exhibition', Old City Library, Rotterdam.

1987
'Foto(con)tekst', Perspektief, Rotterdam.

1988
'Over Fotografie', Van Reekum Museum, Apeldoorn (NL).
'Stipendia 86–87', Ministry of Culture, Amsterdam.

1989
'Tekens van Verzet', Fodor Museum, Amsterdam.

1990
'Art Creates Society', Museum of Modern Art, Oxford.
'Art on Line for AIDS', Paradiso, Amsterdam.

1991
'Stof en Geest', Gymnasium Felisenum, Velsen (NL).

1992
'Wasteland–Fotografie', Biennial Rotterdam III, Rotterdam.
'LUMO Photography Triennial', Jyvaskyla, Finland.
'Fodor Longa, Res Brevis', Fodor Museum, Amsterdam.

1993
'Morgen Gemaakt', Arti et Amicitiae, Amsterdam.

1995
'l'Art du Tampon', Musée de la Poste, Paris.
'Territoria', Triple X Festival, Amsterdam.

1996
'transparentien', Grafisch Atelier Haarlem.

1997
'A Scenic Detour through Commodity Culture', Maastricht.

2001
'Digital Aesthetic Event', Harris Museum and Art Gallery, Preston, England.

2004
'Een boek is een boek is een boek', Apeldoorns Museum.

"I first met Michael in October 1988 at the opening of the exhibition *Man Ray passed twice* in the Amsterdam gallery W139, where I showed the Super 8 film installation 'Choreografie der Bilder' (Choreography of Images). He was enthusiastic about my contribution and he wrote a highly favourable text about my work for a self-published artist's book of mine.

I admired his writing style, his critical views and his concise formulations. His feeling for, and interest in language showed itself in many of his writings but also in his own artistic work. Especially the written word was his muse and gave him space to experiment and communicate; in this he could best show himself and he knew precisely how to express that which engaged his mind. I sometimes had the vague feeling that he himself is the medium who through higher orders wrote the texts.

Michael was proud of his fine collection of rare books and art publications. He liked to consider himself as an intellectual who tackled philosophical and social themes. Often he did not know whether to define himself as an artist or an author as he moved in both fields: as an essayist he had the necessary distance and the gift to phrase his ideas critically; as an artist words were his instruments. In addition, he regularly translated catalogues that dealt with art, photography and new media.

An extensive renovation made our studio in the Wilhelmina Gasthuis, a former hospital in Amsterdam, into a pleasant and productive place. The idea to collaborate on a project was born and in 1992 we made the installation 'Innocence and Experience'. In 1994 we made another installation 'Heaven and Earth'. The accompanying catalogues were published with texts by Andrew Wilson, Heinz Pätzold and Arjen Mulder.

The starting point in our installations is the questioning of both the concept and the perception of the sublime. We were fascinated by this subject and during the process of the many discussions and research that we conducted the installations began to take shape. We made use of several media: photography, texts, and video. The texts were an essential part and here Michael found the right words. At the end of the 1980s I started to combine photos with three dimensional objects. The photographs came from several archives and this concept was also used in the installation 'Innocence and Experience'.

In those days Michael worked as a text editor for the Dutch magazine *Perspektief*, and organised photo exhibitions. He had the requisite knowledge and he closely followed the developments in the field of photography. This influence became visible in his own work, in which he now regularly used photographs, mostly deriving from existing images.

He was very interested in the political changes in Russia, its history and the social consequences. He made several photo works that referred to the October Revolution of 1917. He visited the city that was then still called Leningrad and I remember he returned from this trip very impressed and moved.

Another topic that fascinated Michael in those days was the notion of shopping malls that sprang up in all towns. He, therefore, was fond of quoting from Walter Benjamin's *The Arcades Project*. In 1990 Michael installed a temporary work at a balustrade in a shopping centre in Oxford, a set of names of lifestyle magazines.

Our projects were shown in galleries and art institutes in the Netherlands and abroad. We travelled for example to Newcastle, Stockholm, London, and Glasgow. It was a beautiful and rich period full of experiences and encounters with artists and curators. I gave my first lecture in English and tutored students at various art academies.

Travel was a recurring component: many opportunities made sure that we could go to different places. We stayed, for instance, a longer period in New York, where, in 1990, Michael put together the exhibition *Critical Realism*. We had a great time in New Mexico and took the car along the famous coastal route from Los Angeles to San Francisco.

In 1992 we travelled through Kerala, a state in the southwest region of India. This undertaking also had a personal concern. As a six year-old boy, Michael had visited his father there, who was travelling as a sailor, and on the beach we found the place where he nearly drowned as a child. From there we took a side trip to a holiday resort on the Maldives and enjoyed life. It was an adventurous travel.

My memories of Michael are shaped particularly by the many travels, our projects, and our interest in art and philosophy. I am grateful to him for that inspiring time. It has enriched my life with many colours."

—Claudia Kölgen

Publishing & editing

Editor and publisher of concrete/visual poetry magazine *Kontexts*, 1969–77. Editor *Kontextsound* (Kontexts Publications, 1977). Editor *Deciphering America* (Kontexts Publications, 1978).

Editor and publisher of art journal *Artzien*, 1978–82.

Contributing editor, *Perspektief* photography magazine, Rotterdam, 1986–95.

Editor, *Why not Sneeze?*, Internet art magazine (www.mediahaarlem.nl/sneeze), 1996–99.

Contributor of reviews and articles to various magazines, including *Art Monthly* (London), *Forum International* (Antwerp), *Kunst en Museumjournaal* (Amsterdam), *Metropolis M* (Amsterdam), *Camera Austria*, *HTV de Ijsberg* (Amsterdam).

Member of AICA (Association Internationale des Critiques d'Art) since 1987.

Books

Lifeline (Kontexts Publications, Exeter 1972).

Connotations (Second Aeon Publications, Cardiff 1973).

Extinction (In-Out Productions, Amsterdam 1974).

Speculations (AAA Press, Maastricht 1975).

5 coloured alphabets in black and white (ColleXtion, Antwerp 1975).

Pages (Kontexts Publications, Amsterdam 1976).

Accidence (Daylight Press, Amsterdam 1976).

Limits (Kontexts Publications, Amsterdam 1977).

Selected Pages (Kontexts Publications, Amsterdam 1978).

Pages 2 (Editions Da Costa, Amsterdam 1978).

Wounded Book (Kontexts Publications, Amsterdam 1979).

The Absent Words (Stedelijk Museum, Schiedam 1980).

SomeVolumesFromTheLibraryOfBabel (Editions Ex Libris, Amsterdam 1982).

Ocean Park (Editions Ex Libris, Amsterdam 1983).

Lives of the Artists (Editions Ex Libris, Amsterdam 1985).

Innocence & Experience (with Claudia Kölgen . AIR, Amsterdam 1992).

Heaven and Earth (with Claudia Kölgen . Camerawork/Street Level 1994).

Legend, Selected texts 1966–84 (Boekie Woekie, Amsterdam 2004).

All or Nothing / SomeVolumesFromTheLibrary OfBabel (RGAP, Cromford, 2005).

Teaching

1973
Guest lecturer, Dartington College of Art, England.

1974
Guest lecturer, Exeter College of Art, England.

1974–75
Part-time lecturer, Jan van Eyck Academy, Maastricht (NL).

1977
Guest lecturer, School of Visual Arts, New York.

1981
Guest lecturer, Enschede School of Art (NL).

1987
Guest lecturer and critic, Bezalel Academy, Jerusalem.

1987–88
Part-time lecturer, Camera Obscura, Tel Aviv.

1989–92
Tutor, Art Media Studies, Rijksacademie van Beeldende Kunsten, Amsterdam.

1990
Guest lecturer, School of Visual Arts, New York.
Guest tutor, Hoge School voor de Kunsten, Arnhem (NL).

1992
Guest lecturer, Academy of Fine Art, Helsinki, Finland.

1993
Guest tutor, University of Northumbria, Newcastle-upon-Tyne.

1994
Guest tutor, Glasgow Art School, Glasgow, Scotland.

1995
Guest lecturer, Hoge School voor de Kunsten, Arnhem.

1996
Guest lecturer, Hoge School voor de Kunsten, Utrecht.

1998–
Teacher, The Design Academy, Eindhoven.

1999
Internet website workshops, Split Academy of Art, Zagreb Academy of Art, Croatia.

2004/5
Guest lecturer, MA Photographic Studies, University of Leiden.

Awards

Travel grant, Ministry of Culture, The Netherlands, 1977, 1987.

Stipendium, Ministry of Culture, The Netherlands, 1978, 1979, 1980, 1985, 1991, 1993.

Project Grant, Municipality of Amsterdam, 1982, 1992.

Basisstipendium, Fonds voor Beeldende Kunsten, 1994, 1997, 2001.

Related activities

Organiser of series of exhibitions, presentations and performances at Galerie A+, Amsterdam, 1978.

Speaker on forum on Taal in het Beeld (Language and Art), Makkom, Amsterdam, April 1985.

Speaker on forum on Modernism-Postmodernism, Stedelijk Museum, Amsterdam, December 1985.

Organiser of a 'chain' series of exhibitions at City Art Thoughts, Amsterdam, 1985–86.

Member of selection jury, Young Israeli Photographers, 2nd Israeli Phototgraphy Biennale, Tel Aviv, 1988.

'The Indistinct Image—Some Contemporary Artists' Photography', lecture at the Rotterdam Photography Biennale, September 1988.

Artist in Residence, Light Work, Syracuse (USA), March 1989.

Member of committee, Visual Art Manifestations and Publications, Raad voor de Kunst (Dutch Arts Council), 1989–92.

Curator of the exhibition 'Critical Realism', Perspektief Center for Photography, Rotterdam, Aug–Oct 1990.

Speaker on forum 'Home is where the art is', Teylers Museum, Haarlem, May 1991.

'Dig it all', lecture on digital media, New Visions, Glasgow, May 1994.

Member of committee granting stipendia, Fonds voor Beeldende Kunst, 1994–98.

Speaker at AICA Congress, Belfast and Derry, Northern Ireland, 1997.

Member of jury for new media, 3rd Split International Film and Video Festival, Split, Croatia, 1998.

Teacher, website workshops, Media@ Haarlem, Haarlem, 1997–99.

Speaker at symposium on 'Curating the Web', ICA, London, 1998.

Chairman of the board, Free Media Café, Amsterdam, 1997–2000.

Teacher, website workshops, Open Studio, Amsterdam, 2000–01.

Speaker at symposium on Internet Art, Tate Gallery, London, April 2001.

Speaker at symposium 'Ethiek in de Persfotografie, Gemeentemuseum, Den Haag, May 2004.

Speaker at symposium 'All or nothing? A consideration of blank books', Henry Moore Institute, Leeds, June 2005.

Literature

Interview in *Menu*, The Lunchroom Press, Michigan 1985.

Kees van Gelder, 'Het idealisme van Michael Gibbs en zijn kritiek daarop', *Artzien* 26 (Summer 1982).

Rob Perrée, 'The dialectical view of Michael Gibbs', *Perspektief* 43, Rotterdam 1992.

Arjen Mulder, review of 'Innocence & Experience', *Metropolis M* nr.4 (1992).

Mark Little, 'Innocence & Experience', *Portfolio Magazine* nr,16 (Spring 1993).

Paul Usherwood, 'Michael Gibbs & Claudia Kolgen', *Art Monthly*, March 1993.

Andrew Wilson, review of 'Heaven and Earth', *Art Monthly*, May 1994.

Erwin Wijman, 'XXXL, Digitale prints op gigaformaat', *Capi*, nr.3, najaar 1995.

Friggo Visser, 'Versluierd', *Nieuwsblad van het Noorden*, 6 juni 2001.

"I got to know Michael in Amsterdam in the time we were starting with the In Out Center which was one of the first an artist runned spaces in the early seventies. Right from the beginning Michael made a great impression on me as well as on my artist friend around this enterprise. As a group we were half underground and half intellectual. Michael was super intellectual and his language skill was on a high level. In this time we would always ask Michael to read over our conceptual texts before using them in our works. He also was gifted with a beautiful voice which could easily have been used for the BBC if he had not being part of an underground group of unknown artists in Amsterdam.

In two of my works (performances) Michael read two complete fairy-tales into a tape recording for me, these were Aladdin and the Wonderful Lamp and Little Red Riding Hood and they have been performed in many places in Europe.

Last year Michael, Eva and June visited me to Iceland and stayed with Ineke and me for a few days in our house on the east cost of Iceland. There we spent an intensive time together and now that Michael is no longer with us I am exclusively happy for these few days we spent together in Iceland.

Actually while writing these few words for this publication I would desperately need the language skill of Michael to improve this text."

—Sigurdur Gudmundsson

Contributors

John Byford grew up on a post-war London council estate, attended a south London grammar school and graduated from the University of Sussex. Attracted by working with books and people he entered librarianship and enjoyed a career at the British Library, retiring in 2008. He has published professionally and in football fanzines. He continues to travel, especially in Europe, watches football, not only Crystal Palace, but also teams in Prague where his son lives. Loves libraries and bookshops.

Henriëtte Dingemans was raised in Zimbabwe and South Africa from 1961–1979 by a Dutch father and Irish mother. She lived in Ireland from 1979–1984 to study industrial design, and settled in the Netherlands to study at the KABK and work as an artist. "Place and face are key; voyaging and movement are how I approach the universal aspects of place and people, two inextricable elements. This informs all—my photography, sculpture, painting, installations, and public artworks, even my 'art intervention' in the ecology sphere, 2bnot2b? I address problems and solutions from an aesthetic viewpoint, to engage the viewer to provide answers."

Donald Gardner is a poet and literary translator, resident in the Netherlands since 1979. He has published six collections of his poetry, most recently *The Glittering Sea* (2006) and *The Wolf Inside* (2014). He is known for his readings of his work—in New York, London, Dublin and Amsterdam. In 2015 he was awarded the Vondel Prize for his collection of Remco Campert's poetry, *In those Days* (2014). A previous collection of his Campert translations, *I Dreamed in the Cities at Night*, appeared in 2007.

Sigurdur Gudmundsson lives and works in Xiamen, China. He studied in the 1960s at the Icelandic College of Arts and Crafts and the Ateliers '63 in Haarlem in The Netherlands. Major solo exhibitions include shows at the Baltic, Gateshead (2003), Malmö Konsthall (1992), Kunsthalle zu Kiel (1993) and several shows at the National Gallery of Iceland and Reykjavik Art Museum. His works are in the collections of museums throughout Europe and he has made a number of public sculptures located in the Nordic Countries and Central Europe.

John Held Jr.'s books include *Mail Art: An Annotated Bibliography* (1991), *Rubber Stamp Art* (1999) and *Small Scale Subversion: Mail Art and Artistamps* (2015). He has organised exhibitions at the National Palace of Fine Arts, Havana; the Mayakovsky State Museum, Moscow; and co-curated the exhibition *Gutai Historical Survey and Contemporary Response*, at the San Francisco Art Institute (2013). He is a staff writer for *San Francisco Arts Quarterly*.

Martha Hellion is a graduate of the National School of Architecture, specialising in museum design, visual arts at Goldsmith College and Sir John Cass College of Art London, and the Jan van Eyck Akademie, Maastricht. She was a co-founder of the group of printers and editors Beau Geste Press in Devon in the early 1970s. She organised the first exhibition of Ulises Carrión's work at the Institute of Graphic Arts, Oaxaca in 1998, Mexico City's Library, 1999, and exhibited his complete work at Museum Carrillo Gil, Mexico City, 2003). She currently directs the MH Studio/Center of Research and Documentation on Artist's Publications, publishing and exhibiting with academic institutions, research groups and publishers in Mexico, South America and Europe.

Claudia Kölgen was born in Germany, and has been living and working in Amsterdam since 1983. Her work includes film, installations, photography and drawings and has been shown in the Netherlands and abroad. She has made a number of artists books, most recently: *Wellengang* and *Sehversuche*. From 1991 until 1994 she worked in collaboration with Michael Gibbs on two installations and publications: *Innocence and Experience* and *Heaven and Earth*.

Marga van Mechelen is an art historian and art critic, based at the University of Amsterdam where she teaches the history and theory of contemporary and global art;

conceptual, performance and installation art in particular. Three of her latest books are: *De Appel: Performances, Installations, Video, Projects, 1975–1983* (2006), *Echt Peeters: Realist—Avant-gardist* (2011) and *Art at Large: Through Installation and Performance art* (2013).

Rob Perrée is a writer and exhibition curator, specialising in contemporary American, African American, African and Surinam art and artist's books. He is on the editorial board of *Kunstbeeld* magazine, Amsterdam, and co-founder of the Con Rumore Foundation, Amsterdam. He lives and works in Amsterdam and New York

Gerrit Jan de Rook is a critic and curator. Published in *Metropolis M* and *Museumjournaal*, amongst others. He has made exhibitions in Heden, Gemak, in his home town The Hague, and about Provo and its rebellious successors in the State Museum, Prague. He publishes the utterly obscure magazine *IZ*.

Guy Schraenen is the founder of Galerie Kontakt, Antwerp; Guy Schraenen éditeur, Antwerp/Paris; the Archive for Small Press & Communication (ASPC), Antwerp; and Museum within a Museum in the Museum, Weserburg, Bremen. His activities are mainly focused on collecting, preserving and presenting artists' publications from international and independent art movements between the late 1950s and the 1980s. His *Collected Writings: Essays, Statements, Interviews 1974–2013* was recently published.

Bas Vroege was director of *Perspektief* (Centre for Photography) in Rotterdam, from 1982 to 1992 as well as editor of *Perspektief* magazine, until 1995. He is currently the director of Paradox, a not for profit production platform for documentary, which he founded in 1993. He teaches editorial and curatorial practice in Film and Photographic Studies at the University of Leiden, and is advisor to the Three Shadows Photography Art Centre in Beijing, and Fondazione Fotografia in Modena.

Andrew Wilson is Senior Curator Modern and Contemporary British Art, and Archives at Tate, London. His research has focused on post-war art and culture, often with a specific emphasis on wider countercultures through the 1960s, 1970s and 1980s and the development of conceptual art in the 1960s and early 1970s. In 2016 he curated the major exhibition *Conceptual Art in Britain 1964–1979* at Tate Britain and edited the accompanying catalogue. He is a founding fellow of the London Institute of 'Pataphysics.